DOING REAL WORLD
RESEARCH IN SPORTS STUDIES

Traditional research methods textbooks tend to present an idealized and simplistic picture of the research process. This ground-breaking text, however, features leading international sport researchers explaining how they actually carried out their real life research projects, highlighting the practical day-to-day problems, false starts and setbacks that are a normal part of the research process.

This book focuses on ten pieces of research that have made a distinctive and valuable contribution to the study of sport. For each one the author of that research explains how the project was conducted and the issues that they faced. In addition, each piece of research has a commentary from a leading sports scholar outlining why it is regarded as being an important contribution to the discipline of sports studies and how that research can inform studies being carried out today.

Contributors to the book describe how, in their own real life research projects, they

- initially conceptualized and defined their research projects
- secured funding and/or sponsorship from relevant bodies
- handled enforced changes to the research plans
- confronted/overcame obstacles presented by outside bodies
- managed inter-personal/emotional relationships in the research encounter
- managed possible threats to their personal safety or physical integrity
- managed good luck, bad luck and serendipitous findings
- dealt with favourable and hostile media reaction to research findings.

Doing Real World Research in Sports Studies enables students and researchers to develop a more realistic understanding of what the research process actually involves. It charts the development of key research projects in sport and should be essential reading for any sports research methods course.

Andy Smith is Professor of Sport and Physical Activity and Associate Head of the Department of Sport and Physical Activity at Edge Hill University, where he is also Director of the Social Science of Sport Research Group. He is Co-Editor of the *International Journal of Sport Policy and Politics*.

Ivan Waddington is a Visiting Professor at the Norwegian School of Sport Sciences, Oslo, and the University of Chester. He is a recognised expert on drug use in sport and is the author of *Sport, Health and Drugs* and co-author of *An Introduction to Drugs in Sport* (with Andy Smith).

DOING REAL WORLD RESEARCH IN SPORTS STUDIES

Edited by Andy Smith and Ivan Waddington

Routledge
Taylor & Francis Group

LONDON AND NEW YORK

First published 2014
by Routledge
2 Park Square, Milton Park, Abingdon, Oxon OX14 4RN

Simultaneously published in the USA and Canada
by Routledge
711 Third Avenue, New York, NY 10017

Routledge is an imprint of the Taylor & Francis Group, an informa business

© 2014 Andy Smith and Ivan Waddington

The right of the editors to be identified as the authors of the editorial
material, and of the authors for their individual chapters, has been asserted
in accordance with sections 77 and 78 of the Copyright, Designs and
Patents Act 1988.

British Library Cataloguing in Publication Data
A catalogue record for this book is available from the British Library

Library of Congress Cataloging in Publication Data
[CIP data]

ISBN: 978-0-415-50525-3 (hbk)
ISBN: 978-0-415-50526-0 (pbk)
ISBN: 978-0-203-12780-3 (ebk)

Typeset in Bembo
by Keystroke, Station Road, Codsall, Wolverhampton

MIX
Paper from
responsible sources
FSC
www.fsc.org   FSC® C013604

Printed and bound by CPI Group (UK) Ltd, Croydon, CR0 4YY

For Eric Dunning
Teacher, colleague and friend

Andy would also like to dedicate this book to the memory of his Auntie Bev, who sadly passed away so young.

Ivan would also like to dedicate this book to his grandchildren, Ella and Evan.

CONTENTS

CONTRIBUTORS

Michael Atkinson is Associate Professor in the Faculty of Kinesiology and Physical Education at the University of Toronto. His central areas of teaching and research pertain to non-mainstream physical cultures, suffering, body modification, bio-pedagogical practices in physical cultures, and bioethics. He has published on diverse subjects including ticket scalping, tattooing, transhumanism in sport cultures, Ashtanga yoga, fell running, criminal violence in sport, animal abuse in sport, youth masculinities and health, cosmetic surgery and athletes with critical illnesses. Michael is author/co-author of seven books, including *Battleground: Sports* (2008), *Deviance and Social Control in Sport* (with Kevin Young, 2008), *Boys' Bodies: Speaking the Unspoken* (with Michael Kehler, 2010), *Key Concepts in Sport and Exercise Research Methods* (2011), and *Deconstructing Men and Masculinities* (2010). He is Editor of the *Sociology of Sport Journal* and Director of the Sport Legacies Research Collaborative.

Cora Burnett is a Professor at the University of Johannesburg, lecturing in the sociology of sport and research methodology in the Department of Sport and Movement Studies. She holds two doctorates – a Ph.D. (1984 in Human Movement Studies) and a D.Litt. et Phil. (1996 in Anthropology). She has published more than 90 peer-reviewed research articles, 14 chapters in international academic books and six books or manuals, as well as 41 national and international research reports. Some of her most acknowledged accomplishments include four national studies on: (i) impact assessments of the national community and school mass participation projects; (ii) indigenous games research; (iii) the status of women and girls in South Africa's democracy; and (iv) sport in the higher education sector, as well as several high-profile City Soccer Initiative (CSI) projects (including research and monitoring and evaluation training) for corporates such as the Coca-Cola Foundation, the Absa Foundation, Vodacom Foundation and Rio Tinto (Namibia). Extensive impact assessments have been undertaken for the Australian Sports Commission, the

German Development Corporation and European Union and the Nike Network for Social Change. In 2007, the Sport Development Impact Assessment Tool (S·DIAT) received the Sport Research Intelligence Sportive (SIRC) Africa Research Award. Currently she serves as Vice-President of the International Sociology of Sport Association. Her book, *Stories from the Field* (2012), provides 45 comprehensive case studies of sport-for-development programmes, representing the work of 11 NGOs in eight African countries.

Fred Coalter is Professor of Sports Policy at Leeds Metropolitan University and was previously a Professor of Sports Policy at the University of Stirling. His research interests relate to sport's claimed contributions to various aspects of social policy. His published work includes *A Wider Social Role for Sport: Who's Keeping the Score?* (2007), *Sport-in-Development: A Monitoring and Evaluation Manual* (2006), *Sport-for-Development Impact Study* (2012) – a major study based on fieldwork in Uganda, Tanzania, South Africa, Mumbai and Calcutta – and *Sport-for-Development: What Game Are We Playing?* (2013). Between 2004 and 2012 he was also responsible for compiling Sport England/UK Sport's online research-based Value of Sport Monitor. He is a member of the Scientific Advisory Board of the Swiss Academy Development, a Board member of the Mathare Youth Sport Association's Leadership Academy, a monitoring and evaluation consultant to Magic Bus (India) and recently was a member of the UK-based Centre for Social Justice's working group on sport and social regeneration.

Scott Fleming is Professor of Sport and Leisure Studies at the Cardiff School of Sport, Cardiff Metropolitan University. He has worked at the University of Brighton and the University of Gloucestershire, and holds honorary posts at the Asia-Pacific Centre for the Study and Training of Leisure, Zhejiang University, China, and at Plymouth University. He is also an Associate Member of the Centre for Children and Young People's Health and Well-Being, Swansea University. His research has been broadly concerned with sport and leisure cultures since the late 1980s – his most sustained interest has been around the sociology of sport, racism and ethnicity. More recently he has worked on projects concerned with corporate governance and sports officiating. Throughout his research he has maintained an interest in qualitative research designs and research ethics. He is the author of *'Home and Away': Sport and South Asian Male Youth* (1995) and co-editor of seven Leisure Studies Association volumes of papers. He was the Chair of the Association between 2004 and 2009, and is currently the Senior Managing Co-Editor of *Leisure Studies*.

Ken Green is Professor of Applied Sociology of Sport and Head of Sport and Exercise Sciences at the University of Chester. He is Editor of the *European Physical Education Review* and a Visiting Professor at the Norwegian School of Sports Sciences and the University of Wolverhampton. He is author of *Understanding Physical Education* (2008), *Physical Education Teachers on Physical Education* (2003), *Key*

Themes in Youth Sport (2010), and co-editor of *Physical Education: Essential Issues* (with Ken Hardman, 2005).

John Hoberman has been active in the field of sport studies for many years. His books include *Mortal Engines: The Science of Performance and the Dehumanization of Sport* (1992), *Darwin's Athletes: How Sport Has Damaged Black America and Preserved the Myth of Race* (1997) and *Black and Blue: The Origins and Consequences of Medical Racism* (2012). He has taught courses on 'Race and Sport in African-American Life' and 'Race and Medicine in African-American Life' at the University of Texas at Austin, where he is Professor of Germanic Studies.

Barrie Houlihan is Professor of Sport Policy in the School of Sport, Exercise and Health Sciences at Loughborough University. His research interests include the domestic and international policy processes for sport. He has a particular interest in sports development, the diplomatic use of sport, and drug abuse by athletes. He has authored or edited 19 books and over 50 journal articles. His most recent books are the *Routledge Handbook of Sports Development* (edited with Mick Green, 2011) and *Sport Policy in Britain* (with Iain Lindsey, 2012). In addition to his work as a teacher and researcher, Barrie Houlihan has undertaken consultancy projects for various UK government departments, UK Sport, Sport England, the Council of Europe, UNESCO, the World Anti-Doping Agency and the European Union. He is the Editor-in-Chief of the *International Journal of Sport Policy and Politics*.

Grant Jarvie is Chair of Sport at the University of Edinburgh and visiting Research Professor at the University of Toronto. He served as Vice-Principal and acting Principal at the University of Stirling and most recently, with James Thornton, published *Sport, Culture and Society* (2012). With specific reference to the chapter in this book, he has published several research reports into racism and sport and his first book back in 1985 was titled *Class, Race and Sport in South Africa's Political Economy*.

Dominic Malcolm is Senior Lecturer in the Sociology of Sport in the School of Sport, Exercise and Health Sciences at Loughborough University. His research interests focus upon two empirical themes. The first, the sociology of sports medicine, encompasses athlete experiences of injury and physical and mental illness, the use of performance-enhancing drugs and aspects of the delivery and organization of sports medicine. Most recently this has been consolidated through the production of an edited collection, *The Social Organization of Sports Medicine* (2012) and publication of papers in *Social Science and Medicine, British Journal of Sports Medicine* and the *Sociology of Sport Journal*. The second, the historical sociological analysis of cricket, focuses particularly on national identity, (post)colonialism, race and violence. Most recently this has been consolidated through the publication of an edited collection, *The Changing Face of Cricket* (2010), and the sole-authored monograph, *Globalizing Cricket: Englishness, Empire and Identity* (2013). Through this research he has established an international reputation for his knowledge and application of

Norbert Elias's figurational sociology. In addition to various book chapters and journal articles, his work developing Elias's theoretical ideas has led to the production of two co-edited texts: *Sport Histories: Figurational Studies of the Development of Modern Sports* (2003) and *Matters of Sport: Essays in Honour of Eric Dunning* (2008). His broader contributions to the field include editorship of the international peer-review journal *Soccer and Society* (2000–5), and authorship of *The Sage Dictionary of Sports Studies* (2008) and *Sport and Sociology* (2008).

Lee F. Monaghan obtained his Ph.D. from the Cardiff School of Social Sciences, University of Wales, in 1998. He is currently Senior Lecturer in Sociology at the University of Limerick. His research explores issues relating to the body/embodiment, gender, risk (illicit drug use, sexualities and violence), and neoliberalism and financial capitalism. He has published in journals such as *Sociology of Sport Journal*; *Sport, Education & Society*; *International Review for the Sociology of Sport*; *International Journal of Social Research Methodology*; *Social Science & Medicine*; *Addiction*; *Health, Risk & Society*; and *Body & Society*. His books include *Bodybuilding, Drugs and Risk* (2001), *Men and the War on Obesity: A Sociological Study* (2008), *Debating Obesity: Critical Perspectives* (2011, co-edited with Emma Rich and Lucy Aphramor), and *Key Concepts in Medical Sociology* (2013, co-edited with Jonathan Gabe). Lee is currently working on a book with Michael Atkinson, *Challenging Masculinity Myths: Understanding Physical Cultures*.

Elizabeth C.J. Pike is the Head of Sport Development and Management, and a Reader in the Sociology of Sport and Exercise, at the University of Chichester. She has delivered presentations in universities and conferences throughout Africa, the Americas, Asia, Australasia and Europe critically evaluating risk, injury, ageing, gender and corporeality in sports. Her recent publications include a co-authored book (with Jay Coakley) entitled *Sports in Society: Issues and Controversies*, a co-edited book (with Simon Beames) examining *Outdoor Adventure and Social Theory*, and a number of book chapters on ageing, the experiences of sporting physical activity in later life, gender issues in sport, and the role of complementary and alternative medicines for athlete welfare. Elizabeth is the Chair of the Anita White Foundation at the University of Chichester. She is currently a member of the Executive Board of the International Sociology of Sport Association, and serves as the President of this association and the Sociology of Sport Research Committee of the International Sociological Association. She is a reviewer for several journals and publishers, and is on the editorial boards of the *International Review for the Sociology of Sport*, *Leisure Studies* and *Revista ALESDE*.

Ken Roberts is Professor of Sociology at the University of Liverpool. He is a former Chair of the World Leisure Organization's Research Commission, and also a former President of the International Sociological Association's Research Committee on Leisure. He is a founder member and now honorary life member of the Leisure Studies Association. His books include *Leisure* (1970), *Contemporary*

Society and the Growth of Leisure (1978), *The Leisure Industries* (2004) and *Leisure in Contemporary Society* (2nd edn, 2006). He is also the author of *Key Concepts in Sociology* (2009), *Youth in Transition: Eastern Europe and the West* (2009), *Class in Contemporary Britain* (2nd edn, 2011), and *Sociology: An Introduction* (2012).

Martin Roderick is a lecturer of sociology currently teaching in the School of Applied Social Sciences at Durham University. He has been involved in research focusing on the careers of professional athletes, and specifically on the management of workplace injury in the football industry. He completed his Ph.D. examining the careers of professional footballers in 2003, which was subsequently published as a book: *The Work of Professional Football; A Labour of Love?* (2006). His current research interests concern the problems associated with work and careers in professional sport and the inter connections between family life, issues of work-life balance and athletic careers. His work challenges the orthodox perspective that sports work offers opportunities for self-actualization and sheds light on the way athletes narrate their everyday realities.

Chris Shilling is Professor of Sociology and Director of Postgraduate Research in the School of Social Policy, Sociology and Social Research (SSPSSR) at the University of Kent. His research from the late 1980s has been dedicated to 'embodying' sociology and social theory, and establishing and developing the interdisciplinary field of body studies. He has written on the body in relation to a range of substantive issues (from sport to archaeology, from health, illness and death to music, and from religion to consumer culture) and his work has been translated widely. His major books include *The Body and Social Theory* (3rd edn, 2012), *Changing Bodies. Habit, Crisis and Creativity* (2008), *Embodying Sociology. Retrospect, Progress and Prospects* (ed., 2007), *The Body in Culture, Technology and Society* (2005) and, with Philip A. Mellor, *The Sociological Ambition* (2001) and *Re-forming the Body: Religion, Community and Modernity* (1997). He is currently working on a joint project with Philip on religious body pedagogics and the religious habitus, and is presently Series Editor of the *Sociological Review Monograph Series*.

Andy Smith is Professor of Sport and Physical Activity and Associate Head of the Department of Sport and Physical Activity at Edge Hill University, where he is also Director of the Social Science of Sport Research Group. He is Co-Editor of the *International Journal of Sport Policy and Politics* and co-author of *Sport Policy and Development* (with Daniel Bloyce), *Disability, Sport and Society* (with Nigel Thomas), and *An Introduction to Drugs in Sport: Addicted to Winning?* (with Ivan Waddington).

Karl Spracklen is Professor of Leisure Studies at Leeds Metropolitan University. He is interested in the sociology of sport and leisure and issues around methods and ethics in social science research. His current research projects include whiteness and leisure, Englishness and folk music, extreme metal and mythologies, and authenticity and tourism.

Loïc Wacquant is Professor of Sociology at the University of California, Berkeley, and Researcher at the Centre Européen de Sociologie et de Science Politique, Paris. A MacArthur Foundation Fellow and recipient of the Lewis Coser Award of the American Sociological Association, his interests span incarnation, ethnoracial domination, urban inequality, the penal state and social theory. Wacquant's books have been translated into 20 languages and include *Body and Soul: Notebooks of An Apprentice Boxer* (2004), *Urban Outcasts: A Comparative Sociology of Advanced Marginality* (2008), *Punishing the Poor: The New Government of Social Insecurity* (2009), and *The Two Faces of the Ghetto* (2013).

Ivan Waddington is a Visiting Professor at the Norwegian School of Sport Sciences, Oslo and the University of Chester. He is the author of *Sport, Health and Drugs* (2000) and a co-author of the British Medical Association report, *Drugs in Sport: The Pressure to Perform* (2002). He has also co-edited *Fighting Fans: Football Hooliganism as a World Phenomenon* (2002), *Sport Histories: Figurational Studies of the Development of Modern Sports* (2004), *Pain and Injury in Sport: Social and Ethical Analysis* (2006), and *Matters of Sport: Essays Presented in Honour of Eric Dunning* (2008). His most recent book (with Andy Smith) is *An Introduction to Drugs in Sport: Addicted to Winning?* (2009). His work has been translated into German, French, Italian, Portuguese and Flemish.

Kath Woodward is Professor of Sociology at the Open University and a member of the ESRC-funded Centre for Research on Socio-Cultural Change. She works on feminist, materialist critical theories, embodiment and affect, mostly within the field of sport. Recent books include *Sex Power and the Games* (2012) on the explanatory reach of sex, gender and the idea of enfleshed selves in the Olympics, and *Sporting Times* (2012) on temporalities in sport, using the example of 'real time' in London 2012. She has worked extensively on boxing and is the author of *Boxing Masculinity and Identity, the 'I' of the Tiger* (2006) and *Globalising Boxing* (forthcoming 2013). She teaches first-year social sciences and has taught sociology and women's studies at undergraduate and postgraduate levels. She is the author of the popular introductory social sciences text, *Social Sciences: The Big Issues,* to be published in its third edition in 2013. She has also published on feminist theories and methods with Sophie Woodward, *Why Feminism Matters* (2009). She is currently Principal Investigator on an AHRC-funded project on 'Being in the Zone', in music, sport and the cultural industries, for which she is conducting research on the affective and psychosocial dimensions of the phenomenon of the zone in sport.

Sharon Wray is a Reader in Sociology at the University of Huddersfield. Her research has focused on women's ethnically diverse experiences of ageing and how significant life course events influence health and well-being in later life. She has extensive experience of undertaking research across ethnic and cultural diversity and has published in the areas of ageing, health and physical activity, and ethnic diversity. A key aim of her research is to capture the rich and diverse experiences of older people and make visible those accounts that are often ignored. She is particularly interested in methodological issues relating to the disruption and re-formation of identities during the research process. Recently she has published in the areas of insider and outsider identities in ethnic and migrant qualitative research, and the effects of memory on health and well-being in later life.

PREFACE

As any sociologist will recognize, writing, or – as in this case – editing, a book is a social activity and this book is no exception.

The intellectual origins of this book, as we point out in the introductory essay, are to be found partly in our (largely unsatisfactory) experiences as students on undergraduate and postgraduate research methods courses at various times from the 1960s through to the 1990s and partly in our desire, as teachers, to offer our own students in the sociology of sport an experience in relation to learning about research methods which would be rather more exciting than that which we had received in our own student days.

Our decision to produce a book of this kind – that is, one focusing on the real world process of *actually doing research* as opposed to reading how, in an ideal world, it *should* be done – rests on, and is underpinned by, our conception of sociology as a discipline and, associated with this, our conception of the nature of social scientific research, both of which have been informed by the work of Norbert Elias. Doing research is not the sterilized and mechanical process described in most textbooks of research methods for, as Elias pointed out, humans are both thinking and feeling animals and all social action, including research, necessarily involves both cognition and emotion; it is therefore important, for a more realistic understanding of the research process, not to neglect what has been called the 'human face' of research. It is also important to recognize the limited ability of humans to control complex social processes, to which Elias also drew attention, and, associated with this, the importance of what he called unplanned outcomes as an aspect of all social processes, including research; in this context we have sought to highlight the importance of another common process which is generally ignored within methods textbooks: serendipity, or the process of making discoveries by chance.

The development of our understanding of this particular conception of sociology and of social science research is also a social process in which many people have played a part and to whom we are indebted. In particular we would like to thank our former colleagues at the University of Leicester and former and current colleagues at the University of Chester and, in particular, Eric Dunning, Patrick Murphy, Ken Sheard, Dominic Malcolm, Martin Roderick, Ken Green, Ken Roberts and Daniel Bloyce, all of whom have offered continual support, encouragement and advice and, most importantly (bearing in mind that we are thinking *and* feeling animals), good friendship.

We would also like to thank all the contributors to the book, not least for meeting our deadlines for submission which has enabled us to deliver the manuscript (more or less) on time. We would also like to thank Simon Whitmore and Joshua Wells at Routledge for their efficiency and helpfulness.

Finally, we would like to thank all our current and former students of research methods for responding so enthusiastically to stories of real world research!

INTRODUCTION

Real life research: The inside story

Ivan Waddington and Andy Smith

In his Introduction to Riley's 1963 *Sociological Research I: A Case Approach*, Robert K. Merton, one of the leading sociologists of the twentieth century, noted that 'textbooks have managed to earn a dubious reputation for being dull and plodding' and he added that this was the case 'especially when they deal with the methods of inquiry employed in an academic discipline' (Merton, 1963: xiii). Merton hinted that one of the reasons for this was that students do not learn from most textbooks of research methods how to conduct sociological research; rather, they learn 'only to talk learnedly about how it *should* be conducted' (Merton, 1963: xiii; emphasis added), with little appreciation of the 'difficulties that turn up in actual investigation' (Merton, 1963: xiii). Riley's book sought to overcome these problems partly by including methodological commentaries on some classic sociological studies such as William Foote Whyte's *Street Corner Society* and Thomas and Znaniecki's *The Polish Peasant in Europe and America*, and partly by the addition, in a second volume, of research exercises for students to undertake (Riley, 1963).

Since this early attempt to make the teaching of research methods more interesting, exciting and realistic, there have been, from time to time, other attempts to achieve the same objective, one of which – Frost and Stablein's *Doing Exemplary Research* (1992) – provided the model for this book. But by and large, textbooks of research methods in social sciences have retained a traditional and, in our view, rather uninspiring format. This is not a view which we, as editors, have reached lightly, or indeed without personal – and often unsatisfying – experiences of research methods courses. Since we are of rather different ages – one young(ish) and one (to use a sporting analogy) very much a veteran – we were students on undergraduate and postgraduate courses in research methods at various times from the mid-1960s through to the late 1990s. The experience was one that we recall as something that we had to do as a course requirement rather than something that gave us any sense of intellectual excitement or engagement. And as teachers working together on the M.Sc. degree in the Sociology of Sport and Exercise at the University of Chester, we sought to offer our own students an experience in relation to learning about research methods which would be rather more exciting than that which we had received in our own student days. This book is an out-growth of that teaching.

Conventional texts on research methods in the social sciences tend to follow a long established format. They often begin with a general discussion of the role of theory in research and, in particular, in formulating the research problem and research design, typically followed by a discussion of ethical issues in research. The central chapters of most books are then given over to detailed discussions of the major methods used in social scientific research such as surveys and sampling, case studies, questionnaires, interviews, participant and non-participant observation, ethnography and the use of documents. Finally, many texts include advice about data analysis and writing up the research. This is, more or less, the general structure followed by some of the most widely used recent texts such as Babbie's *The Basics of Social Research* (2005), Gilbert's *Researching Social Life* (2008), Bryman's *Social Research Methods* (2008) and Denscombe's *The Good Research Guide* (2010).

We do not, of course, claim that such texts are without value, for there is clearly an important place for 'how to' guides of this kind. What we do claim is that, although such guides are useful in many respects, they also present a very partial − and therefore misleading − picture of the process of doing research. More precisely, they describe how research *ought* to be done in an ideal world, rather than how it is *actually* done in the real world. In most textbooks, students are thus presented with a view of research as a process which moves smoothly and unproblematically from the initial conceptualization and definition of the research problem through to the development of research methods, data collection, interpretation and writing up and presentation of the project. In the course of this process there are no hiccups and nothing ever goes wrong; researchers never have bad luck and never make mistakes; members of the research team and/or key interviewees never fall ill or become unavailable for other reasons; there are never disagreements within the research team; the relationship between observers and observed never breaks down; researchers never experience threats to their personal integrity or physical safety in the course of conducting their research; research objectives never change or have to be revised as unanticipated problems arise or the original objectives become less relevant or impossible to investigate; difficulties never arise in relation to sponsors or funding organizations (such as interference from, or hostile reactions from, sponsors in relation to research findings, attempts at censorship, etc.); and there are never problems in dealing with (both favourable and hostile) media reaction to the research findings. And, of course, researchers' personal lives never get in the way of research!

The partial and misleading picture of the research process as presented in most textbooks may be illustrated by reference to the role of chance, and in particular serendipity, in the research process. Serendipity is sometimes referred to as a 'happy accident' or, more precisely, the process of making discoveries by chance. Merton, who has perhaps done more than any other social scientist to highlight the importance of serendipity as part of the research process, defined serendipity as 'the discovery through chance by a theoretically informed mind of valid findings which were not sought for' (Merton, 1957: 12). Serendipitous findings of this kind can generate important new problems for investigation and also lead to radical changes in the original research methods in order to examine the new problems which arise in the course of the research. Serendipity is therefore a 'chance' process which can radically alter both the objectives and the methods of a research project as the project develops; because of this, an understanding of serendipity is, as Merton recognized, an essential part of the sociology of science and, in particular, it is central to an understanding of how science develops (Merton and Barber, 2006).

Examples of serendipity in science are numerous, with one of the most famous being the discovery by Alexander Fleming of penicillin. Examples are also commonplace in social science and, indeed, in social studies of sport. In this volume, for example, Waddington (Chapter 1) provides no fewer than three examples of serendipitous findings in the study of the management of injuries in English professional football, one of which, relating to the way in which football club doctors are appointed, added a major new dimension to the project; he also notes that the project would probably never have got off the ground had it not been for a chance meeting with an ex-professional footballer whose personal contacts with the Deputy Chair of the Professional Footballers' Association helped to secure the support of that organization for the project. Even more striking is Waquant's description (Chapter 3) of the remarkable series of chance events which radically changed the nature of his research project for, having set out with the intention of writing a historical anthropology of colonial domination in New Caledonia in the South Pacific, he ended up writing a classic study of boxing on the South Side of Chicago!

It is important to emphasize that, as Merton pointed out, serendipity is not unusual. Dunbar and Fugelsang (2005: 61) have noted that several studies of scientific discovery 'have all given unexpected, anomalous, or serendipitous findings a central role in scientific discovery', while their own study of scientists working in three biology laboratories found that over half their findings were unexpected (Dunbar and Fugelsang, 2005). But serendipity is rarely, if ever, mentioned in textbooks of research methods. None of the four widely used textbooks cited earlier list 'serendipity' in their index; neither do any of them list 'chance', 'luck', or 'unexpected findings'. It would seem that researchers, at least in the pages of textbooks, do not need good luck and, equally significantly, always manage to avoid bad luck. And since research (in textbooks) always goes to plan, there are presumably never any unexpected findings.

Among the very few social science books on methods to address the issue of serendipity is Townsend and Burgess's *Method in the Madness* (2009) and it is not without significance that they go to some length to emphasize the differences between the approach to understanding the research process offered in their book and that to be found in conventional textbooks of research methods. Thus they state that their book 'should not be seen as a textbook' (Townsend and Burgess, 2009: 2) and, most significantly, their book is subtitled *Research Stories You Won't Read in Textbooks*.

It was the omission from methods textbooks of important aspects of the research process, such as the elements of chance and serendipity described above, which led Frost and Stablein (1992: xi–xii) to conclude that:

> The research act as depicted in many research texts seems to us to be somewhat idealized, abstract, and mechanical. When we look at the research product in journals it resembles a rather stylized and even sterile product. There is rarely much more than a hint to the reader in texts and in published articles of what went on behind the scenes when the research was being done, of the human face of research ... doing research is a much messier and more imperfect endeavor than most official sources of information about the process recognize or admit. It is also more personal. People doing research become intrigued, excited, frustrated, and depressed along the investigation trail. They experience despair and exhilaration. They are often puzzled and surprised by what they find.

Just occasionally, authors of methods textbooks give some recognition of the fact that the picture they paint of research is in some respects misleading. For example, in the introductory chapter to his *Social Research Methods*, Bryman writes:

> There is one final point I want to register before you read further. It is to alert you to the fact that social research is often a lot less smooth than the accounts of the research process you read in books like this ... In fact, research is full of false starts, blind alleys, mistakes, and enforced changes to research plans ... If social research is messy, why do we invariably not get a sense of that when we read reports of research in books and academic journals? Of course, research often does go relatively smoothly and, in spite of minor hiccoughs, proceeds roughly according to plan. However, it is also the case that what we read in reports of research are often relatively sanitized accounts of how the research was produced, without a sense of the sometimes difficult problems the researcher(s) had to overcome.
>
> *(Bryman, 2008: 15)*

This recognition of the 'messiness' of research is welcome, though it is worth emphasizing that this is Bryman's only reference to the messiness of research and it occupies little more than one page in a textbook of over 700 pages. But that is still one page more than one finds in most other methods textbooks!

It was their dissatisfaction with conventional methods texts which led Frost and Stablein to produce *Doing Exemplary Research* (1992), in which they selected seven pieces of exemplary research and invited the authors of those studies to write about the personal 'journeys' that they undertook in actually carrying out their projects. Significantly, these 'journeys' highlight many aspects of the research process usually ignored in textbooks. For example, in the description of their research on aspects of organizational culture (the book is about research on organizations), Meyer, Barley and Gash provide a story of what Frost and Stablein describe as '"whole" people, people with complex combinations of personal, professional, and intellectual motivations' (Frost and Stablein, 1992: 20). In this context, the authors' description of the interpersonal dynamics between Barley, who was a junior faculty member at Cornell University, and Meyer and Gash, who were both graduate students at Cornell, is particularly interesting. They note that, at the outset, they 'underestimated the arduousness of the task in which they were about to engage' and that important aspects of their personal lives affected key aspects of the organization of the research. For example, they met for three to five hours on one or two evenings per week, but these meetings rarely began before Barley and Meyer had put their children to bed and Gash had returned from her nightly dance class; as a consequence, the meetings typically ran late, were 'both physically and mentally draining' and, partly because all three researchers were stubborn, the meetings generated not just heated intellectual debates but, occasionally, inter-personal conflict. The three had also decided that all decisions would be made on the basis of consensus and Barley revealed that, as the senior member of the team, he frequently felt that he had to 'bite his tongue' in order not to pull rank and impose a decision on the others (Meyer *et al.*, 1992: 31). They also note that, as Simmel pointed out long ago, triads are inherently unstable social structures, in that two members of a triad typically align more frequently with each other than they do with the third and, in the case of their own triad, 'even though each of the authors took his or her share of abuse, the most frequent alignment was clearly Barley and Meyer against Gash' and they add that, from time to time, 'Meyer and Barley discussed their regret at "ganging up" on Gash'. They note that this alignment probably reflected the fact that Gash was a 'solo' on a number of dimensions, for in contrast to Meyer and Barley, both of whom were married men with children, Gash was single, female, more interested in psychology and less committed to some aspects of the project (Meyer *et al.*, 1992: 35).

Textbooks rarely (and perhaps surprisingly, since the authors of these texts are themselves social scientists) have much to say about relationships between researchers, though, as the paper by Meyer *et al.* indicates, these are often critical to the research process. In their description of their project on the expression of emotions within organizations in the same book, Robert Sutton and Anat Rafaeli reveal that although they had previously 'had fun working together', when their project ran into difficulties they responded by avoiding each other which, they say, was notable because 'we had developed a style of working that involved detailed and nasty arguments peppered with personal insults'. They became so frustrated by the lack of progress of their research that they 'began to talk seriously about giving up the paper, and were so depressed that we talked a bit about abandoning future research on expressed emotion. Anat even had private thoughts about turning motherhood into a full-time career' (Sutton and Rafaeli, 1992: 120–1). Fortunately for Sutton and Rafaeli, they enjoyed some good luck at appropriate points in their research for they note that, at one stage of the project, when they 'weren't making any progress toward the development of a solid, publishable empirical paper', 'a happy accident happened' which provided them with an unanticipated source of valuable empirical data (Sutton and Rafaeli, 1992: 119).

In her description, also in *Doing Exemplary Research*, of her research on small groups, Gersick similarly points out that in her project, 'something unexpected happened' which led her to make some unexpected discoveries. However, she reports that she became so engrossed in following her new line of enquiry that she was blown 'off the track' and completely ignored the original objectives of the project and had to be redirected back on course by a senior colleague (Gersick, 1992: 52–5). She also notes that, at a later stage of the project, 'some fortunate events occurred' which helped her to develop a theoretical context for her work (Gersick, 1992: 61).

Since the publication of *Doing Exemplary Research*, a few other texts have included some chapters in which researchers write about how their research was actually done and these essays confirm the frequently 'messy' character of research. For example, Bryman and Burgess's *Qualitative Research* (1999) includes an essay by Roy which, suggest Bryman and Burgess, 'demonstrates the role of good fortune and sheer tenacity in gaining access in many organizations' (Bryman and Burgess, 1999, vol. 1: xvi). Roy investigated union organization and industrial conflict in the South of the USA in the 1960s, a topic which was then considered 'not respectable', and Roy writes that 'my choosing a taboo subject for research was not due to any deliberate boldness on my part. The investigation wasn't planned. I stumbled into it quite by chance' (Roy, 1999: 256). In the same volume, Morgan reflects on the rather less good fortune which characterized his study of female workers in a factory in England. Morgan's presentation of his research at a meeting of the British Association for the Advancement of Science generated some media interest and two national newspapers identified and named the factory which was the centre of the research, even though Morgan himself had properly refused to provide this information to the papers. Morgan writes that his essay is not an account of a research project which 'went wrong' – though in the unwelcome public identification of the factory the project did 'go wrong' – but a description of how he dealt with the personal embarrassment this caused and how it altered the project in certain respects (Morgan, 1999: 292–3). It might be noted that at the time that Morgan was already an experienced sociologist who later became President of the British Sociological Association; if such unfortunate mishaps can occur in the research of a senior scholar then they can certainly occur in the research of younger and less experienced social scientists.

Interestingly, Bryman and Burgess's book also contains one example of research into sport. In his paper, appropriately titled 'The sociologist as celebrity: The role of the media in field research', Adler describes the evolution of his research which focused on his university's highly successful basketball team. The study was based largely on participant observation and his close involvement with the team led to a barrage of media publicity as a result of which, and quite unexpectedly, Adler himself became a celebrity, and his paper focuses on the effect of this on his own sense of self and the ways in which it affected the research.

A few other sociologists of sport have also reflected, in academic journals and elsewhere, on how they actually conducted research projects on aspects of sport. Sugden and Tomlinson (1999), for example, have described their 'investigative mode of sociological inquiry' and the unorthodox methods which this sometimes entailed in their study of football's world governing body, Fédération Internationale de Football Association (FIFA). They describe how, for example, in order to gain access to key FIFA officials at the World Cup in South Africa in 1996, one of them passed himself off as a newspaper reporter in order to secure a press pass. They also describe how they made contact with a group of ticket touts, a process which they correctly note was not without some personal risk:

> They were big boys, engaged in an illegal operation and, so the researcher thought, probably wouldn't take too kindly to being spied upon, particularly on their day off, by someone who carried a press pass. But investigative research demands risks – some calculated, others not.
>
> *(Sugden and Tomlinson, 1999: 385)*

They add that they 'have taken many gambles in the service of ... investigative research' (Sugden and Tomlinson, 1999: 391) and note that 'Getting at deep, insider information in the manner described above, is not usually advocated in graduate school research methods courses or manuals of acceptable research practice. We think it should be' (Sugden and Tomlinson, 1999: 386).

Such risk-taking, which may involve possible threats to the researcher's physical well-being, is not unusual in some forms of research, particularly research into the lifestyles of those involved in activities which are illegal and/or heavily stigmatized; as Sugden and Tomlinson note, 'People with something to hide do not routinely invite social commentators and confirmed sceptics into their inner sanctums' (Sugden and Tomlinson, 1999: 390). The present volume contains two papers which deal with this particular problem, for Atkinson (Chapter 4) and Monaghan (Chapter 5) provide fascinating accounts of how they negotiated – not without some difficulties – access to two such groups: ticket scalpers in Canada and steroid-using bodybuilders in Wales.

Brackenridge (1999) has also reflected on the process of 'managing herself' as a lesbian engaged in sensitive research, in this case research into sexual abuse in sport. Brackenridge notes that the process of 'managing herself' involved three aspects:

> first, *managing* myself, coping with the strains and stresses of the research; second, managing *(by)* myself as being alone in the research; and third,

> managing my *self/selves*, deciding which of several possible selves or agendas – the personal, the scientific or the political – is being addressed at any given time.
>
> (*Brackenridge, 1999: 399*)

Brackenridge has also, elsewhere, described some of the difficulties she and her team experienced when researching child welfare in football, a project which had been commissioned by the English Football Association (FA). Among problems described by Brackenridge (2007) are organizational inertia in the FA, a lack of cooperation and rudeness by some people within the FA, budget cuts which required major revision and reduction of the research programme in the course of the project and even a refusal by the FA to pay Brackenridge's consultancy fees, which were only paid after Brackenridge initiated legal action against the FA. The fact that 'real life' problems such as those listed above rarely feature in research textbooks provides the essential rationale for this volume.

How, then, can we best characterize the papers in this volume? Sparkes (2002) has distinguished three rather different modes of 'telling tales' about sport and physical activity. The first of these is the 'scientific tale', which is the dominant tale in the physical and biological sciences and, to some extent, also in the social sciences. Typically it requires researchers to write up their work for publication in scientific journals in a highly stylized format: aims, methods, results and discussion. The structure of the scientific tale is formal and logical but also mechanical, sanitized and altogether lacking in the messiness which is characteristic of much 'real life' research; as Waddington notes in his essay in this volume (Chapter 1), this style of writing often presents a distorted and misleading picture of how the reported research was actually done. We learn about the results of the research but the sanitized statements of methods give few clues about the process of actually *doing* the research, of what Frost and Stablein call the 'human face of research'.

The second kind of tale identified by Sparkes is the 'realist tale', which is often used in the writing up of qualitative research – for example research based on fieldwork or in-depth interviews – and which is frequently found in social science of sport journals. As Sparkes has noted, such tales are often characterized by extensive, closely edited quotations which are 'used to convey to the reader that the views expressed are not those of the researcher but are rather the authentic and representative remarks transcribed straight from the mouths of the participants' (Sparkes, 2002: 44). Such tales may make a valuable contribution to our understanding of social aspects of sport for, as Sparkes notes, 'realist conventions connect theory to data in a way that creates spaces for participant voices to be heard in a coherent text' (Sparkes, 2002: 55). But realist tales also tend to be what Sparkes calls 'author-evacuated and methodologically silent':

> In realist tales, the voice of the researcher, if heard at all, tends to be found in the methods section of the article. Here, there may be hints that the author is concerned about various issues associated with the fieldwork, such as the

ethics of different relationships as they develop between the researcher and the participants in the course of an inquiry. Such concerns, however, are not dealt with in any great depth in realist tales.

(Sparkes, 2002: 57)

In contrast to both scientific and realist tales are 'confessional tales', which foreground 'the voice and concerns of the researcher in a way that takes us behind the scenes of the "cleaned up" methodological discussions so often provided in realist tales' (Sparkes, 2002: 57):

Confessionals, therefore, explicitly problematize and demystify fieldwork or participant observation by revealing what actually happened in the research process from start to finish. Therefore, the details that matter in confessional tales are those that constitute the field experience of the author.

(Sparkes, 2002: 58)

Sparkes goes on to cite Van Maanen to the effect that these field experiences include such things as 'stories of infiltration, fables of fieldwork rapport, mini dramas of hardships endured (and overcome), and accounts of what fieldwork did to the fieldworker' (Van Maanen; cited in Sparkes, 2002: 58).

It is clear that the essays in this volume, in which researchers describe how they actually undertook their research – that is, their personal 'research journeys' – approximate most closely to Sparkes's 'confessional tales'; they are stories about good luck and bad luck; of unanticipated findings; of twists and turns in the research process; of obstacles encountered and (sometimes) obstacles overcome; of managing difficult problems of access and interpersonal relations; of risk-taking in sometimes potentially dangerous and threatening situations; of favourable and hostile public reactions to one's findings. They are, in short, stories of doing 'real life' research in sports studies.

A final word about how we have organized the book. We have selected ten research projects which, in our view, have made important contributions to understanding social aspects of sport, and we asked experts within each of these areas to write short commentaries explaining why those research projects were important: that is, what contribution each of them has made to our understanding of a particular problem area within sports studies. We then asked the authors of those research projects to describe how they actually carried out those research projects. We did not specify in advance the issues we wanted them to deal with so that the ways in which they have described their own 'research journeys' represent how they themselves have reflected on their own research projects. As a result, different contributors have chosen to focus on different aspects of the research process. Some have highlighted the personal, social and intellectual origins of their projects; others have focused on the problems, opportunities, mishaps and changes of course as their projects developed; still others have focused on managing (and sometimes surviving!) the public reaction to research findings. But whatever the focus within individual essays, all the contributions describe 'real life' research. We hope that the accounts of these personal 'research journeys' will help to give students and other researchers a better understanding of what the process of doing research actually involves and, bearing in mind our own experiences as students on research methods courses, we hope that they will also make the process of learning about research both more interesting and more enjoyable.

1

RESEARCHING THE WORLD OF PROFESSIONAL FOOTBALL

Ivan Waddington

Introduction

> I think that sports medicine and the care of players in this country is appalling . . . It doesn't add up, with football players becoming more and more valuable assets. It is like buying a four-and-a-half million pound car and taking it down to your local garage for servicing by a guy who may or may not know what he is doing.
>
> *Premier League club doctor*

> You're not meant to be injured. You should be playing. You get paid to play. He [the manager] totally ignored you when you were in the treatment room. His attitude was: 'You're no use to me anymore'.
>
> *Premier League player*

> Everything has to be done yesterday. The players have to be fit yesterday. If they miss a week, it's like a month to anyone else. The players will play when they're injured. You tend not to get the player injury-free. You . . . manage the level of injury irritation to play 90 minutes of football.
>
> *First Division club physiotherapist*

The above comments, transcribed from interviews undertaken for our study *Managing Injuries in Professional Football: A Study of the Roles of the Club Doctor and Physiotherapist* (Waddington *et al.*, 1999), provide a brief flavour of some of the key findings of that study.

This chapter traces the development of that study, which would probably never have got off the ground had it not been for a chance meeting with an ex-professional footballer who facilitated the initial contact with the Professional Footballers'

Association (PFA), which proved essential in gaining access to the relatively closed world of professional football. The research process also developed in several unanticipated directions, partly as a result of a series of serendipitous findings. This paper describes the origins of the project, the initial difficulties in securing an interview sample of professional footballers, club doctors and physiotherapists, how these problems were overcome and how the nature of the research problem, and the methods, changed in the process of doing the research. The difficulties in doing the research were compounded by the hostility of the English Football Association (FA), which refused any cooperation, and these problems are also described. Since the research documented what was generally perceived as a 'scandal' of poor medical care in professional football clubs, it generated a huge amount of media interest – it was the subject of a 30-minute programme on BBC radio and also received widespread television (TV) and newspaper coverage – and some aspects of the dissemination of our findings, and their consequences, are discussed.

Origins of the project

For many years before I became interested in the sociology of sport, my main area of interest, both for research and teaching, had been the sociology of medicine; indeed I had for several years taught the sociology of medicine in the medical school at the University of Leicester. I was, of course, familiar with the literature on doctor-patient relationships and, as a football fan, I had frequently thought that one aspect of this relationship might be particularly problematic in relation to the situation of club doctors in sports such as professional football.

The relationship between doctor and patient is normally underpinned by three fundamental assumptions:

(i) the doctor's skill is used exclusively on behalf of the patient;
(ii) the doctor is not acting as an agent on behalf of anybody else whose interests may conflict with those of the patient; and
(iii) the doctor may be trusted with private or intimate information which he/she will treat confidentially and not divulge to others.

I had, over many years, often thought that these assumptions may not apply in the same way, or to the same degree, in the work situation of the club doctor or physiotherapist in professional sports such as football. The central problem was this: if the team doctor and physiotherapist are employed by, and are therefore acting as agents of, the club, how can they simultaneously act as agents for, and on behalf of, the individual player-as-patient? How, in their day-to-day practice, do club doctors and physiotherapists resolve the potential conflicts of interest between their responsibility to their employer (the club) and their responsibility to the individual player-as-patient? What happens if the interests of the club and the player do not coincide, as inevitably is the case from time to time? For example, do the normal rules of confidentiality apply, or do team doctors and physiotherapists routinely pass on to team managers information which would normally be considered confidential, such as information about a player's drinking habits, or other aspects of their lifestyle? And what is the role of club medical staff in return-to-play decisions after injury?

Although I had often turned this problem over in my mind, I had never thought seriously about trying to initiate a research project along these lines, largely because the world of English professional football is a notoriously closed world which is hostile to 'outsiders', defined as those who have never played, or otherwise been involved in, the professional game at a high level. I thought the process of trying to gain access to key personnel within football clubs – players, doctors and physiotherapists – would not just be difficult but also, probably, ultimately fruitless.

All this changed as a result of a chance meeting with an ex-professional foot-baller, Graham Parker, who was also a lecturer at Coventry University Business School. Graham was taking a distance learning M.Sc. in the Sociology of Sport which we offered at the University of Leicester at that time (late 1990s) and I was allocated Graham as one of my tutees at a weekend conference for our distance learning students. Graham mentioned that he had formerly been a professional footballer and I raised with him some of the issues concerning club doctors, indicating that I thought it would be difficult to get the necessary support for a research project from within the world of professional football. However, Graham said that he had good contacts with the then Deputy Chief Executive of the PFA, Brendon Batson, and that he would informally sound out Batson about supporting the project. This resulted in an invitation to submit a written proposal to the PFA and this led, in turn, to a meeting with Batson at the PFA offices in Birmingham at which he pledged PFA support for the project. Batson clearly recognized the importance of the proposed project to his members; I was aware of the fact that his own career had been brought to a premature end as a result of injury, and this may have predisposed him in favour of the proposal.

We asked the PFA for minimal funding for the project – just £1,500 to help cover our travelling expenses to carry out the interviews – with the remainder of the costs, most notably the salary costs and the costs of secretarial support, being borne by the University. We might note, as an aside, that for this very modest outlay the PFA received a 68-page report which reflected nine months intensive work and which made 19 recommendations for improving the structure of club medical practice; in terms of value for money, this must represent just about the best ever bargain in commissioned research! However we were not interested in seeking major funding from the PFA, or carrying out the project on a commercial basis; what was critical for the success of the project was not the limited funding from the PFA but the fact that the support of the PFA would give us access to clubs and players.

With the support of the PFA, we were now in a position to move ahead with the project. The research team consisted of myself and Martin Roderick, then a young research associate at Leicester who had played professional football with Portsmouth in the late 1980s and who at the time was playing semi-professional football. I carried out the interviews with doctors and physiotherapists and Martin did most of the interviews with players. We agreed that he could build in additional questions to players about other aspects of professional football and this enabled him to complete a Ph.D. on footballers' careers which resulted in the production of his book, *The Work of Professional Football: A Labour of Love?* (Roderick, 2006a) which is essential reading for anyone who wants to understand the reality of professional football as work. Graham Parker also did some interviews, mainly with retired players.

Obtaining a sample

The initial plan was to conduct interviews with players using purposive sampling. We agreed with Brendon Batson that we would draw up a list of players with 'interesting' injury histories whom we wished to interview. That list was submitted to Batson and he contacted the players; if they agreed to be interviewed, he passed their phone numbers to us so we could agree a time and place for the interview. However, of the initial list of some 20 players whose names we submitted, only two or three agreed to be interviewed. We repeated the process twice more but each time only two or three players were prepared to be interviewed. This was a disappointing response, not least because the research was being conducted on behalf of the PFA, the players themselves were potential beneficiaries, in health terms, of the research findings and some of those whom we wished to interview, but who refused, were actually the PFA representatives in their clubs.

As a result, we had to supplement our purposive sample by the use of convenience sampling. As indicated earlier, Martin had played with Portsmouth and we were able to build up a sample of players in all four divisions of English professional football through his personal contacts. Graham also conducted several interviews with former players, based on his personal contacts in the game. In all, we interviewed 19 current players and eight retired players.

Access to club physiotherapists was less problematic. At the time, another young researcher at Leicester, Julian Harrison, was teaching an evening course in sports science in Loughborough and his students included physiotherapists from two professional clubs in the Midlands region of England. They both agreed to be interviewed and they also gave us the names of colleagues in other clubs who they thought would be (and who generally were) prepared to be interviewed. This snowballing technique was continued in each club in which we interviewed and we quickly built up a sample of ten physiotherapists spread evenly across the four divisions of the Premier League and the Football League.

To secure a sample of club doctors, I initially wrote to all club doctors within a radius of about 100 miles of Leicester, explaining the project and requesting an interview. This generated just seven replies, all of which came from doctors at Premier League clubs; the fact that these club doctors were more willing to be interviewed than their colleagues in lower division clubs probably reflected the fact that, as we found out in the course of the research, they spend more time at the club and are generally more involved in the club than are doctors in lower league clubs, some of whom may only go to the club on home match days. Although we knew that interviewing all seven doctors would be likely to bias our sample towards Premier League doctors, we did not feel that we could afford to turn down any offers of interviews. But once we had conducted these interviews we targeted doctors working outside the Premier League. Our targeted doctors included two women who worked in non-Premier League clubs, whom we wanted to interview because there are few women who hold such positions and we wanted to find out how these women became involved in what is a very macho world. We also interviewed three other non-Premier League doctors, partly by using Batson's contacts and partly by writing directly to the doctors at the clubs. In all we interviewed 12 doctors, seven of whom were with Premier League clubs, while two were with clubs in the first division, two were with second division clubs and one was with a third division club.

While our sample was biased towards doctors working in the Premier League, this turned out to be no bad thing because it gave us an effective defence against one potential criticism of our work. Our research revealed a host of bad – in the sense of unprofessional – practice within football clubs and, as the evidence of bad practice mounted up in the course of the research, we began to fear that critics might suggest that we had deliberately chosen clubs in which we were likely to find bad practice. However, since our interviews with doctors were biased towards those in Premier League clubs, our data reflected an abundance of bad practice not in the poorest clubs with fewest resources but in the largest and most affluent clubs, where one might reasonably have expected the best facilities and, perhaps, the best practice. Had our interviews with doctors included more interviews with clubs in lower divisions, we might well have discovered even more bad practice than we did.

Guaranteeing anonymity

In the course of an interview, interviewees may reveal 'insider' information which some of their colleagues may prefer was not revealed to 'outsiders', they may discuss sensitive issues, such as difficulties in their relationships with colleagues, and they may even be prepared to act as 'whistle blowers', that is to reveal information about wrongdoing of one kind or another. Quite clearly, interviewees will be much less likely to reveal such information if they feel that their remarks may be traced back to them. Because of this it is common practice, when conducting interview-based research, to offer interviewees a guarantee of anonymity, i.e. that the researchers will not reveal the identity of their interviewees or provide any information which might enable them to be identified.

Although the issue of anonymity is always important, we felt that it was likely to be an issue about which many of our interviewees might be particularly sensitive, given their often high-profile roles within professional football. Many of our interviewees were celebrated footballers who were nationally, and in some cases internationally, famous while those who were not well known to the general public – such as the team doctors and physiotherapists – worked for football clubs, all of which were well known within their local community and some of which were known throughout the world. In addition, the interviews with players inevitably focused, in part, on their personal injury histories (which could affect their prospects for future transfers to other clubs) and their relationships – which were not always good – with club doctors, physiotherapists, managers and other players, while the interviews with club medical staff also raised what might be considered sensitive issues, such as relationships with injured players and managers – the latter not infrequently difficult or problematic – or how they had dealt with players who had consumed drugs or who regularly consumed large amounts of alcohol. Given this situation, we anticipated that our interviewees would require an unambiguous assurance that neither they nor the clubs for which they worked would be identified in the report for the PFA or in any other publication which might come out of the research. In a word, it was important that we were able to provide a guarantee of anonymity. But how could we do this, other than by simply saying that we would not reveal the identity of any person or club? How could we provide a more secure – in effect a cast iron – guarantee about which our interviewees could feel more secure?

The answer was provided by a colleague at the time, Patrick Murphy, who came up with an idea which we felt worked very well. It is usual practice when interviewing to record the interview in order that the conversation can be transcribed and analyzed later; in other words, it is recorded for the benefit of the researcher. Patrick's idea was wonderfully simple: make two recordings, one for the researcher, the other for the interviewee. This is what we did. We took two tape recorders (this was before digital recorders came into general use) into the interview and then we explained, on tape, that we would not reveal the identity of the interviewee or provide any information which might enable him/her to be identified. It was explained that, at the end of the interview, one copy of the tape would be given to the interviewee so that, if we were to do anything improper or unprofessional, such as revealing their identity, misquoting them or misrepresenting what they had said, they would have all the evidence they needed to make a formal complaint against us with our employer, the University of Leicester, or with the British Sociological Association. All our interviewees seemed happy with this procedure and, though we cannot be sure, this may have contributed to their willingness to talk openly and candidly about their experiences. But whether or not this was the case, it may be regarded as a useful means of effectively underpinning the guarantee of anonymity in situations where this is of particular importance. It might be added that our initial thought that anonymity might be an issue of particular importance in this research proved to be correct because, as we shall see, when the report was made public there were several requests from the media for us to reveal the identities of some of our interviewees; we of course refused to do so.

Serendipity

Merton (1957: 12) has defined serendipity as 'the discovery through chance by a theoretically informed mind of valid findings which were not sought for'. As Merton noted, serendipity is a fairly common experience in research; it involves an observation which is unanticipated, anomalous or surprising and which stimulates the investigator to 'make sense of the datum', to fit it into a broader frame of knowledge (Merton, 1957: 104). There were several examples of such serendipitous findings in our research.

One of these arose from our attempt to generate a sample of doctors for interview. As noted earlier, we used a snowballing technique with club physiotherapists and this proved extremely successful in generating a sample of physiotherapists. We also tried to use this technique with club doctors but in this context it proved entirely unsuccessful, for club doctors told us they could not give us the names of colleagues in other clubs whom we could contact. After three or four such interviews, I realized that club doctors were telling us more than that they simply could not help us to build up our sample: they were telling us that *they did not know – because they did not come into contact with – other club doctors.* This led us to probe the reasons for this. It quickly became clear that, unlike club physiotherapists, who were always present at club matches, home and away, club doctors rarely travelled to away matches. Most club doctors were general practitioners working in the community; they spent most of their time working in general practice and it was this which generated almost all of their income and travelling to away matches was very disruptive in terms of the impact on their work in general practice. Club physiotherapists told us that they always made a point of talking with the physiotherapists of opposing teams in order to compare notes on the best way to manage injuries, but the fact that club doctors rarely met other club doctors meant that they did not have a similar opportunity to share and discuss common problems in this way. Because of this serendipitous discovery, we recommended in our report that the FA and Football League 'should be encouraged to organize more regular meetings for club doctors, perhaps on a regional basis, so that doctors can explore common problems, whether in relation to clinical issues or in relation to issues concerned with their conditions of employment' (Waddington *et al.*, 1999: 67).

A second serendipitous finding concerned the use of creatine supplementation by players. Creatine is a naturally occurring compound which, in relation to specific kinds of activity, may help to improve performance, postpone fatigue and improve speed of recovery. Martin interviewed a player who had been admitted to hospital following an injury in a game and who, while in hospital, became acutely ill with what initially appeared to be a kidney stone; the illness was eventually diagnosed as a kidney malfunction caused by excessively high doses of creatine. This led us to ask questions about players' use of creatine. We found that practice in relation to creatine use was haphazard. Many players were using creatine supplementation with very little knowledge of creatine; some used it on the basis of advice from local gym users, while many were using it on their own initiative and without medical advice. We were concerned that some players may have been given advice which encouraged them to use excessively high and potentially dangerous doses of creatine and, as a consequence, we included in our report an appendix in which we suggested that where creatine was given to players, its use should be supervised by club medical staff and the players' health regularly monitored to ensure that creatine levels did not exceed maximum recommended levels.

But the most striking and significant serendipitous finding concerned medical career structures and the process of appointing club doctors. As outlined earlier, the project, as originally defined, had centred on potential conflicts of interest in the role of club medical staff. I conducted the very first interview of the project, with a doctor at a Premier League club, and following usual interviewing practice, I decided to ask a few gentle and undemanding questions as a way of putting my interviewee at ease before moving on to what might prove to be more sensitive questions. My first question – which was not even part of the original interview schedule – and his reply added an important new dimension to the research:

IW: Could you tell me how you got the appointment at [the club]?

Doctor: I was phoned up by [the previous club doctor]. He just said to me that he wanted to retire and he was looking for a successor and would I mind coming along and watching a few matches with him as he got to know me.

IW: And you knew him professionally before?

Doctor: No. I didn't know him at all.

IW: So why did he contact you?

Doctor: I don't know. I think I met his brother at a conference and I think his brother must have spoken to him.

IW: So you hadn't been involved in sports medicine before?

Doctor: No, I hadn't.

(Waddington et al., 1999: 12)

This was, it should be emphasized, my very first question in the very first interview and it threw up an unexpected and astonishing fact. Was this really, I wondered, how people got jobs as club doctors in Premier League clubs? I discussed this with Martin and we decided that we should add to our interview schedule a series of questions about how club doctors were appointed and about their career structures more generally. This led to several key findings: most club doctors obtained their posts on the basis of personal contacts with the previous club doctor, who had often been the senior partner in the practice in which they worked or, quite frequently, a relative, usually a father or uncle; the post of club doctor was rarely advertised; doctors were often appointed without formal interview; if there was an interview, there was not normally a doctor on the interviewing panel; and very few doctors had a qualification in sports medicine. It was on this basis that we described the process of appointing club doctors as 'a catalogue of poor employment practice … [which] … is unlikely to be in the best long-term interests of the club or the players' (Waddington *et al.*, 1999: 13). These key findings provide a good example of serendipity; they were not originally sought for and were not part of the original research design.

One further point arises in relation to such serendipitous findings, namely, the way in which the process of writing up research for publication often presents a misleading picture of how research is actually done and, more specifically, of how projects may change in the course of doing the research. This is particularly the case in those (normally non-social science) journals which have a rigid format with which authors have to comply. For example, we published a paper on the methods of appointment and qualifications of club doctors in the *British Journal of Sports Medicine*, which requires authors to organize their material under the following headings: Objectives, Methods, Results, Conclusions. We accordingly felt constrained to describe the key objective of the research as to 'examine the methods of appointment, experience, and qualifications of club doctors and physiotherapists in professional football' (Waddington *et al.*, 2001: 48), even though this was *not* one of our objectives when we began the research. The format adopted by journals such as the *British Journal of Sports Medicine*, creates a misleading picture of the process of doing research as an almost mechanistic, orderly and unproblematic process in which one moves smoothly from formulation of the problem to data collection to analysis, a process in which everything goes to plan and there are no surprises, no serendipity. The reality is that very often, as in the situation above, what becomes a major theme of the research may not be present at the beginning of the project, and only emerges in the course of actually doing the research. Such is the nature of serendipity.

The evolution of the research project

We noted earlier a number of serendipitous findings that led us to ask new questions which had not been part of our original project. But the project also changed radically in relation to methods. At the outset, and in the research proposal which we originally presented to the PFA, we had envisaged the research as being entirely interview based; however, as we neared the end of the planned interviews, we saw a need to build in a postal questionnaire to club doctors in order to provide an additional data source. Our thinking in this regard was shaped by what many of our interviewees had told us about their own and others' unprofessional practice in football clubs.

One of the most difficult aspects of interviewing club medical staff proved to be the need to control my surprise – sometimes my astonishment – when doctors and physiotherapists, in a remarkably unreflexive way, described shockingly unprofessional aspects of their practice; examples included deliberately withholding information from players, sometimes as a matter of club policy, about the nature and extent of their injuries, in order to persuade them to continue playing while injured; the punishing (or 'inconveniencing' as physiotherapists called it) of injured players – for example, keeping them at the ground until late afternoon and then releasing them into the rush-hour traffic jams – as a way of reminding them that being injured was not regarded as an acceptable status; and frequent breaches of medical confidentiality, in which club medical staff would convey to coaches/managers information which would normally be considered confidential to the doctor-patient relationship, such as information relating to a player's lifestyle – in the worst breach of medical confidentiality, we were told about a club doctor who threatened to make a player's injury history public in order to undermine that player's desired transfer to another club. What was perhaps most surprising was the fact that many of the club medical staff who described their own unprofessional practice seemed largely or wholly unaware of just how bad the practice was that they were describing.[1] For this reason, it was important that I did nothing to reveal, either in my face or in my tone of voice, my own shock at the bad practice they were disclosing, for I did not wish to say or do anything which might have made them reluctant to provide such information.

Nevertheless, controlling my astonishment and maintaining a calm exterior was a difficult aspect of many interviews. On many occasions, as I listened to the taped interview in my car on the drive back to Leicester, I could still hardly believe what many of my medical interviewees had told me. And as the evidence of bad practice mounted, we began to rethink the original decision to base the study just on interviews.

Our main concern in this respect was that much of the practice that we documented was so unprofessional that we were afraid that potential critics might claim that our findings were based only on a limited number of interviews, or perhaps that we had deliberately sought out or looked for bad practice and that we had hand-picked our interviewees accordingly. Because of this, Martin and I agreed that we needed additional data on club doctors and it was this which led to the decision to send a questionnaire to all club doctors whom we had not interviewed. Of course, questionnaires normally yield rather different kinds of data than do interviews, but it was nevertheless possible to use questionnaires to check some of the information which we had gathered in the interviews and which pointed to bad practice, particularly in the process of appointing club medical staff. To this end we designed a questionnaire which asked for information about whether the doctor's position had been publicly advertised, whether there had been a formal interview for the post, whether there were doctors on the interview panel, and also information about the doctor's career, their qualifications and experience in sports medicine, and about the amount of time they spent at the club.

We were, of course, aware of the fact that doctors are busy people and that they receive a great deal of mail, particularly from pharmaceutical companies, and we were concerned that our questionnaires might simply end up in the doctors' waste bins. Because of this we decided to contact Alan Hodson, then the FA's Head of Medicine and Sports Science, to ask him for his support. I accordingly telephoned him, explained what we were doing and asked him whether, if I sent him a copy of our questionnaire for him to consider, he would be prepared to write a covering letter to club doctors, encouraging them to complete and return the questionnaire. The FA were, at that time, conducting their own national audit of injuries in professional football and I thought that our sociological study would nicely complement their more clinically oriented study and that my proposal would therefore be welcomed by Hodson.

I could not have been more wrong! I was wholly unprepared for Hodson's response to my request, which was one of undiluted hostility; indeed, I remember walking, almost shell-shocked, into Martin's room after putting the phone down and saying 'You will not believe the conversation I have just had with Alan Hodson!'. Hodson left me in no doubt that he considered us unwelcome trespassers on his territory. Why, he demanded, had he not been told about the research before? Why had I not asked his permission to do the research? When I explained we were doing the research on behalf of the PFA, I was asked why the PFA and in particular Brendon Batson had not asked for his permission? I was told very firmly that no one in any football club would speak to us without his permission and that no club doctor or physiotherapist would do anything which was not in the best interests of the players, to which I replied that we had already completed more than 40 interviews, that we had found many situations in which medical staff had acted unprofessionally and in ways which were not in the best interests of players, adding that he clearly stood to learn a great deal from our research about the ways in which club medical staff actually worked. It was not a pleasant conversation.[2]

Quite clearly the possibility of Hodson providing support for the project was out of the question. But this left us with a problem: could we get an acceptable response rate from club doctors without his support, or would our questionnaires simply end up in the doctors' waste bins? If we were to avoid the latter scenario, we would need to think very carefully about the design of the questionnaire, the best way to contact doctors and what information to provide in our covering letter.

Given that doctors are busy people, it was important that they could complete the questionnaire quickly and that meant that it had to be designed so that respondents could answer questions simply by ticking the appropriate box. We also thought that club doctors might be more likely to respond if, rather than sending out an anonymous 'Dear Club Doctor' letter, we personalized it by addressing the envelope and the covering letter to each club doctor by name. Since there is no available list of club doctors, one of our secretaries spent a day on the phone, ringing around all 92 league clubs and explaining that we wished to send a research questionnaire to the club doctor and asking for his/her name. All clubs obliged by providing this information.

We were also convinced that the construction of the covering letter would be likely to have a major influence on the response rate and we therefore spent a great deal of time and thought in constructing this letter. The covering letter was, in effect, our one chance to persuade club doctors to take time out of their busy schedules in order to complete and return the questionnaire and this meant that while the letter had to be brief – in order to ensure that it was read – it also had to contain a number of items of vital information designed to assuage any reservations that doctors might have about completing the questionnaire: that the study was being undertaken on behalf of a key organization within the game, the PFA; that the questionnaire was very simple and mostly involved ticking the appropriate box; that it would not take more than two to three minutes to complete; that a reply paid envelope was enclosed; that the questionnaire was about career structures and did not ask for any information which might be considered confidential, e.g. in relation to the clinical treatment of players; and that the questionnaire should be completed anonymously, a point which we emphasized by stressing that we did not wish respondents to identify either themselves or the club for which they worked.

After sending out the questionnaires there was, of course, a delay of a few days before replies started to come in. During this period, we discussed between ourselves, with some trepidation, what the likely response rate might be. Our fear was that, despite our efforts to get club doctors on board, most questionnaires might still end up in doctors' waste bins and that we would get too few returned questionnaires to be of use. However, the response rate exceeded our most optimistic expectations.

We sent out a total of 90 questionnaires to club doctors, of which 58 were returned, a response rate of 64 per cent. Moreover, the responses were spread over all four divisions, with 13 replies from Premier League doctors, 13 from doctors in first division clubs, 15 from second division club doctors and 16 from doctors at third division clubs; one respondent did not indicate the division in which the club played. The questionnaires provided an invaluable means of data triangulation and meant that, when taken together with the interview data, we had data from over 70 of the 92 league clubs; significantly, the questionnaire data provided strong supporting evidence for several key themes which had emerged from the interviews. We were delighted, not only because we had managed successfully to overcome what we had feared might be a real problem in relation to the response rate but also because – and having made the phone call described earlier, I took some satisfaction from this – we had done it without any assistance from – indeed, despite the objections of – the FA!

Disseminating the findings

As is usual practice, we published our findings in academic journals (in sports medicine and sociology) but our work also proved of considerable interest to a much larger, lay, audience. While we welcomed this wider interest in our work, it did raise some unanticipated problems.

We delivered our report to the PFA in the autumn of 1999 and we agreed with Brendon Batson that we would not make the report public until the PFA had had a proper opportunity to study the report and consider their response. The report was, we were told, sent by the PFA to the FA Medical Committee for their consideration, but we were not told anything about their response or whether they intended to implement any of our recommendations. In November 1999, we informed the PFA that we needed to make our findings public because, if we delayed any longer, the report would soon become 'last year's report'. I was on friendly terms with a reporter from the local radio station, BBC Radio Leicester, and had mentioned to him that we were doing this research. He had repeatedly asked to have a look at the report and eventually I delivered a copy to him on the morning of Tuesday 16th November 1999. Later that day, he phoned me to say that he had read the report and had contacted BBC Radio Five in London and, on the basis of what he had told them, they had decided immediately to make a radio programme about what quickly came to be seen as a scandal regarding the provision of medical care in English clubs.

At that time, BBC Radio Five ran a series of investigative sports journalism programmes called *On the Line*. The programmes, which lasted 30 minutes, were broadcast on Thursday evenings and each programme focused on one particular issue. There was just one programme left in that series and the BBC took an immediate production decision to shelve the final programme which had been made for the series and to make a new programme focusing on our findings. The new programme was put together in just two days and was broadcast on Thursday 18th November 1999. The BBC put out a press release the day before the programme was broadcast and this resulted in extensive coverage in several national newspapers, including *The Guardian, Daily Telegraph, Independent, Daily Mail* and *Daily Star*, while many local newspapers all over the country ran syndicated articles. In addition, ITV ran a major feature on their *Tonight with Trevor McDonald* programme, while our research even featured in an edition of *Heart of the Matter*, a long-running BBC religious affairs programme broadcast on Sunday evenings and hosted by Joan Bakewell, in which the focus was on ethics in football. In a hectic few days, Martin and I did dozens of media interviews.

We were, of course, pleased with this extensive coverage – and even sought it – not least because we were ourselves genuinely shocked by many of our findings, and a colleague in another department at Leicester, who specialized in risk management, advised us that the most effective way of changing dangerous or bad practice is by public exposure. But almost inevitably, this media exposure brought new problems, not least that we were continually being asked by less responsible sections of the media to identify some of the key interviewees, with various incentives being offered if we did so. These demands focused particularly on the identification of the player who was, as some newspapers described it, 'blackmailed' into abandoning his possible transfer by the club doctor who threatened to make public his medical history. Perhaps not surprisingly, a journalist from the tabloid paper, *The Sun*, was particularly insistent in asking for the identification of this player; more surprisingly, and perhaps even more disgracefully, we were even asked by the editor of an academic journal to identify some of our interviewees. Needless to say, we refused to comply with all such requests.

As part of our attempt to generate a public debate on our findings, we also sent copies of the report to the General Medical Council (GMC), which is the regulatory body for medical practitioners in the UK. In our covering letter to the GMC, we drew attention to the many breaches of confidence, which constitute a clear breach of medical ethics, which we documented in the report. In their reply, the GMC indicated that they were concerned about these issues and that, if they were provided with more information about the player who was 'blackmailed' by the club doctor, they would investigate with a view to possible disciplinary proceedings against the club doctor concerned. However, we indicated that we would not identify the player involved or the club for which he played, since this would have involved breaking our own guarantee of anonymity.

There is no doubt that the publicity which the report received heaped a great deal of pressure on the FA to improve the organization of club medical services and Alan Hodson, the spokesperson for the FA in this area, struggled in media interviews to defend a system which was riddled with bad practice. And the assessment of our colleague in risk management about the effectiveness of publicity proved correct; just two months after the report was published, the *Sunday Times* (30th January 2000) reported that, in the wake of the PFA report, the FA had announced that it was intending to introduce new guidelines, to be distributed to clubs, dealing with potential conflicts of interest and medical confidentiality. One year later, in February 2001, the FA published their *Guidelines for Medical and Support Staff,* which focused in particular on issues relating to medical confidentiality (Football Association, 2001).

Two years later, the British Medical Association, in the section on sports medicine in its handbook, *Medical Ethics Today,* drew upon the PFA research with particular reference to the problems which we had documented in relation to medical confidentiality and it emphasized that:

> Ethically, sports doctors need to be aware that their chief loyalty is to their patients, and that, contractual obligations notwithstanding, the duty of medical confidentiality remains unchanged.

In a further reference to the PFA research, it noted that players 'who have sustained injuries may come under pressure from managers to continue to play' and that this 'may be the case even when continuing to play may exacerbate injuries or incur risks of long term damage'. In this context, it emphasized that:

> the doctor's chief obligation must be to the long term health and wellbeing of individual players. In such a situation, doctors must inform both the player and manager of the risks involved so that both parties can make an informed decision about whether play should continue
>
> *(British Medical Association, 2003: 596)*

It was of course pleasing to see that our research had had some impact on policy, but as we wrote shortly after the FA announced its new guidelines, they represented a 'welcome first step' but no more than that, because while creating the guidelines is relatively easy, implementation is more difficult and we identified several structural obstacles to effective implementation (Waddington and Roderick, 2002). Perhaps it is time, a decade later, for a re-study.

Notes

1   I have tried elsewhere to theorize the structural context of sports medicine in order to explain why medicine is practised differently, more competently and/or more ethically in non-sports contexts (Waddington, 2012).

2   It is interesting to note that, several years after our research, Celia Brackenridge reported many problems with the FA when carrying out research on child welfare in football on behalf of the FA. She notes that while 'the football community was, in the main, helpful and cooperative ... there were also occasions where our fieldworkers faced rudeness, including from people in paid positions and/or positions of significant authority within the FA' (Brackenridge *et al*, 2007: 192).

SPORTS MEDICINE GOES UNDER THE KNIFE: THE DISSECTION OF ATHLETE HEALTHCARE

Dominic Malcolm

I remember 1998 very vividly. It was during this time that Ivan Waddington and Martin Roderick led a research project (with contributions from Graham Parker and Rav Naik) funded by the Professional Footballers' Association (PFA). The project consisted of interviewing current and former professional footballers, football club doctors and physiotherapists, and a postal questionnaire sent to football club doctors. The research not only came to form the basis of an impressive range and number of publications (Roderick, 2006a, 2006b, 2006c, 2004; Roderick *et al.*, 2000; Waddington, 2000, 2002; Waddington and Roderick, 2002; Waddington *et al.*, 1999; Waddington *et al.*, 2001), but was a significant stimuli for a body of research into what might broadly be defined as the social organization of sports medicine (Malcolm and Safai, 2012). Like Waddington and Roderick, I worked at the University of Leicester's Centre for Research into Sport and Society (CRSS) at this time. I share(d) with them a commitment to the figurational sociology of Norbert Elias. I would become one of those researchers inspired to explore this area further.

These memories are vivid partly because of the context in which the research took place, and partly because of the nature of the research itself. The CRSS was a small and tight-knit group, numbering in the region of a dozen academic and administrative staff. We regularly had lunch together and talked about sport and sociological matters. As 'the PFA research' gathered momentum, it came to dominate our discussions. While careful to protect interviewees' anonymity, Waddington and/or Roderick would discuss snippets of the research data with an eager and attentive audience – the sometimes shocking details of player prognoses, coaching coercion and medical mismanagement. Our interest was not only stimulated by the sociological significance of the emerging data, or even the potential social impact of the research, but also because of the resonance of some genuinely moving stories. Unlike the vast majority of 'risk-pain-injury' research, this focused on the lived experiences of *professional* sportspeople. Moreover, the research exposed the precarious nature of the 'dream' of being a professional athlete. It remains personal to me as a formative period in my development as an academic.

I relay this background as a way of addressing a key epistemological point which has particular resonance for me as a figurational sociologist. Critics of figurational sociology (e.g. Hargreaves, 1992; Giulianotti, 2004) have tended to position the perspective as essentially underpinned by a positivist epistemology. In part, this perception stems from Elias's (1987) use of the concept of involvement and detachment. While Elias used these terms as a way of circumventing traditional social science debates polarizing researchers into two oppositional groups – those who attempt to re-create natural science methodologies and those who reject such an 'aspiration' as unobtainable – this goal is frequently overlooked. Rather, greater emphasis has been placed on Elias's attempt to demonstrate that 'more adequate' human knowledge has developed in conjunction with greater human capacity for 'detachment'. There is not scope to fully flesh out or to evaluate the veracity of this position here (see instead Malcolm, 2011). The more significant point for present purposes is that this position has led other aspects of Elias's argument to become obscured. In particular, Elias strongly recommended that researchers focus their efforts on areas of social life with which they are (already) personally engaged and, following a 'detour via detachment', undertake 'secondary involvement' in order to use their research to improve social conditions. To this end, it is important to note Waddington and Roderick's close personal involvement with football, the latter briefly playing in the pre-Premiership first division, before 'retiring' to pursue higher education and ultimately an academic career. Waddington and Roderick would not – could not – have generated such research had they not cared a great deal.

What did Waddington *et al.* find? The conclusion to the preliminary report (Waddington *et al.*, 1999) highlighted the widespread failure of professional football clubs to invest adequately in the medical services provided to players. This was exemplified by the propensity within football clubs to employ former players as physiotherapists. For many, their highest professional qualification was the English Football Association (FA) 'Diploma in the Treatment of Injuries'. Consequently, around half of all football club physiotherapists were not eligible to work in the British National Health Service. (Indeed on reflection it is a moot point whether the term 'physiotherapist' was always appropriate in this context.) It further pointed to the absence of a clearly defined role for medical personnel in football clubs and the non-standardized nature of the division of labour between medical and coaching staff. These factors led to variations in the ethical standards maintained by healthcare professionals in the sport. The initial tranche of publications explored the social relations in professional football which conspired to produce a culture of 'playing hurt', the methods of appointment and qualifications of football club doctors and physiotherapists, and the problems and issues raised in managing medical confidentiality in the football club setting. Subsequently, the authors explored the importance of 'uncertainty', 'stigma' and 'careers' in understanding the working lives of professional footballers.

Like all good research, the work of Waddington *et al.* was also to have an important academic legacy. Their research took place in a context where: (a) an interest in the bodies of athletes; (b) a questioning of the *a priori* assumption that sport participation unproblematically improved health; and (c) disquiet over the widespread tolerance of pain and injury, were all developing. Their work added to and fuelled this field.

Most significantly for me, however, the research was amongst the first to radically critique the 'practice' of sports medicine and to introduce a fundamental principle of the sociology of medicine to the sociology of sport; namely, that medical professionals do not necessarily do what they say, or live up to their own self-proclaimed standards. My own work with Ken Sheard (Malcolm and Sheard, 2002) transposed the scrutiny of football doctors and physiotherapists (as well as the athletic subculture) onto their rugby union counterparts. Shortly after, Parissa Safai (2003), whose supervisor Peter Donnelly was a frequent visitor to the CRSS in the late 1990s, published work from her Ph.D. illustrating the negotiations which characterized relations between athletes and clinicians in Canadian college sport. Nancy Theberge (2008; 2009), Lynley Anderson (2009) and Andrea Scott (2012; Malcolm and Scott, 2011) all produced work which could only emerge (at least in the particular form that it did) in the aftermath of the PFA report. The legacy of Waddington *et al.* therefore extends geographically from British to New Zealand and Canadian sport, and theoretically to questions of occupational development, multi-disciplinary working practice and professional ethics. That is to say, it is my view that the most enduring academic legacy of this body of work is the 'revelation' that medical care in sport simply did not function in accordance with the principles more generally accepted for this, or related, professions.

But what also marks out this research project as distinctive is the social impact it would subsequently have, pre-empting by a decade the 'impact' agenda for academic research in the UK. Waddington and Roderick actively sought publicity. They did so precisely because of their 'involvement' (in the Eliasian sense) in the research. That is to say, they courted media attention because they thought that their findings were socially significant and that the human condition would be improved by knowledge dissemination. Consequently the day the report was launched was frenzied. The findings were covered in all the English national daily newspapers. BSkyB's television news channel ran the story every 30 minutes throughout the day. Unfortunately, one of the physiotherapists BSkyB chose to highlight *had* been a participant in the research and angrily (and wrongly) assumed that the researchers had reneged on their promise of confidentiality and given his name to the press. Journalists from various papers (and indeed subsequently the editor of one academic journal) wanted to know the names of the players whose cases were discussed in the report, and some began to offer not insignificant amounts of money to have those names exclusively revealed. Waddington and Roderick's commitment to the research ethics of their own professional body (the British Sociological Association) meant that all such approaches were rejected.

The FA's initial and public response was predictably defensive. Their 'defence' was that the report exaggerated the poor, and overlooked the good, practice in football. It was 'predictable' in that this position was premised on the mentality that 'only "football people" understand football'. But away from the glare of publicity, the response within the sports medicine community was rather more measured. Letters published in the *British Journal of Sports Medicine* were largely supportive. Those practising in the area were receptive to the obvious implications for reform. Indeed I suspect that some significant remedial action was either directly instigated or accelerated by this research. Sports physiotherapy in the UK has developed exponentially since the late 1990s and I doubt that many, if any, leading football clubs are now primarily served by such poorly qualified 'physiotherapists'. I similarly think that it could not be a coincidence that the British Olympic Association's medical committee published guidelines regarding medical confidentiality issues in the sporting workplace just a year after the PFA report was released. I would also think that the report's criticisms galvanized the efforts of many British Association of Sport and Exercise Medicine members to have their sub-discipline recognized as a speciality by the state (as it subsequently was in 2005).

While I have no doubts about the scholarly and societal value of this research it would be remiss of me not to ask what researchers can learn from its design and methodology. I do not say this because I want to undermine the good work that has been done. Rather, I do so because all social scientists should seek to build on and develop existing research. I think that two points can be made in this regard. First, a key finding of the research – one which gained considerable media attention and probably had the most significant long-term impact on professional footballers' health – was the 'under-qualification' of many physiotherapists. This finding essentially stemmed from the survey responses of club doctors. While it was corroborated through interviews with physiotherapists, I think on reflection that a survey of physiotherapists would also have been valuable. A cornerstone of assessing validity is to ask whether the information obtained is derived in the most appropriate way and/or from the most appropriate source. Second, one could ask whether other aspects of the behaviour of managers and players should have been considered. What are the pressures on managers which lead them to curtail medical autonomy? Similarly, in what ways do athletes contribute to their own medical mismanagement? How does athletes' behaviour contribute to the disempowerment of those charged with their healthcare? These were among the questions which Ken Sheard and I posed as we set out on a research project that closely drew upon the design of the 'PFA research', but we did so only because of the (sometimes serendipitous) findings of Waddington and colleagues. Whilst we learnt a lot from incorporating physiotherapists and coaches more directly in our research, we only did so because Waddington *et al.* had inadvertently discovered something about the division of labour within sports medicine, and within sports clubs, that no one had anticipated.

Reconsideration of this research leads me to one final reflection on the importance of teamwork in academic research. This project was the product of the unintended and unforeseen convergence of various career trajectories. Ivan Waddington had started his academic career as a sociologist of medicine before developing an interest in the sociology of sport and sports medicine in particular (e.g. Waddington, 1996). Post-playing career, Martin Roderick was exploring ideas about pain and injury in sport in the development of a Ph.D. (Roderick, 1998). Graham Parker was a former professional footballer and a member of the PFA who met Waddington and Roderick when he enrolled as a student at the CRSS. Rav Naik was a doctor working with Sheffield Wednesday Football Club whose clinic was highlighted in the PFA report as a model of good practice. Each brought different skills, attributes and resources to the project. It was surely this interesting mix of practitioner, former professionals and academics from different backgrounds that made this research socially and intellectually valuable.

2

DARWIN'S ATHLETES:
A RETROSPECTIVE AFTER 15 YEARS

John Hoberman

Introduction: The origins of *Darwin's Athletes*

This essay is the author's account of the origins, reception, and afterlife of *Darwin's Athletes: How Sport has Damaged Black America and Preserved the Myth of Race* (Hoberman, 1997). The purposes of the book, according to the first Preface, were to explore 'the cultural complexities of race inside the sports world', to dissolve the 'taboo' that wrapped the topic of racial athletic aptitude in 'a shroud of fear', and 'to produce a socially useful analysis of black subjugation to white institutions and the racial folklore that sustains it' (Hoberman, 1997: xii). This account of the stated goals of the book was followed by some brief reflections on what cultural anthropologists today would call my 'positionality' in relation to what and whom I was writing about. Who was I to be offering a public analysis of contentious social issues that were loaded with racial tensions? Was I sufficiently trained to take on the responsibility of carrying out a project that might somehow exacerbate the already troubled state of American race relations? I might have replied that two decades of research and writing in sports studies, and having twice taught a racially integrated university course on 'Race and Sport in African-American Life', qualified me to write this book. But this response would have been inadequate, since formal qualifications alone do not produce ambitious or interesting books. One can speculate about factors that make interesting research possible. The author who embarked upon *Darwin's Athletes* was a broadly educated person whose interests and publications included history, literature, biological science, and the social studies any sports scholar must engage with. Formal, as opposed to autodidactic, study of African-American history and culture might have been a good preparation for writing *Darwin's Athletes*. Still, I am not convinced that formal study in this field would necessarily have been an advantage. Creative research is a profoundly autodidactic activity that can benefit from not having absorbed standard doctrines and perspectives. I was deeply involved in an African-American studies curriculum, but it was a course of study I formulated on my own. Fifteen years later, the major deficit I see in this author is a lack of understanding of American racial etiquette a less segregated life might have taught him.

A retrospective search for the origins of *Darwin's Athletes* must naturally go deeper than the author's stated intentions. I wrote *Darwin's Athletes* more quickly, and with greater emotional intensity, than any of my other books. There was something urgent about this project which I saw no need to analyze at that time. The deeper sources of the book I would describe as follows: the first was my racially segregated life as a child during the 1950s. The second was the experience of being in Berkeley, California, during the late 1960s and early 1970s at a time of social upheaval; Berkeley made critical thinking a habit. The third development that occurred many years later was my decision in 1993 to teach 'Race and Sport in African-American Life' at the University of Texas (UT) at Austin. My interactions with these racially integrated groups of students amounted to my belated racial integration into American society.

Some personal background

Many white adolescents at this time experienced their morsels of racial integration with black age-group peers in the context of sports. In my case, there were no black team-mates because there was exactly one black student in our high school by 1960. As a member of the track and cross country teams, I competed in races which included black runners from high schools in other towns, and I remember that our star had a comradely relationship with a top black runner from another school. My friend Steve, who was more talented than I was, had a friendly rivalry with a black teenager whose ability matched his own. As Steve's best friend, I would have known if he and his black rival did any socializing, and I am sure they did not. This was event-appropriate racial mixing. What is more, the difference in socio-economic levels could have made for awkward home visits. These sporting rivalries promoted instead a transitory bonding that lasted as long as the competitions in which they originated. Our family lived in a prosperous suburban bubble about 15 miles north of Harlem, which I remember as a mysterious and dangerous fantasyland of mesmerizing squalor and awe-inspiring black music. The other black people I had personal contact with were the black women who at times worked and lived in our home, at a time when the middle-class could still afford (coloured) domestic 'help'.

The humiliation that results from having relationships with servants became an indelible part of my childhood. Our parents were racial liberals, so the fact that these women were black servants made these feelings of shame that much deeper. Small wonder that I was emotionally crippled about race relations for decades afterwards. It was the 1990s, namely, teaching the race and sport course, along with the *Darwin's Athletes* experience, that finally liberated me from those early feelings of shame and humiliation about my distorted relationship to black people. In fact, a need to exorcize those feelings may well have been the reason I was able to write

Darwin's Athletes as quickly and with such emotional urgency. I do not remember thinking in 1995 about why this project possessed me the way it did. In this sense, I was one more white man seizing an opportunity to work off his feelings about blacks, although I do not think that was the only force that drove the writing of the book. As for motives, one of the ironies of the *Darwin's Athletes* experience is that, during the 1980s and 1990s, I somehow managed (although not by conscious design) to avoid reading the anthropological and multicultural literatures that are filled with caveats about how professional white observers of non-whites have an obligation to scrutinize their own motives and show the requisite humility when claiming that they understand the Other. Today I am in a position to appreciate the consequences of that period of ignorance.

It is difficult for me to describe in a coherent way the impact of the Berkeley scene while I lived there as a graduate student from 1966 to 1972. In 1966 the choice between Harvard and the University of California at Berkeley was an easy one. The Berkeley Free Speech Movement of 1964 had conferred legendary status on the university and the counter-culture that proliferated inside Berkeley spilled into the black precincts of Oakland to the south, and made San Francisco the mecca of hippies, the celebrated drug culture, and the vanguard of rock 'n' roll. Berkeley combined a frothing politics of anti-establishment dissent with self-deluding fantasies of communal harmony, a ragtag swarm of adolescents and older vagrants living on the margins, the marijuana and LSD culture, cultic devotion to local musicians, the chic hooliganism of the Hells Angels, and a bohemian squalor that arose out of drug dealing, the phony importuning beggars lining Telegraph Avenue, and a vague sense that in this unhinged place just about anything was possible.

Young black men were one part of the scene along Telegraph Avenue, the counter-cultural thoroughfare that covered four blocks and then became light-urban sprawl before it disappeared over the horizon into working-class Oakland. But the young blacks who hung out on Telegraph did not constitute a racial group in a political sense. They were tourists like everyone else, looking, amidst the restless and anomic crowds, for whatever it was they wanted to find. The black man I remember was known on the street as Super Spade, a dark Hercules who paraded his sculpted torso down Telegraph with two fancy dogs on a leash. The rumour was that a Hells Angel who had taken offence at Super Spade's flamboyant style went after him and wound up taking a thorough beating in the process. One day in 1968 or 1969 there was a rumour that the brutal and racist Oakland police were about to carry out a raid on the Black Panthers' stronghold across the city line in Oakland. I wondered whether a real slaughter was going to occur, and a call was heard for volunteers to interpose themselves between the besieged Panthers and the blood-thirsty police. I remember deciding that I was not going to be participating in this event that, as it turned out, never happened at all.

For me and for many others immersion in this world was a transformative experience that changed one's outlook on life. It altered one's understanding of what life was for and what it could be. It called into question the conventional wisdom that had dictated the courses of many well-ordered lives like my own.

And it radically altered the course of my intellectual life. It was in Berkeley that I met the pioneering and courageous sports radical Jack Scott. And it was in Berkeley that I followed the exploits of the young and courageous Harry Edwards and his campaign for a black athletes' boycott of the 1968 Mexico City Olympic Games. I spent the summer of 1968 in Mexico City and witnessed the huge political demonstrations that preceded the pre-Olympic massacre of 2 October 1968. These experiences were preparing the ground for redirecting the course of my life into the field of sports studies.

In January 1971, while enrolled in a graduate programme in Scandinavian Languages and Literatures, I walked into the university library resolved to embark upon a journey into the world of sports studies, or what there was of it more than 40 years ago. Making this crossing into the realm of the sweat and physicality of the jock culture required that I overcome a revulsion against the world of the locker room and the vulgarity and stupidity it represented to me. The gratifications of my own experience as a high-school athlete somehow existed in another dimension. The decision to devote myself to sports studies meant crossing over into alien territory, but that was what I wanted. The final conversion occurred five years later while I was an assistant professor at Harvard, where I would eventually teach a seminar called 'Sport and Political Ideology' that several years later turned into my first book.

I do not remember when I decided to teach 'Race and Sport in African-American Life' for the African-American Studies Programme at UT. By this point I had done enough research to include a chapter called 'Darwin's Athletes' in *Mortal Engines: The Science of Performance and the Dehumanization of Sport* (Hoberman, 1992), and it is reasonable to assume that this initial work on the history of ideas about racial athletic aptitude helped to catalyze my interest in teaching in this area. By the time I first taught 'Race and Sport' in the spring of 1993, I had also served on a couple of racially integrated committees connected to a multiculturalism initiative at UT that was encountering significant resistance from about half of the faculty. There was, in fact, a reason for my unawareness of the multicultural and anthropological literatures that I should have been absorbing at that time. During this period I was immersed in acquiring the knowledge of performance-enhancing drugs that went into *Mortal Engines* and subsequent publications.

I taught 'Race and Sport' in 1993, 1995, and 1998. Later on the African-American Faculty who devised their own syllabi taught this material in their own ways. Teaching classes composed of more-or-less equal numbers of black and white students was a transformative experience. For the first month of the 1993 semester I experienced anxiety pains in my stomach while walking to class. This physical discomfort signalled a new and stressful situation that was caused, not by overt student resistance to the white instructor, but by anxiety about my reception that was rooted in what I have called the 'crippling' racial syndrome I had acquired as a child. Over time the psychosomatic symptom disappeared and my comfort in the classroom increased. While I did not know a lot about what was going on inside the heads of my black students, there was at least some interest in what was going on inside of mine. A most memorable encounter occurred in a small room where seven young black women had arrived for a review session. They sat on one side of a table, and I sat across from them. The first words from one of these unsmiling faces were: 'Why are you doing this?'

How *Darwin's Athletes* became controversial

Darwin's Athletes became a controversial book largely because a small and vocal group of African-American academics bitterly objected to a white author's demoralizing interpretation of what black involvement in sport had meant for African Americans. The severity of this criticism was due in part to the fact that *Darwin's Athletes* is a one-sided book; my purpose was to reveal and explore negative effects of African-American involvement in sport that had been neglected by virtually all commentators other than the famous sports activist and sports sociologist Harry Edwards, who eventually retired from an academic career at the University of California, Berkeley. Edwards' (1973) argument that African Americans had become over-invested in sports and its purported benefits for black Americans dates from the early 1970s.[1] He continued to promote this view for more than two decades, until he eventually concluded that the situations of many young black men had become so desperate that they should be encouraged to pursue *any* potentially useful activity, including sports (Ryan, 1998).

Black academics who specialize in the study of sport have not publicly embraced Edwards' original argument about the detrimental effects of sport on the black community. This group is much more inclined to accentuate the assumed positive effects that *Darwin's Athletes* briefly acknowledges but mostly neglects by design. The book's one-sidedness was a polemical stratagem that succeeded in provoking readers to take a hard look at Edwards' neglected thesis about the social costs of sports to black America. More specifically, some black sports scholars want to believe in the political potential of the black athlete. The sheer numbers of elite black athletes in high-profile roles tempt these academics (and some sportswriters) to believe that there must be a way to convert black athletic achievement into social advancement for black people. For these people the unrelenting scepticism of *Darwin's Athletes* was a provocation that merited a full-throated reply.

There is a temptation to reduce the response to *Darwin's Athletes* to the voices of its angriest critics. This was the public drama that helped to animate discussion of the book and both amazed and appalled more sympathetic white colleagues (Guttmann, 2003).[2] In fact, the book received a mixed response and provoked a wide range of published assessments about which one can generalize in the following way. Whites approved of the book more than blacks, but not unanimously. Similarly, while blacks disapproved of the book more than whites, black opinion was split in a way white opinion was not. Black sports scholars presented a united front of opposition to the book. While a few black journalists praised the book, others tended to be cautious without expressing the hostility that unified the academics.

Conspicuously absent from the hostile discussion of *Darwin's Athletes* were Harry Edwards and the scepticism about sport's benefits for blacks that he had broadcast for years in mass-circulation publications such as *Psychology Today* (Edwards, 1973) and *Ebony* (Edwards, 1988, 1992). It is not surprising that Edwards' dissent from the more optimistic doctrine of sports' benefits did not expose him to the hostility and resentment that greeted *Darwin's Athletes*. He had already earned credibility as an advocate for black athletes as an activist who deserved much of the credit for the Black Power demonstration at the 1968 Mexico City Olympic Games. He has remained active for many years as a speaker and as a consultant on race relations for professional sports organizations. No white man could have occupied these roles. Similarly, one lesson of the *Darwin's Athletes* controversy is that no white man would be allowed to play Edwards' spoiler role as a sports sceptic without paying a price for his discouraging message.

The historical context of *Darwin's Athletes*

The *Darwin's Athletes* controversy is best understood in its historical and comparative contexts. From an historical standpoint, this racial controversy had been preceded by others involving white authors who had provoked strong reactions from black critics. Any attentive historian of American race relations could have predicted much about the response to the book as well as the specific accusations that would be directed against its author. Like other white intellectuals who had preceded me in the role of perceived interloper, I was resented as an overbearing white man who, in the words of one critic, was 'telling black folks what to do'. From a comparative perspective, critical responses to my book about race in the sports world resemble in significant ways the collective denunciation of William Styron's (1967) novel *The Confessions of Nat Turner* and black commentators' criticisms of Richard Sudhalter (1999) and his book *Lost Chords: White Musicians and Their Contribution to Jazz, 1915–1945*. In this sense, it does not matter whether the white author has produced a social analysis of race and sport, an historical novel about a black protagonist, or music history that argues for the inclusion of white musicians in the jazz pantheon. These white interpretations of black lives and race relations engender a deep resistance among many blacks that needs to be understood as something other than a reflexive hostility to anything 'white'.

The expectation of hostile or incompetent interference in their lives by whites is all but universal among African Americans. A more sophisticated author would have understood this and might have adjusted his presentation of ideas and evidence accordingly. Lacking this understanding, I made the choice, in conformity with my Berkeley-trained intellectual temperament, to be as direct and confrontational as my notion of decency would allow, in the service of persuading an interracial audience that it had much to learn about the ultimate consequences of imposing an athletic identity on black human beings. Given the bitter history of American race relations, it was inevitable that black critics would call into question that sense of decency along with my intellectual competence.

The historical context for understanding the response to *Darwin's Athletes* is the emergence during the 1960s of a self-assertive African-American intelligentsia that was finally able to challenge the liberal politicians and social scientists who had monopolized the formulation of policies to advance black interests. The unprecedented public profile of these black intellectuals was one of the achievements of the Civil Rights movement of this era. Their relationship with the white liberal establishment was dramatically transformed in 1965 by the unintended public release of a US government document that became known as the Moynihan Report.

The publication in 1965 of Daniel Patrick Moynihan's 55-page report titled *The Negro Family: The Case for National Action* ('the Moynihan Report') ignited an enormous controversy over the ethics and propriety of discussing the African-American condition in a public forum (Moynihan, 1965). It also raised fundamental questions about the motivations and methodologies of the social scientists who were conducting research on the African-American population. Following the initial controversy it became clear that the relationship between African Americans and the sociologists and anthropologists who studied them was both problematic and widely resented. Black and white liberal resistance to the Moynihan Report marked a turning point in American race relations within the intelligentsia, because it produced a crisis in the racial politics of the public representation and discussion of African Americans. This new era of African-American self-assertion complicated relations between black intellectuals and the white liberal intellectuals who had long thought of themselves as indispensable allies of their black counterparts.

A profound effect of the Moynihan Report was to bring to public attention the fact that many white 'experts' had made careers out of studying blacks. 'The study of human behavior by various disciplines', a black psychiatrist had noted in 1938, 'is essentially one dominated by the more academic minds of the white races' (Prudhomme, 1938: 190). This consequence of the enormous imbalance of power between blacks and whites has received less attention than it deserves, but not because black intellectuals have not recognized their predicament. Frantz Fanon wryly observed in 1952: 'For some time there has been much talk about the Negro. A little too much. The Negro would like to be dropped, so that he may regroup his forces, his authentic forces' (Fanon, 1952). Like the Committee on the Study of the Negro of the 1920s, the April 1964 conference on the Negro in America was an all-white affair (see also Harris, 1982). A year later James Farmer of the Congress for Racial Equality (CORE) declared that he had had enough, and 'that the cocktail hour on the "Negro Question" is over and that we are sick unto death of being analyzed, mesmerized, bought, sold and slobbered over while the same evils that are the ingredients of our oppression go unattended' (Farmer; cited in Rainwater and Yancey, 1967: 410). At the November 1965 White House conference on race and social policy, one long-time observer of the Civil Rights movement noted that the Moynihan Report had created what he called 'a new mood' among black militants:

> There was a total refusal by most of the Negroes [I heard] to discuss *anything* that might remotely imply that there was anything whatsoever that Negroes,

individually or collectively, should be doing or needed to do. [One leader's] formulation, which was repeated *ad nauseam*, was that race is entirely a white man's problem that could only be solved by white men, and that it was intolerable that the government had all these white men sitting around discussing 'our problem'.

(*Rainwater and Yancey, 1967: 252*)

The other problem, of course, was that the vast majority of 'experts' on racial matters were white.

African-American scepticism about white social scientists has a long tradition. James Baldwin, the great predecessor of the militant black intellectuals of the 1960s, was protesting against the sociological dehumanizing of black people in 1951 (Baldwin, 1955: 25–8). An important difference between Baldwin and the rejectionist 'new mood' of the 1960s is evident in Baldwin's discussion of 'the Negro in America' from the perspective of a collective American 'we' that represents both Baldwin and his white readers. Ten years later Baldwin wrote: 'The [early black] student movement depends, at bottom, on an act of faith, an ability to see, beneath the cruelty and hysteria and apathy of white people, their bafflement and pain and essential decency. This is superbly difficult' (Baldwin, 1961: 69–70). This brave attempt to make an accommodation for the sins of white folk lived on in the work of Martin Luther King, Jr., but it had no role to play in the work of the militant black intelligentsia of the 1960s. Black resentment of white social scientists fitted the 'new mood' perfectly and finally began to redress the grotesquely skewed relationship between white experts and their black subjects. If anyone grasped the force of the 'new mood', it was the much-abused Daniel Patrick Moynihan. 'Now, with only a few exceptions', he commented in 1968, 'social science studies of Negroes are carried out by whites, and we are not to wonder that more and more the cry goes out from the slums that they are tired of that white magic and will listen no more'. He even went so far as to advise that social scientists be trained like psychiatrists 'to anticipate and accept hostility' from the people whose lives they studied (Moynihan, 1968: 40).

The Moynihan scandal was the Big Bang event that did more than any other single factor to create the universe of political correctness we inhabit to this day. Moynihan, then Assistant Secretary of Labor to President Lyndon Johnson and a political liberal, composed a private memorandum on what he called 'the deterioration of the Negro family' and its role in preventing the social advancement of black Americans. Any document of this kind required an intimate look at the lives of black people, including 'disintegrating Negro marriages' (Moynihan, 1965: 5), illegitimacy rates, and fatherless children. The fateful concept he used to encapsulate these misfortunes and misbehaviours was 'the tangle of pathology' (Moynihan, 1965: 29) that had imprisoned black people in their desperate predicament. Magnifying the social impact of the Report was its implicit refutation of a Black Power movement emphasizing black strengths. In addition, the major media were broadcasting its contents in a selective and sensationalizing manner. The full text of the Report was not even available to the public until 1967. By this time the ideo-logical battle lines had hardened, and for many blacks and white liberals, mention-ing the Report took on the character of an epithet.

The Moynihan Report remains the most important chapter in the history of the estrangement between African Americans and the social sciences, defined as sociology, anthropology, and history. The history of its reception and eventual rehabilitation is at the same time a history of the 'politically correct' norms that developed in its aftermath and have exerted a profound influence on our social and intellectual lives. As the sociologists Douglas S. Massey and Robert J. Sampson (2009: 9) recently noted, the Report was quickly 'consigned to the netherworld of the politically incorrect, where it would remain for decades', although not until it had left 'several unfortunate and entirely dysfunctional legacies'. William Julius Wilson and others have lamented the stunting effects of the Moynihan controversy on the development of social scientific research on race relations in the United States. The influence of the racially conservative social scientist Charles Murray derives in part from the sociological vacuum that was left behind in the wake of liberal social scientists' abandonment of the study of African-American social pro-blems. As Wilson stated in 2009, the 'backlash against the report essentially shut down meaningful conversation about the role of culture in shaping racial outcomes' (Wilson, 2009: 96).

Post-Moynihan racial discourse

Darwin's Athletes was launched into a post-Moynihan world that had rewritten the rules of American racial etiquette for the intelligentsia. Three years after the Report erupted into the American racial drama, Irving Howe deplored the ferocity of the attack on Moynihan: 'It was as if, somehow, to discuss the Negro family in public were a breach of good manners' (Howe, 1968: 14). Howe saw this sort of fastidiousness as condescension toward blacks. What he did not see were the decades of racially offensive social science that blacks had been expected to accept without complaint. From now on, however, full-throated complaints about white misbehaviours would be the order of the day. In their famous sociological study *Beyond the Melting Pot* (1963), Nathan Glazer and Moynihan had conceded this very point: 'The defense of a minority group and its interests may legitimately be shrill and insistent when it is powerless and weak and there is no one to listen; thus much may be excused the Negroes' regarding their loud protests of the early Civil Rights period (Glazer and Moynihan, 1970: 177). Little did Moynihan suspect that this eminently fair standard would soon be applied to him.

The post-Moynihan world of racial discourse attempts to enforce two kinds of political correctness. The first forbids racially defamatory speech, such as racial epithets, that are regarded as dehumanizing and of no possible social value; this prohibition has a long history that antedates the Moynihan controversy. The second, and more problematic, type has condemned sociological and, especially, 'cultural' interpretations of minority values and behaviours that minorities or their defenders may find unflattering, denigrating, or 'pathologizing'. While the Moynihan controversy did not create this kind of political correctness, it played an enormous role in establishing its authority for regulating the relationship between black people and the white social scientists or policymakers whose thinking and behaviour affect black lives. Mitchell Duneier has called the enforcers of these norms 'politically correct stereotype guardians' who elevate their own 'innocence over evidence as an entitlement to generalize' about race matters in American society (Duneier, 1992: 138). These are the people who went after Moynihan and his alleged racism in 1965. The historian Stanley M. Elkins, who had taken an ideological beating similar to the one inflicted on Moynihan following the publication of his *Slavery* (1959), disparagingly called Moynihan's critics 'prehensile white liberals who were beginning to try on "radical" attitudes' (Elkins, 1975: 42). How much did these critics really care about black people and their feelings, and to what extent was Moynihan serving as a surrogate for the residual racist who often dwelled in the heart of a white liberal of this era? This was a time (1965) when a popular liberal journalist could write in a best-selling book about the 'biological anarchy' (White, 1965: 227) taking place in 'the zoological tenements' of Harlem (White, 1965: 229). A year earlier a liberal Democratic former mayor of Philadelphia had declared that: 'The time has come for the Negro to stop feeling so damned sorry for himself' (*US News & World Report*, 1964: 6). In fact, vocal black disdain for the white liberal became a defining characteristic of the post-Moynihan era. For years afterwards white 'liberal' authors writing about black problems enjoyed no ideological immunity from black criticisms of their competence or their motives. The author of *Darwin's Athletes* found in time that this rule applied to him, along with some other white intellectuals who aspired to illuminate, or even ameliorate, race relations in the United States.

It is important to recognize that 'post-Moynihan' racial discourse did not just appear overnight after the Report was leaked from the White House in the summer of 1965. A number of more humane white observers of black life were publishing before the Moynihan controversy, but they were exceptional when compared with more typical white liberal views of blacks. What is more, most of these relatively insightful people demonstrated their own limited understanding of black–white relations even as they exceeded the modest societal race-norms of their times. The white psychiatrist Frederic Wertham may have been an exception to this rule. 'We're not here to make a study of the Negro', he said in his Harlem clinic in 1940, thereby demonstrating a striking degree of personal and professional modesty (Martin, 1940: 798). The psychoanalysts who published the influential study *The Mark of Oppression: Explorations in the Personality of the American Negro* (Kardiner and Ovesey, 1951) were very conscious of what they were undertaking, but not so sure about what its effects would be. 'In times as troubled as ours', they write, 'the impact of some types of sociological investigation is extremely uncertain and, by the same token, the role of the investigator is correspondingly uneasy'. These authors, like other white authors (including this writer) are, for whatever reasons, willing to take the risk that their 'efforts will be misused for ends [they do] not approve' (Kardiner and Ovesey, 1962: v). This is, when one thinks about it, a curious calculus, and black observers may have questions about how carefully white authors will weigh the perceived risks and benefits of publishing what they have found.

The 'post-Moynihan' racial discourse that continued to evolve after 1965 into what we call 'political correctness' thus became a politically self-conscious genre of writing. Non-black authors would now start respecting black 'sensitivities' and become aware of black people's intellectual self-confidence. 'White intellectuals', Stanley Elkins wrote in 1975 of the pre-Moynihan era, 'had not yet reached the point at which they would feel the need to weigh everything they said for its effect on an emergently aggressive black audience' (Elkins, 1975: 41). White intellectuals and policymakers were to show more modesty and less presumption regarding what black people wanted and needed. In 1968 Moynihan expressed disapproval of 'a certain elitist impulse to manage the lives of the less fortunate' that had become identified with his own career (Moynihan, 1968: 35). White authors sometimes anticipated that their writing would offend black readers.

The most critical reviewers of *Darwin's Athletes* argued that the book violated important 'post-Moynihan' norms to the point of giving offence. In this way, *Darwin's Athletes* offered its own re-enactment of the rupture between white liberals and black activists that had become irreparable by the end of the 1960s. Describing in 1970 the historian Eugene Genovese's defence of William Styron against his black opponents, one observer concluded that: 'In this kind of dispute the middle ground of moderation virtually disappears' (Cunliffe, 1970: 30–1). The demolition of this middle ground was accelerated by the Moynihan Report, and the absence of middle ground is evident in the categorical rejection of *Darwin's Athletes* by certain black reviewers. From their uncompromising perspective, *Darwin's Athletes* revels in (rather than analyzes) unflattering racial folklore about black people, fails to understand important aspects of African-American lives, demonstrates a 'hatred' for black intellectuals, constitutes 'a diatribe of insulting warmed-over racism', and 'is methodologically weak, theoretically suspect, and substantially vacuous and develops no policy recommendations of any worth' (Shropshire and Smith, 1998: 109).[3] As one reviewer put it:

> Essentially, Hoberman has written a 341-page opinion piece. Packed with 53 pages of footnotes and 22 pages of bibliographic references, and filled with academic-sounding jargon from the medical anthropology literature, the book might at first glance appear to be honest scholarship. Ultimately, however, it is nothing more than amusing speculation, imaginative guesswork, and fanciful fiction . . . The book is biased, one-sided, and invidious.
>
> *(Myers, 1998: 881)*[4]

The categorical condemnation of *Darwin's Athletes* can be summarized as follows: the book is racist either by accident or design; the white author is possessed by an unwholesome fascination with racial biology; he does not understand black people or their culture; he presumes to be able to speak on behalf of black people; his work is inferior and receives far more attention than it deserves; he ignores significant black authors and fails to take black sensibilities into account; he ascribes to black people 'pathological' traits that stigmatize them as inferior or damaged beyond repair (see below).

The authors of the Moynihan Report and *Darwin's Athletes,* like so many other white analysts of black-white relationships, offered certain arguments that had originated with black scholars. While academic experts were aware that Moynihan's portrayal of the black family had drawn heavily on the pioneering work of the sociologist E. Franklin Frazier, the media and the public it served had no idea this was the case. The sociologist Orlando Patterson pointed out that some historians who disapproved of Frazier's portrait of the black family, fearful of attacking an Afro-American scholar directly, pilloried Frazier through the surrogate target of the unfortunate Daniel Patrick Moynihan (Patterson, 1998: 46).

Another black thinker who was spared at Moynihan's expense was Dr Kenneth Clark. In 1965 James Farmer wrote:

> As if living in the sewer, learning in the streets and working in the pantry weren't enough of a burden for millions of American Negroes, I now learn that we've caught 'matriarchy', and 'the tangle of Negro pathology' ... a social plague recently diagnosed by Daniel Moynihan in his celebrated report on 'The Negro Family'.
>
> *(Farmer; cited in Rainwater and Yancey, 1967: 409)*

But it was not Daniel Patrick Moynihan who had diagnosed this social plague – it was the famous black psychologist Kenneth Clark, whose *Dark Ghetto* (1965) makes the Moynihan Report read like upbeat reporting by comparison. The 'tangle of pathology' Moynihan's critics wrapped so firmly around his neck came straight out of the black psychologist's grim description of the mean streets of Harlem (Clark, 1965: 106).

In a similar vein, virtually all of the critics who faulted *Darwin's Athletes* for its tactless and misguided intrusions into the black experience simply ignored the book's debt to Harry Edwards, along with his critical analysis of African Americans' feelings about athletic achievement and its purported value to black social advancement. Edwards had complained in 1973 about the 'substantial lack of black expertise and serious black analytical perspectives' that had limited African Americans' understanding of their involvement with sports (Edwards, 1973: 43). Athletics, he said, 'stifles the pursuit of rational alternatives by black people' (Edwards, 1973: 44). Fifteen years later he deplored 'the tragedy of the personal and cultural underdevelopment that afflicts so many among both successful and unsuccessful Black sports aspirants' (Edwards, 1988: 138). Many young blacks, Edwards wrote in 1992, 'emerge from the athletic experience seriously impaired relative to their abilities to compete or to make their way as responsible, productive adults in the broader society' (Edwards, 1992: 128). The critics' refusal to mention Edwards had a transparent motive. Erasing the roles black thinkers have played in the work of white social scientists or cultural historians makes it that much easier for black critics to ascribe racially motivated bias or ignorance to the white authors they have targeted.

It should be noted that Harry Edwards has not reciprocated *Darwin's Athletes'* appreciation of his early writings. Reminded by an interviewer in 1998 that his most conspicuous ideological ally was now the controversial author of *Darwin's Athletes*, Edwards responded by announcing that the position he had argued for 20 years was now irrelevant: 'Those who are calling for the de-emphasis of sports are behind the times or seriously misreading the facts of black life and reality' (Ryan, 1998). In 1997 Edwards had told the audience of a Houston radio station that *Darwin's Athletes* was 'a hoax'; years later he disparaged the book before an audience at the University of Kentucky, thereby joining the camp of the categorical rejectionists.[5] Edwards moderated his criticism in published interviews in 1997 (Cose, 1997) and 2000 (Leonard, 2000). To the best of my knowledge, he has never published a review of the book.

The Confessions of Nat Turner (1967)

The publication of William Styron's novel *The Confessions of Nat Turner* (Styron, 1967) catalyzed a major re-enactment of the Moynihan scandal, including a passionate stigmatizing of the prominent white author by his black critics. Once again a white man had interpreted an intimate dimension of black life, even if in this case the intimate sphere was limited to the inner life of a fictional character. The novel is an account of a slave revolt that occurred in Virginia in 1831, as narrated by its leader in a literary prose Styron has provided to his slave protagonist. Styron and his book enjoyed a brief honeymoon before the storm hit: the book received excellent reviews and won a Pulitzer Prize. Styron received an honorary degree from an historically black college and 'felt gratitude at their acceptance of me', as he later wrote (Row, 2008). What Styron did not understand at that point was that the Moynihan cataclysm had transformed race relations among the intelligentsia, and that what had once appeared to be the normal interracial courtesies were now destabilized and could no longer be counted upon to sustain dialogue. As two white observers put it in 1968, the publication of *Nat Turner* 'dramatically exposes the degree to which communication and dialogue between the black and white communities has completely broken down' (Sitkoff and Wreszin, 1968: 11). Years later Styron lamented that his critics had disregarded 'the gentlemanly rules of polemics' (Styron, 1992: 5).

The assault on Styron arrived in 1968 in the form of *William Styron's Nat Turner: Ten Black Writers Respond* (Clarke, 1968), a short and uncompromising book that wound up on the front page of *The New York Times Book Review*. The condemnation of Styron was even more categorical than the attack on Moynihan, in the sense that a number of prominent black figures had defended Moynihan against the charge of racism when the uproar over the Report broke in 1965 (Rainwater and Yancey, 1967). Styron, however, had no black support.[6] 'No event in recent years has touched and stirred the black intellectual community more than this book', one of his black opponents proclaimed (Hamilton, 1968: vii). One of the charges the writers directed against Styron was that he had appropriated – in effect, stolen and distorted – a black folk hero who had played an important role in sustaining the morale of black Americans. In fact, at the time Styron's novel appeared, the Nat Turner who had been hanged after leading the insurrection was not widely known among the black population (Gross and Bender, 1971: 487). It was Styron's notorious book that made Nat Turner a household name among the black people from whom he had allegedly been 'stolen'.

Styron eventually concluded that rehabilitating his name among African Americans was an impossible task. The fate of Moynihan's reputation among many blacks had been sealed when the tsunami of sensationalized coverage of the Report inundated the American media during the latter half of 1965. For Styron the analogous campaign of defamation occurred during the widespread coverage of *Ten Black Writers Respond* in 1968. In both cases the crude but effective process was to exaggerate the invidious content and character of documents most people had not read and would never read, in part because they had been rendered taboo. In the absence of more accurate information, the verdicts were in before corrective action had any chance to reframe or rehabilitate the authors and their work. A quarter-century after the novel's publication, Styron reflected on what he had not known at that time:

> It would have been inconceivable to me that within a short time I would experience almost total alienation from black people, be stung by their rage, and, finally, be cast as an archenemy of the race, having unwittingly created one of the first politically incorrect texts of our time.
>
> *(Styron, 1992: 435)*

Lost Chords (1999)

The three case studies we have examined so far all involve the written word and the messages or doctrines words can convey. Written media are fertile ground for ideological conflicts as well as the misunderstandings and hostilities they can engender. We have seen the traumatic effects of the Moynihan scandal and other events of that era exacerbate racial tensions in the social sciences and in the literary world, provoking some angry reactions from black critics that have shocked white intellectuals who did not foresee the alienating and even enraging effects white portrayals of black lives could have on black audiences. While the jazz world might seem an unlikely venue for racial dramas and recriminations of this kind, its image as a racially harmonious subculture is deceiving. Public disputes over the origins and quality of jazz played by black and white musicians have been fought out since they began in earnest during the Moynihan era. LeRoi Jones' *Blues People: Negro Music in White America* (1963) set a high standard for pursuing some bitterly contested disputes that continue to this day.

The publication in 1999 of *Lost Chords: White Musicians and Their Contribution to Jazz, 1915–1945,* by the respected white jazz trumpeter and musical biographer

Richard Sudhalter, provoked a mixture of anger and discomfort among both black and white commentators. Prominent black commentators such as Branford Marsalis, Robin D.G. Kelley, and Gerald Early were dismissive. The 900 pages of *Lost Chords*, Marsalis said, did 'not deserve the dignity of a response' (Kelley, 1999; Nelson, 2004). 'At public forums, where he gamely tried to defend his work, Mr. Sudhalter was sometimes mocked and jeered' (Schudel, 2008).

Lost Chords can be understood as an attempt to promote the racial integration of the jazz canon before 1945. But many respondents to the book, and especially musicians, saw another agenda at work. Sudhalter's (1999: xxi) argument that 'the music may not be so much a black American experience as an *American* experience' did not sit well with black practitioners and some jazz aficionados, despite his attempts to acknowledge the black contribution to jazz. Anticipating the political reaction that awaited him, Sudhalter disclaimed any political motive of his own:

> Such a study is anything but an exercise in one-upmanship or retaliation: any attempt to look at the music without regard to such seminal figures as Armstrong, Ellington, Coleman Hawkins, Lester Young, Henry Allen, Sid Catlett, Benny Carter, and the rest would be folly. Their primacy, and the reverence in which they are held, belong to the unquestioned foundation on which the entire edifice rests.
>
> *(Sudhalter, 1999: xxi)*

Yet Sudhalter's homage to the great black jazzmen was not quite enough to neutralize the racial politics that haunts this book. Multiple readers, some or all of whom may be white, detect an undertone of reticence, a qualified rather than unconditional acknowledgement of black artistic primacy, an ultimate refusal to accept their status as immortals. Given the giant reputations at stake, even the appearance of doubts about the sanctity of the jazz pantheon might be construed as disrespect for all that black musicians have meant for the development of jazz. The hostile responders – I doubt that some critics of *Lost Chords* can accurately be called readers – appear to have come to this conclusion.

In March 2001 Sudhalter participated in a three-day symposium at the Masonic Auditorium in San Francisco on the topic of 'Jazz and Race: Black, White and Beyond'. He and his co-panellists, who included the 1960s radical Angela Davis and the jazz critic Nat Hentoff, hoped for 'a lively, civil discussion'. Moderating the event was none other than Harry Edwards, the sports sociologist and jazz aficionado, who, while acknowledging the multi-racial character of jazz, suggested that it was African Americans who had provided 'the leading-edge creativity' (Hamlin, 2001).

Narrative 'tone' and the controversy over 'pathology'

The post-Moynihan era revealed a profound dissatisfaction among black people regarding how white social scientists and other writers had portrayed the black experience. This dissatisfaction now coexisted with the emergence of a black intelligentsia determined to redress the traditional imbalance of power and influence that had promoted what they (often correctly) regarded as the misrepresentation of black people. More equitable forms of black–white dialogue transformed the racial etiquette that now governed most public discussions of racial topics. White commentators became more self-conscious about what they said and how they said it. The 'how' referred to here can be called narrative 'tone'. 'Tone' in this sense can include a multitude of offences, intended or unintended, some of them resulting from authorial temperaments that reject racial etiquette, modify its requirements to suit their own standards, or indulge in stylistic habits that can offend by exaggerating or intensifying what are already discomfiting portrayals of fraught situations. Friends and neutrals alike saw abrasive qualities in Moynihan's prose: 'his weakness for the tantalizing phrase' (*Time*, 1970: 16) such as the 'murderous slum population' (*US News & World Report*, 1970: 58); his 'catalytic approach' (Patterson, 2010: 49) to discussion; his 'fondness for dramatic language, memorable images'; 'Moynihan wanted his statistics to "bleed"' (Rainwater and Yancey, 1967: 176). Such stylistic habits are problematic when it becomes difficult to distinguish between style that sharpens an argument and style that expresses self-indulgence.

A number of reviewers, black and white, hostile or receptive, found the authorial 'tone' of *Darwin's Athletes* problematic or offensive. The *Library Journal* reviewer said the book 'challenges established beliefs in *a thought-provoking, albeit disturbing manner*, offering arguments that are convincing, controversial, and guaranteed to spark debate' (*Library Journal*, cited in Hoberman, 1997; emphases added). 'Much in this book', a white journalist wrote, 'is repugnant by design; Hoberman "scraped the bottom of the racist barrel to show where ethnic folklore comes from"' (Wilkens, 1997). One black reviewer faulted my 'naive ignorance of the sensibilities of African Americans', a criticism with which I must agree if we recognize that the offended group consisted primarily of black sports scholars whose views of sport I should have taken more seriously than I did (Myers, 1998: 880). Once again we must resist the temptation to reduce the response to the book to the commentaries that simply denounced it. Many black readers either did not object to the 'tone' of the book or were willing to accept some discomfort while absorbing its contents. We should also keep in mind that some books *ought* to make readers uncomfortable. What, after all, is the difference between 'thought-provoking' and 'disturbing' or 'offensive'? It is a fact that many white authors have offended many black audiences out of malice or insensitivity or just plain stupidity. But feeling offended is not an infallible indication that an offence originating in malice, insensitivity or stupidity has been committed.

The word 'pathology' has still not recovered from the effects of the Moynihan Report. Half a century after Moynihan borrowed the 'tangle of pathology' image from Kenneth Clark, it still carries associations with the Report's alleged defamation of black people. The term 'pathologizing' is still used as an epithet to signify insensitivity toward or a desire to denigrate black or other vulnerable people. In a similar fashion, the Report that gave the term 'pathology' its toxic celebrity continues to be denounced by many commentators who have never read it.

That being said, it is a fact that an inclination or wish to find pathology is always latent in white diagnoses and interpretations of black lives. This bias is rooted in the invidious comparisons that inhabit the traditional Western racial hierarchy. Primitive forms of racist pathologizing appear in the writings of antebellum plantation physicians and colonial era European travellers to Africa for whom black life itself is a form of pathology. In contrast, the alleged pathologizers of our own era display scholarly or therapeutic motives in a context where the objects of study are always black and a hint of voyeurism is often present. For example: 'What Ghetto Males Are Like: Another Look' (Hannerz, 1972).

Black readers have always had two options when confronted by white texts that offend them: either assume that a white author's interest in presenting unpleasant racial folklore serves a decent and ultimately antiracist purpose, or challenge the author's motives for serving up this sort of material at all. Following the Moynihan scandal, blacks in particular became more aware of this dilemma and were able to address it in blunt or even ironic terms. For example, when in late 1965 black leaders were trying to decide how much attention a conference should devote to the problems of the black family, the veteran NAACP lobbyist Clarence Mitchell commented: 'Some of the brainy Negroes thought perhaps it should be looked at. I didn't. My reaction was more visceral than brainy' (*Newsweek 66*, 1965: 40).

The harshest criticisms of *Darwin's Athletes* have claimed that the book 'pathologizes' African Americans. An angry Gerald Early reported in 1998 that the author of *Darwin's Athletes* had gotten 'into deep trouble with black intellectuals . . . for suggesting that blacks have a "sports fixation" that is tantamount to a pathology, a word that rightly distresses African-Americans' (Early, 1998: 17). In his damning 1998 review of the book, S.L. Myers argued that *Darwin's Athletes* 'contributes to the reinforcement of negative imagery of black mental inferiority through an unbalanced and hostile analysis of blacks in sports' (Myers, 1998: 881). As late as 2010 Ben Carrington saw in *Darwin's Athletes* a 'pathologizing of black communities which ends up reproducing a conservative narrative of how black people are themselves to blame for their own conditions, thus negating the structural determinants of both poverty and white racism' (Carrington, 2010: 177ftn). None of these commentators offered specific evidence or an argument to support their claims. By this point 'pathologizing' had become such an authoritative cliché among anti-racists that no explanation was required.

The sense of indignation that motivates 'pathology' accusations tends to make accusers less attentive to the history of the 'pathology' concept than they should be. Early, for example, equates my use of the term 'fixation' with pathologizing. First, one might ask whether calling this state of mind a 'syndrome' or a 'complex' might have been less offensive, or whether it is the author's presumed motives which are the real issue. Second, not all African Americans see the term 'fixation' in the same way. The African-American authors of *The Color Complex: The Politics of Skin Color Among African Americans* (Russell *et al.*, 1993) state that their book examines 'a psychological fixation about color' that produces discrimination within the black community. Their use of the term went unremarked; four years later, a white author's use of the term offended Gerald Early and no doubt some other black readers, as well.

But the larger questions regarding use of the term 'pathology' concern (a) whether it belongs in the social sciences vocabulary at all, and (b) what the consequences of banning it from the social sciences would be. Stigmatizing the word 'pathology' in this context erases the difference between defining a human predicament and defaming the people who are caught up in it. Kenneth Clark addressed this distinction when in 1965 he defended Daniel Patrick Moynihan against the charge of racism: 'Is the doctor responsible for the disease simply because he diagnoses it?' (*Newsweek* 66, 1965: 40). The real issue here is the presumed motive of the person who has used the term 'pathology'. This is why a number of prominent black figures, who saw Moynihan as a 'doctor' rather than as an exploiter of the black predicament, did not object to his use of the term 'pathology' in 1965. It became, however, so tainted a word that even today social scientists 'practically never use the term "pathology"' (Small *et al.*, 2010: 8), even as the Moynihan Report has undergone a partial academic rehabilitation (Massey and Sampson, 2009). Unaware of this proscription, the author of *Darwin's Athletes* used the word 'pathological' once and was called to account by his ideologically vigilant readers.

The opponents of 'pathology' language should also be aware of how many influential black and white commentators have used 'damage imagery' that implies 'pathology'. It is, therefore, misleading to imply that 'pathologizing' is a specifically white mental habit. As for motives, the historian Daryl Michael Scott has argued that the accusations of racism provoked by the use of 'damage imagery' by social scientists have been largely misplaced. 'Their manipulation of damage imagery, far from reflecting their racism, was most often a moral critique of racism' (Scott, 1997: 94).

The stigmatizing of the term 'pathology' that began in 1965 occurred in tandem with the stigmatizing of the 'culture of poverty' thesis launched by the anthropologist Oscar Lewis in 1966. Critics of this concept saw it as a form of insensitivity that branded the poor as fatally flawed and beyond social redemption (e.g. Valentine, 1968). Researchers who embarked upon such studies were often accused of 'blaming the victim'. The politically correct ban on the study of culture and poverty lasted until the mid-1980s, as 'many liberal social scientists tended to avoid describing any behavior that could be construed as unflattering or stigmatizing to people of color' (Wilson, 2009: 99). These inhibitions have been dissipating as a younger generation of scholars, less burdened by the ideological traumas of the post-Moynihan era, pursues research into the relationship between the vast and protean realm of 'culture' and the lives of the poor (e.g. Cohen, 2010; Small *et al.*, 2010).

In retrospect, it is hard to imagine how any social scientist could have believed that studying *any* group of people could exclude an examination of their 'culture'.

One way to appreciate the necessity of including 'culture' in the territory covered by *Darwin's Athletes* is to listen to how Harry Edwards made his case about the social costs of sports to the black community. African-Americans' disproportionate channelling of black youth into athletic endeavours, he wrote in 1973, was a 'black cultural tendency' (Edwards, 1973: 52) that should be resisted. In 1988 he saw black youth 'in obsessive pursuit' (Edwards, 1988: 138) of sports goals that would 'elude the vast and overwhelming majority of them'. In 1992 he wrote of an 'exaggerated emphasis upon athletic achievement in the Black family' (Edwards, 1992: 128) and the resulting impairment of 'personal and cultural development' (Edwards, 1992: 130). All of these remarks should provoke disapproval among certain critics of *Darwin's Athletes*. Edwards talks of a dysfunctional 'black cultural tendency', a distorted ('obsessive') relationship to sports, and the black family as a source of impaired 'personal and cultural development' (Edwards, 1992: 130). But for the author of *Darwin's Athletes,* Edwards' terminology amounts, not to defamation, but to a black sociologist's attempt to describe the real world.

Epilogue

Darwin's Athletes produced numerous media appearances and two public events. The first indication of a black backlash against the book appeared during an interview on the FOX television network in February 1997, only weeks after the book had been published. My interlocutor was Kenneth Shropshire, an African-American attorney and faculty member at the Wharton School of Business at the University of Pennsylvania. (At this point I was unaware that he had written two books of his own on race and sport.) When asked by the moderator for a comment, Professor Shropshire replied: 'One thing we need is fewer white men telling black people what to do'.

The ideological mobilization against the book manifested itself with considerable emotional force at the annual meeting of the North American Society for the Sociology of Sport (NASSS) that was held in Toronto in November 1997. My keynote speech was an inept and ineffective defence of the book. A better grasp of the racial politics of the Moynihan era would have helped me understand the situation into which I had gotten myself.

The collective mood of this event was absolutely unique to my experience and to that of other attendees with whom I have spoken since then. To this day Canadian colleagues refer to it as 'The Rumble in Toronto'. An atmosphere of latent ideological violence hung in the air, as if we were all waiting for something awful to happen. What I sensed was an incipient race riot aimed, not at the few black people attending the meeting, but at the conspicuous violator of the NASSS ethos of political correctness. After the keynote, during which I was heckled from the back of the room, came a follow-up discussion. I and a few of my (white) critics sat behind a table in a small seminar room that was packed with an audience awaiting – who knew what? As I recall it, the questioning was animated but civil, and it is a certainty that none of the issues were resolved to anyone's satisfaction. In fact, my appearance at that meeting accomplished nothing other than demonstrating that the field of sports studies could generate a degree of racial animosity comparable to that of other social venues.

The other event was an (almost) all-black conference titled 'Sport Matters: Black Intellectuals Respond to and Transcend *Darwin's Athletes*'. It was held at New York University, 2–4 April 1998, and was co-sponsored by NYU and the National Basketball Association (NBA). On 16 January 1998, I received a call from one of the conference organizers. He was extending an invitation to the conference. He offered me travel expenses, a $500 honorarium and, at the very end of the conference, a 45-minute response to three days of presentations attacking the book. At the end of the call he said: 'I hope you don't come'. Given the miniscule role I had been offered, I was happy to oblige him.

I believe now that my decision not to participate was a mistake. I am certain that the emotional discomfort would have been outweighed by what I could have learned by attending. And how much discomfort would I have actually suffered? One thing the *Darwin's Athletes* experience has taught me is that critics who will flay you in print can turn out to be the most reasonable and cordial people one could hope to meet. This curious discrepancy between public and private behaviour suggests that there is a ritual aspect embedded in such public condemnations of white interlopers. What can sound like hysteria turns out to be a socially mandated reflex, a defensive gesture directed at resented white men who symbolize the collective harm that whites have done to blacks over the past 500 years.

Notes

1 See Edwards (1973: 44): 'First, far from being a positive force in the development of the black masses, integrated big-time sport in its present form is perhaps a negative influence'; 'Sports provide the black fan with the illusion of spiritual reinforcement in his own life struggles'; 'Athletics, then, stifles the pursuit of rational alternatives by black people'.

2 See, for example, Guttmann (2003: 368): 'Equally absurd are the accusations of racism directed against John Hoberman, whose exemplary study, *Darwin's Athletes*, restates a truth spoken decades earlier by Arthur Ashe: concentration on sports performance to the neglect of academic achievement has been a disaster for the African-American community'.

3 See Shropshire and Smith (1998). These reviewers' critical statements about *Darwin's Athletes* also include the following assertions: 'It is our opinion that Hoberman has written a book that takes us back to the days when African Americans were referred to as less than human being' (p. 103); 'Any sincere analysis of Hoberman by African American academics must make mention of his views about us, for his view of us, as humans, may in fact affect our view of him or what may stand behind his written text' (p. 103-104); 'his condemnation of African American athletes and intellectuals is not welcome; moreover, the assertions are not true' (p. 104); 'Repeatedly, Hoberman takes out of context many aspects of African American life and culture. Apparently, he just does not get it when it comes to understanding African Americans and especially African American life chances' (p. 104); 'Hoberman's insistence on speaking for African American intellectuals. His strongest and most deeply entrenched hatred is for African American intellectuals' (p. 105); 'a diatribe of insulting, warmed-over racism that is being applauded in high places such as *The New York Times*, *US News and World Report*, and the *Chronicle of Higher Education*' (p. 105); 'Hoberman synthesizes

these racist beliefs with racial biology. He does so broadly and not with clear-cut condemnation. In some ways, his discourse provides fuels for the racist fires of others' (p. 106); 'Every 3 to 5 years, there comes along a White male who attempts to dabble in the race/ethnicity arena. Most fail' (p. 109).

4   See Myers (1998) whose comments also include among others the following claims: 'If you believed that blacks were more violent than whites, that black families are more apt to abuse their children, that the myth of black physical and athletic superiority has contributed to the elevation of sport over intellectual pursuits in black America, then you will find all of the arcane evidence that you could ever hope to amass in this book' (p. 879); 'The writer of this review concludes that the book does nothing more than excite the fantasies that indeed blacks are intellectually inferior, while simultaneously giving hope to whites that blacks may not be genuinely athletically endowed in the superior manner supposed by the old-style racists the book's author attempts to confront' (p. 879–80); 'Whether intentionally or out of naive ignorance of the sensibilities of African Americans, Hoberman has managed through his pseudoscientific analysis of sport to reinforce ideas of black intellectual inferiority and to preserve the myth of race' (p. 880).

5   These comments were reported to me directly by first-hand witnesses.

6   Styron's friend, James Baldwin, supported him but played no significant role in the public controversy of 1968.

RACISM, SPORTS RESEARCH AND POLITICAL FAILURE

Grant Jarvie

Introduction

While sport may be judged to have had a number of political successes it is possible that the failure of sport to eradicate racism is one of its greatest political failures. Policies, practices and legislation by governments and sporting organizations have regularly flagged up the fact that racism and xenophobia remain important social and political issues to be resolved within sport. While governments, policies and the contexts change, those involved in sport and other institutions, including education, have much work to do.

A number of texts have tried to explain and expand upon certain aspects of what is a large body of research. *Darwin's Athletes: How Sport has Damaged Black America and Preserved the Myth of Race* (Hoberman, 1997) was certainly controversial at the time, even dangerous and while this author did not politically or intuitively agree with the book's central thesis, it was certainly a brave stance and an important contribution to the field of sport, racism and ethnicity. As a researcher, perhaps naively at the time, wanting to tackle forms of inequality, I read Hoberman's book alongside a number of other research interventions that were seen at the time as key references that had to be covered. Others that specifically addressed sport included: Edwards (1969), Cashmore (1990), James (1963), Vertinsky (1998), Lapchick (1975) and Hain (1971) but they all had different ideas about change agendas and the possibilities of social and political change were nuanced by the particular context and politics of the respective researchers.

Research into sport, racism and ethnicity

Enquiries into sport, racism and ethnicity have taken a number of starting points which have involved differences in terms of both their politics and their approach to research. Arguments about the relationship between sport, racism and ethnicity have tended to reflect a variety of arguments (Carrington, 2010; Eitzen, 2003; Jarvie, 2000; Jarvie and Thornton, 2012; Kjaerum, 2012; Markovits, 2003; Spaaij, 2011; Wigginton, 2006) which have included the ideas that sport: (i) is inherently conservative and helps to consolidate patriotism, nationalism and racism; (ii) has some inherent property that makes it a possible instrument of integration and harmonious ethnic and race relations; (iii) as a form of cultural politics has been central to processes of colonialism, imperialism and post-colonialism in different parts of the world; (iv) has contributed to unique political struggles which have involved black and ethnic political mobilization and the struggle for equality of and for black peoples and ethnic minority groups; (v) is an important facet of ethnic and racial identities; and (vi) has produced stereotypes, prejudices and myths about ethnic minority groups which have contributed both to discrimi-nation against and an under-representation of ethnic minority peoples within certain sports. In addition, it is held that race and ethnicity are factors influencing choices that people make when they choose to join or not join certain sports clubs and that we need to develop a more complex set of tools for understanding the limits and possibilities that influence sport, racism and ethnicity and in particular the way that such categories historically articulate with other categories and social divisions.

For researchers addressing such issues, it is important to acknowledge that racism in and through sport is not a form of universalism in which the experiences and solutions are the same. As an activist and researcher in the late 1980s campaigning against apartheid in South Africa, I was often conscious of the fact that while solidarity existed between some black Americans and an oppressed majority in South Africa, the world of black Americans and black South Africans was very different. Research into sport and racism should in the first instance be sensitive, sophisticated and nuanced enough to recognise specific problems, specific issues and specific solutions. At the same time it should be acknowledged that while racism is continually reframed and conceptualized in different situations it is still, as a social political problem, pervasive.

The terminology involved in understanding sport, racism and ethnicity research is dominated by the use of certain terms such as *black, white, Afro-Caribbean, African, African-American, Asian, people of colour,* and many other terms that are used in campaigns to symbolize and assert differences between people in sport and in other areas of life. Any researcher working in the area needs to quickly decide starting points, concepts and research questions, all of which are not neutral.

The Hoberman thesis and key research questions

The Hoberman thesis presented in *Darwin's Athletes* was published in 1997 at a time when the USA was still almost a decade away from electing its first black President and at a time when black American golfers still struggled to have access to golf clubs. In 1997, when Tiger Woods won the Masters and donned the green jacket that accompanied the winning of the coveted title, golf became thrilling to watch for an entirely new audience. On the hallowed putting greens of Augusta, where Woods would not have been allowed membership a few years earlier, history had been made. Social change through sport occurred and at the time America did not have the language to deal with the change. Not since Lee Elder squared off against Jack Nicklaus in a sudden death playoff at the American Golf Classic in 1968 had a black golfer gained so much televised attention (Bass, 2002).

The sports press at the time cast the feat of Woods as breaking a modern colour line, yet no one, including Woods himself, could fully describe exactly what colour line had been broken. The press conveyed his parental heritage as variously African-American, Asian and Native American; overwhelmingly others portrayed Woods as a black athlete, a golfer who had brought about change in the same way attributed to the likes of Jesse Owens, Tommie Smith, John Carlos, Muhammad Ali, Tydie Pickett, Louise Stokes, Vonetta Flowers and Alice Cochrane. Woods himself did not consider himself in such terms but embraced a more nuanced racial heritage more representative of the melting pot imagery associated with American history and a determining demographic factor of so-called Generation X (Bass, 2002: xvi).

This background is important because the task that has been set is to consider why *Darwin's Athletes: How Sport has Damaged Black America and Preserved the Myth of Race* was viewed as an important contribution to understanding race and sport in African-American life – the title of a course taught by the author John Hoberman for many years. To his credit the author acknowledges the challenge of universalism early on when he states that the purpose of the project was to 'understand the cultural complexities of race inside the sports world . . . a racialized universe that is seldom brought to life by the sportswriters that cover it' (Hoberman, 1997: xii). Therefore Hoberman himself recognizes the need to be specific and as such he is not presenting a thesis on sport and racism *per se* but rather the life and expectations of certain groups of athletes in the USA. It is wrong in my view to draw corollaries with other situations and contexts.

The research questions set out in the preface are many and are worth mentioning in full since they set the agenda for the thesis. They are 'Why are many African Americans' feelings about athletic achievement so intense that they amount to a fixation that almost precludes criticism of its effects? How do white-controlled institutions profit from the perpetuation of the sports fixation? Finally, how has the cult of the black athlete exacerbated the disastrous spread of anti-intellectual attitudes among African-American youth facing life in a knowledge-based society?' (Hoberman, 1997: xiii).

The central argument put forward by Hoberman is that in some respects sport has been damaging for certain groups of people by stereotyping them as good at physical culture and, by implication, less proficient in other aspects of university life. Hoberman was in effect taking up and developing a theme of the earlier work into racism and sport that had suggested that sport is yet another social arena within which racial stereotyping takes place. It is, of course, just as important here not to replace one form of universalism with another, particularly if it is an avenue for improving life chances amongst any disproportionately disadvantaged groups in America. This does not mean to say that other avenues or pathways to success are supported, acknowledged, and broadened. One of the greatest disappointments and frustration of any researcher or university teacher working in this and related areas is that far too many people in the second decade of the twenty-first century still do not get a fair chance of access to education or sport or other avenues of social mobility which can facilitate a route out of poverty.

Richard Lipsyte in *The New York Times* favourably reviewed the book but academic hostility to the thesis was voiced in different ways and from different political positions. Some of the arguments were that: (i) black working-class African Americans are no more obsessed with athletics than white working-class Americans, (ii) it lacked the depth of understanding of African-American history or athletic experience that might have been expected; and (iii) activists and academics had long since discredited biological-racially orientated studies as racist and condemned to the past and so should the author. It is interesting to read, some 13 years later, Hoberman's colleague at the University of Texas, Ben Carrington (2010: 174), asserting that Hoberman's account is 'provocative, partial and in the end a distortion of the black experience of sport'. He goes on to argue that 'Hoberman's diagnosis of the dark side of black involvement in sport . . . ends up replacing one exaggerated and naïve paradigm namely that sport erases racism and racial discourse with its conceptual opposite that sport can reproduce certain racial ideologies' (Carrington, 2010: 174). Finally, Carrington argues that what he describes as Hoberman's pathologizing of black communities forgets to negate the structural determinants of poverty and white racism and their impact upon the quest for pathways out of poverty, including sport (Carrington, 2010).

Conclusions

While it is important to explain and understand sport, racism and ethnicity, the more important questions emanate from questions relating to social change. Hoberman presents a thesis, draws upon a range of written evidence but does not suggest fully what is to be done but rather leaves a range of inferences and implications. It is certainly important to ask what empirical evidence can we draw upon to substantiate aspects of sport, racism and ethnicity? (What is happening?) Or what theories, ideas and concepts can we draw upon to explain and analyze this substantive evidence? (How can we make sense of what is happening?) Or what capacity does sport have to produce social change? (What can be done to produce change?) Or what is the contemporary role of the student, intellectual, or researcher, in the public arena attempting to develop anti-racism policies? (What are you going to do about it?) Yet it is the interplay between these questions that is, in my mind, what is more important. It is the constant interplay between theory, explanation, evidence and intervention that is one of the hallmarks of the best research into sport, racism and ethnicity.

We need evidence to combat racism in sport but we also need advocacy. On the question of advocacy to combat racism and to make the bridge between other forms of sporting inequality the Hoberman thesis remains silent, but then that is not what the author or the research set out to do in the first place. This research has the voice of the author but not many other voices are presented in the book and perhaps the thesis might have benefited from voices or interview material on nearly all of the sensitive issues raised.

3

HABITUS AS TOPIC AND TOOL: REFLECTIONS ON BECOMING A PRIZEFIGHTER

Loïc Wacquant

In this essay, I recount how I took up the ethnographic craft; stumbled upon the Chicago boxing gym that is the main scene and character of my ethnography of prizefighting in the black American ghetto; and designed the book *Body & Soul* that reports on its findings so as to both deploy methodologically and elaborate empirically Pierre Bourdieu's signal concept of habitus (Wacquant, 2004a).[1] I draw out some of the biographical, intellectual and analytic connections between this research project on a plebeian bodily craft, the theoretical framework that informs it, and the macro-comparative inquiry into urban marginality of which it is an unplanned offshoot. I sketch how the practicalities of fieldwork led me from the ghetto as implement of ethnoracial domination to embodiment as a problem and resource for social inquiry. Through this reflection on becoming a prizefighter, I argue for the use of fieldwork as an instrument of theoretical construction, the potency of carnal knowledge, and the imperative of epistemic reflexivity, as well as stress the need to expand the textual genres and styles of ethnography so as to better capture the *Sturm und Drang* of social action as it is manufactured and lived.

The concept of habitus supplied at once the anchor, the compass, and the course of the ethnographic journey recapped in *Body & Soul*. It is the *topic* of investigation: the book dissects the forging of the corporeal and mental dispositions that make up the competent boxer in the crucible of the gym. But it is also the *tool* of investigation: the practical acquisition of those dispositions by the analyst serves as technical vehicle for better penetrating their social production and assembly. In other words, the apprenticeship of the sociologist is a methodological mirror of the apprenticeship undergone by the empirical subjects of the study; the former is mined to dig deeper into the latter and unearth its inner logic and subterranean properties; and both in turn test the robustness and fruitfulness of habitus as guide for probing the springs of social conduct. Contrary to a commonly held view that it is a vague notion that mechanically replicates social structures, effaces history, and operates as a 'black box' that obviates observation and confounds explanation (see Jenkins, 1991), it emerges that Bourdieu's sociological reworking of this classic philosophical concept is a powerful tool to steer social inquiry and trace out operant social mechanisms. Properly used, habitus not only illuminates the variegated logics of social action, it also grounds the distinctive virtues of deep immersion in and carnal entanglement with the object of ethnographic inquiry.

From the South Pacific to the South Side of Chicago

Since the notion of habitus proposes that human agents are historical animals who carry within their bodies acquired sensibilities and categories that are the sedimented products of their past social experiences, it is useful to begin with how I came to ethnographic research and what intellectual interests and expectations I brought with me to the South Side of Chicago. My initiation to fieldwork predates my entry in graduate school at the University of Chicago in 1985. To fulfil my military duties (as every French male had to do back then) I was assigned by a stroke of luck to do a civilian service in the South Pacific as a sociologist in a research centre of ORSTOM, France's former 'office of colonial research'. So I spent two years in New Caledonia, a French island northeast of New Zealand, in a small research team – there were only three of us – at the time of the Kanak uprising of November 1984. This means that I lived and worked in a very brutal and archaic colonial society, because New Caledonia in the 1980s was a colony of the nineteenth-century type that had survived virtually intact to the end of the twentieth century (see Bensa, 1995). It was an extraordinary social experience for an apprentice sociologist to carry out research on the school system, urbanization, and social change in the context of an insurrection, under a state of emergency, and to observe in real time the struggles between the colonials and the independence forces, and to have to reflect in a concrete way about the civic role of social science. For instance, I was privileged to participate in a closed congress of the Kanak Socialist National Liberation Front in Canala at the height of the clash, and I also travelled all the way around the *Grande Terre* (the main island) and made several sojourns in Lifou island at the home of friends who were long-time Kanak militants at a time when practically no one was moving about in the territory.

The New Caledonian crucible sensitized me to ethnoracial inequality and to spatial consignment as a vector of social control – the Kanaks were largely relegated to isolated rural reservations and hyper-segregated neighbourhoods in the capital city of Nouméa. It also alerted me to the variegated workings of rigid hierarchies of colour and honour in everyday life and to the crucial place of the body as a target, receptacle, and fount of asymmetric power relations. And it exposed me to extreme forms of deprecative racial imagery: the Native Melanesians were typically pictured as 'super-primitives' devoid of culture and history, even as they were rising to seize their historical fate (Bourdieu and Bensa, 1985). All of this would prove immensely useful later, on the South Side of Chicago, where germane treatments of African Americans were current. It is in New Caledonia that I read the classics of ethnology, Mauss, Mead, Malinowski, Radcliffe-Brown, Bateson, etc. (especially works on the South Pacific: the Trobriand Islands were just nearby) and that I kept my first field notebooks. The very first was scribbled among the tribe of Luecilla, in the Bay of Wé, at Christmas 1983, about a year before the independentist uprising (its highlight was a section on going bat-hunting and having to eat the roasted proceeds of our expedition at dinner that evening). Field notations found their way into my first publications on educational inequality, colonial conflict, and the transformation of Melanesian communities under the press of capitalist expansion and French rule.

At the close of my Caledonian sojourn, I got a four-year fellowship to do my doctorate at the University of Chicago, the cradle of US sociology and home of the main tradition of urban ethnography. When I arrived in Upton Sinclair's town, my intention was to work on a historical anthropology of colonial domination in New Caledonia, but I got unexpectedly derailed and detoured into America's dark ghetto. On the one side, the New Caledonian gates were abruptly shut after I filed a complaint against the mediocre bureaucrat who was my supervisor in Nouméa and had forced his name as co-author of a monograph on the school system that I had carried out by myself (Wacquant, 1985). The directors of the Institute in Paris hastened to cover up for the cheater and effectively banned me from the island. On the other side, I found myself confronted day-to-day with the gruesome reality of Chicago's ghetto, or what was left of it. I was assigned the last student-housing unit available on campus, the one no one had wanted, and so lived on 61st Street, at the edge of the poor black district of Woodlawn. It was a constant tremor and puzzlement to have right under my window this quasi-lunar urban landscape, with its unbelievable decay, misery and violence, backed by a hermetic separation between the white, prosperous and privileged world of the university and the abandoned African-American neighbourhoods all around it. Coming from Western Europe, where such levels of urban blight, material destitution and ethnic segregation are unknown, this questioned me profoundly on a quotidian level, intellectually and politically. It is at this point that the second decisive encounter of my intellectual life took place, the one with William Julius Wilson (the first was with Pierre Bourdieu, five years earlier, when I decided to convert from economics to sociology after hearing a public lecture by him, see Wacquant, 2002a).

Wilson is the most eminent African-American sociologist of the second half of the twentieth century and the foremost expert on the nexus of race and class in the United States – his analysis of 'Blacks and American Institutions' in *The Declining Significance of Race* (Wilson, 1978) set the parameters for that subfield of social research in 1978. He was one of the faculty who had initially attracted me to Chicago, and so when he asked me to work with him on the big research project on urban poverty he had just started (roughly, the agenda marked out by his book *The Truly Disadvantaged*, Wilson (1987)), I jumped at the chance, and I quickly became his close collaborator and co-author. This afforded me the opportunity to get straight to the core of the subject and also to get a close-up look at how this scientific and policy debate operated at the highest level, especially in the philanthropic foundations and think tanks that shaped the resurgence of the problematic of race, class and poverty in the inner city. That is how I started my investigations, first as an acolyte of Wilson and then by myself, on the transformation of the dark ghetto after the riots of the 1960s, by striving to break with the pathologizing vision that pervaded and distorted research on the question.

I owe a huge personal and intellectual debt to Bill Wilson, who was a mentor at once demanding and generous: he stimulated and supported me and he also gave me the freedom to diverge from his analyses, and at times to go in a direction diametrically opposed to his. By example, he taught me intellectual courage: to pursue the big picture, to dig deep into the details, to ask the hard questions, even when this entails ruffling a few social and academic feathers along the way. He also invited Pierre Bourdieu to speak to his research team on his Algerian research on urbanization and proletarianization from the early 1960s (Bourdieu et al., 1963). As it turns out, Bourdieu had tried to get *The Declining Significance of Race* translated into French a few years earlier. This meeting and the ensuing discussion solidified my sense that I could make a link between Bourdieu's early anthropological inquiries into the life paths of Algerian sub-proletarians and the contemporary predicament of the residents of Chicago's black ghetto which preoccupied Wilson. But I did not know just how yet.

Ethnography played a pivotal role at that juncture, on two counts. On the one hand, I took more anthropology than sociology courses because the sociology department at the University of Chicago was very dull intellectually and because I was viscerally committed to a unitary conception of social science inherited from my French training. The courses, works and encouragements of John and Jean Comaroff, Marshall Sahlins, Bernard Cohn and Raymond Smith pushed me towards fieldwork. On the other hand, I wanted to find quickly a direct observation post inside the ghetto because the existing literature on the topic was the product of a 'gaze from afar' that seemed to me fundamentally biased if not blind (Wacquant, 1997). That literature was dominated by the statistical approach, deployed from on high, by researchers who most often had no first-hand or even second-hand knowledge of what makes the ordinary reality of the dispossessed neighbourhoods of the Black Belt, and who fill this gap with stereotypes drawn from common sense, journalistic or academic. I wanted to reconstruct the question of the ghetto from the ground up, based on a precise observation of the everyday activities and relations of the residents of that *terra non grata* and for this very reason *incognita* (see Wacquant [1992], 1998a).

I deemed it epistemologically and morally impossible to do research on the ghetto without gaining serious first-hand knowledge of it, because it was right there, literally at my doorstep (in the summer time, you could hear gunfire going off at night on the other side of the street), and because the established works seemed to me to be full of implausible or pernicious academic notions, starting with the scholarly myth of the 'underclass' which was a veritable intellectual cottage industry in those years (see Gans, 1995; Katz, 1993; Wacquant, 1996). As a white Frenchman, my formative social and intellectual experiences made me a complete foreigner to this milieu and intensified the need I felt to acquire some practical familiarity with it. After a few aborted attempts I found, by accident, a boxing gym in Woodlawn, some three blocks from my apartment, and I signed up saying that I wanted to learn how to box, quite simply because there was nothing else to do in this context. In reality, I had absolutely no curiosity about or interest in the pugilistic world in itself (but I did want to get good exercise). The gym was to be just a platform for observation in the ghetto, a place to meet potential informants.

Habitus comes to the gym

But, very quickly, that gym turned out to be not only a wonderful window into the daily life of young men in the neighbourhood, but also a complex microcosm with a history, a culture and a very intense and rich social, aesthetic, emotional and moral life of its own. In a matter of months, I formed a very strong, carnal, bond with the regulars of the club and with the old coach, DeeDee Armour, who became a sort of adoptive father to me. Gradually I found myself attracted by the magnetism of the 'Sweet Science' to the point where I spent most of my time in and around the gym. After about a year, the idea grew on me to dig into a second research subject, namely, the social logic of a bodily craft. What is it that thrills boxers? Why do they commit themselves to this harshest and most destructive of all trades? How do they acquire the desire and the skills necessary to last in it? What is the role of the gym, the street, the surrounding violence and racial contempt, of self-interest and pleasure, and of the collective belief in personal transcendence in all this? How does one create a social competency that is an embodied competency, transmitted through a silent pedagogy of organisms in action? In short, how is the *pugilistic habitus* fabricated and deployed? That is how I found myself working on two connected projects simultaneously – two projects ostensibly very different from each other but in fact tightly linked: a carnal microsociology of the apprenticeship of boxing as sub-proletarian bodily craft *in the ghetto*, which offers a particular 'slice' of this universe from below and from inside (Wacquant, 2004a); and a historical and theoretical macrosociology *of the ghetto* as instrument of racial closure and social domination, providing a generalizing perspective from above and from the outside (Wacquant, 2008).

I had started writing a field diary after every training session from my first afternoon at the gym, initially to overcome the overpowering sense of being out of place on the pugilistic scene on so many levels and not knowing really what I would do with these notes. Now I shifted to taking systematic notes and to exploring the various facets of the Sweet Science. The notion of habitus immediately came to me as a conceptual device to make sense of my personal experiences as a boxing apprentice and a scaffold to organize my ongoing observation of pugilistic pedagogy. I had read Bourdieu's anthropological works front and back during my Caledonia years, so I was fully familiar with his elaboration of the notion, intended to overcome the antinomy between an objectivism that reduces practice to the mechanical precipitate of structural necessities and a subjectivism that confuses the personal will and intentions of the agent with the spring of her action (Bourdieu [1980], 1990; see Wacquant, 2004b). The author of *Outline of a Theory of Practice* had retrieved habitus from a long line of philosophers, stretching from Aristotle to Aquinas to Husserl, to develop a dispositional theory of action recognizing that social agents are not passive beings pulled and pushed about by external forces, but skilful creatures who actively construct social reality through 'categories of perception, appreciation and action'. But, unlike phenomenology, Bourdieu insists that, while being resilient and shared, these categories are not universal (or transcendental, in the language of Kantian philosophy), and that the generative matrix they compose is not unchanging. Rather, as the embodied sediments of individual and collective history, they are themselves socially constructed:

> As the product of history, habitus produces individual and collective practices, and thus history, in accordance with the schemata engendered by history. It ensures the active presence of past experiences which, deposited in each organism in the form of schemata of thought and action, tend, more surely than all formal rules and all explicit norms, to guarantee the conformity of practices and their constancy across time.
>
> *(Bourdieu [1980], 1990: 91F)*

Four properties of the concept of habitus suggested its direct relevancy for disclosing the social making of prizefighters. First, habitus is a set of *acquired* dispositions, and no one is born a boxer (least of all, me!): the training of fighters consists precisely in physical drills, ascetic rules of life (concerning the management of food, time, emotions and sexual desire), and social games geared toward instilling in them new abilities, categories and desires, those specific to the pugilistic cosmos (Wacquant, 1998b). Second, habitus holds that practical mastery operates *beneath the level of consciousness and discourse*, and this matches perfectly with a commanding feature of the experience of pugilistic learning, in which mental understanding is of little help (and can even be a serious hindrance in the ring) so long as one has not grasped boxing technique with one's body (Wacquant, 1995a). Third, habitus indicates that sets of dispositions *vary by social location and trajectory*: individuals with different life experiences will have gained varied ways of thinking, feeling and acting; their primary dispositions will be more or less distant from those required by the Sweet Science; and thus they will be more or less invested in and adept at picking up the craft. This certainly accorded with my personal experience and notations on the disparate behaviours of my gym mates over time, as they tangled with the competing lure of the street and the gym, adapted to the authority of our coach, and sought to remake their self in accordance to the exacting demands of the trade. Fourth, the socially constituted conative and cognitive structures that make up habitus are malleable and tranmissible because they result from *pedagogical work*. If you want to pry into habitus, then study the organized practices of inculcation through which it is layered (Wacquant, 1995b).

The 'magical moment' of fieldwork that crystallized this theoretical hunch and turned what was initially a side-activity into a full-blown inquiry into the social logics of incarnation was a rather inglorious one: it was getting my nose broken in sparring in May 1989, about nine months into my novitiate. This injury forced me to take a long 'time out' away from the ring, during which Bourdieu urged me to write a field report on my initiation for a thematic issue of *Actes de la recherche en sciences sociales* in preparation on 'The Space of Sports'. The result was a long article that showed me that it was both feasible and fruitful to convert the theory of action encapsulated by the notion of habitus into an empirical experiment on the practical production of prizefighters at the Woodlawn gym (Wacquant, 1989, 2002a). This article was soon augmented by more direct engagement with habitus on the theoretical front.

While I was carrying out my investigations on boxing and on the ghetto, I was in constant contact with Bourdieu who encouraged and guided me. Upon learning that I had signed up to learn how to box at the Woodlawn Boys Club, he had written me a note that said essentially, 'Stick it out, you will learn more about the ghetto in this gym than you can from all the surveys in the world.' (Later on, as I got deeper into my immersion, he got a bit scared and tried to get me to pull back. When I signed up to fight in the Chicago Golden Gloves, he first threatened to disown me as he feared that I would get hurt, before realizing that there was no need to panic: I was well-prepared for this trial by fire.) Bourdieu came to Chicago several times, visited the gym, and met DeeDee and my boxer friends (I introduced him to them as 'the Mike Tyson of sociology'). During one of these visits, we hatched the project of a book that would explicate the theoretical core of his work, aimed at the Anglo-American readership, since it was on this front that there were the strongest distortions and obstacles to a fertile grasp of his models. We devoted three years to writing this book across the Atlantic (by fax, phone, letters and meetings every few months), entitled *An Invitation to Reflexive Sociology* (Bourdieu and Wacquant, 1992), in which we disentangle the nexus of habitus, capital, and field. During those years, I led a sort of Dr Jekyll-and-Mr Hyde existence, boxing by day and writing social theory by night. In the afternoon, I would go to the gym, train, hang out with my buddies and 'conversate' on end with our coach DeeDee before driving him home at closing time. And, later that evening, after having typed my field notes, I would turn to the book manuscript with Bourdieu. It was in turns intoxicating, invigorating and exhausting. But the daytime sessions as a student of pugilism offered both a respite from theoretical cogitation and powerful stimuli for thinking through the abstract issues tackled in the book in very mundane empirical terms. The sociology of the ghetto (which I had extended to encompass a comparison with the post-industrial transformation of the French urban periphery), the carnal ethnography of the skilled body, and theoretical work with Bourdieu: all these strands were elaborated together and at the same time, and they are all woven together.

The boxing project is an ethnography in a very classic mould in terms of its parameters, a sort of village study like the ones British anthropologists conducted in the 1940s, except that my village is the boxing gym and its extensions, and my tribe the fighters and their entourage. I retained this structural and functional unity because it encloses the boxers and carves out a specific temporal, relational, mental, emotional and aesthetic horizon which sets the pugilist apart, pushes him to 'heroize' his life-world, and thereby raises him above his ordinary environs (Wacquant, 1995c). I wanted, first of all, to dissect the cloven relation of 'symbiotic opposition' between the ghetto and the gym, the street and the ring. Next, I wanted to show how the social and symbolic structure of the gym governs the transmission of the techniques of the 'Manly Art' and the production of collective belief in the pugilistic *illusio*. And, finally, I wished to penetrate the practical logic of a corporeal practice that operates at the very limits of practice by means of a long-term apprenticeship in 'the first person'. For three years, I melted into the local landscape and got caught up in the game. I learned how to box and participated in all phases of the preparation of the pugilist, all the way to fighting in the big amateur tournament of the Golden Gloves. I followed my gym buddies in their personal and professional peregrinations. And I dealt on a routine basis with trainers, managers, promoters, etc., who make the planet of boxing turn and share in the spoils of this 'show-business with blood' (Wacquant, 1998c). In so doing, I was sucked into the sensuous and moral coils of pugilism, to the point where I seriously envisaged interrupting my academic trajectory to turn professional.

But, as the foregoing should have made clear, the object and method of this inquiry were not of the classic mould. *Body & Soul* offers an *empirical and methodological radicalization of Bourdieu's theory of habitus*. On the one hand, I open the 'black box' of the pugilistic habitus by disclosing the production and assembly of the cognitive categories, bodily skills and desires which together define the competence and appetence specific to the boxer. On the other hand, I deploy habitus as a methodological device, that is, I place myself in the local vortex of action in order to acquire through practice, in real time, the dispositions of the boxer with the aim of elucidating the magnetism proper to the pugilistic cosmos. This allows me to disclose the powerful allure of the combination of craft, sensuality and morality that binds the pugilist to his trade as well as impresses the embodied notions of risk and redemption that enable him to overcome the turbid sense of being super-exploited (Wacquant, 2001). The method thus tests the theory of action which informs the analysis according to a recursive and reflexive research design.

The idea that guided me here was to push the logic of participant observation to the point where it becomes inverted and turns into *observant participation*. In the Anglo-American tradition, when anthropology students first go into the field, they are cautioned, 'Don't go native.' In the French tradition, radical immersion is admissible – think of Jeanne Favret-Saada's ([1978], 1980) *Deadly Words* – but only on condition that it be coupled with a subjectivist epistemology which gets us lost in the inner depths of the anthropologist-subject. My position, on the contrary, is to say, 'go native' but '*go native armed*', that is, equipped with your theoretical and methodological tools, with the full store of problematics inherited from your discipline, with your capacity for reflexivity and analysis, and guided by a constant effort, once you have passed the ordeal of initiation, *to objectivize this experience and construct the object*, instead of allowing yourself to be naively embraced and constructed by it. Go ahead, go native, but come back a sociologist! In my case, the concept of habitus served both as a bridge to enter into the factory of pugilistic know-how and methodically parse the texture of the work(ing) world of the pugilist, and as a shield against the lure of the subjectivist rollover of social analysis into narcissistic story-telling.

From flesh to text

Some of my critics, conflating the narrative form of the book for its analytic contents and mistaking my work for an extension of the 'study of occupations' in the style of the second Chicago School (Hughes, 1994), did not even notice the double role which the concept of habitus played in the inquiry and even complained about the absence of theory in the book (Wacquant 2005b). In fact, theory and method are joined to the point of fusion in the very empirical object whose elaboration they make possible.

Body & Soul is an *experimental ethnography* in the original meaning of the term, in that the researcher is one of the socialized bodies thrown into the socio-moral and sensuous alembic of the boxing gym, one of bodies-in-action whose transmutation will be traced to penetrate the alchemy by which boxers are fabricated. Apprenticeship is here the means of acquiring a practical mastery, a visceral knowledge of the universe under scrutiny, a way of elucidating the praxeology of the agents under examination, as recommended by Erving Goffman (1989) in a famous talk on fieldwork – and not the means of entering into the subjectivity of the researcher. It is absolutely not a fall into the bottomless well of subjectivism into which 'auto-ethnography' joyfully throws itself (Reed-Danahay, 1997), quite the opposite: it relies on the most intimate experience, that of the desiring and suffering body, to grasp *in vivo* the collective manufacturing of the schemata of pugilistic perception, appreciation and action that are shared, to varying degrees, by all boxers, whatever their origins, their trajectory and their standing in the sporting hierarchy (Wacquant, 2005a). The central character of the story is neither 'Busy' Louie, nor this or that boxer, and not even DeeDee the old coach, in spite of his central position as conductor: it is the gym as a social and moral forge.

Indeed, I hold that, with this project, I did in an explicit, methodical and above all *extreme* manner that which every good ethnographer does, namely, to give herself a practical, tactile, sensorial grasp of the prosaic reality she studies in order to shed light on the categories and relations that organize the ordinary conduct and sentiments of her subjects. Except that, usually, this is done without talking about it or without thematizing the role of 'co-presence' with the phenomenon being studied, or by making (herself and others) believe that this is a mental process, and not a bodily and sensual apprenticeship which proceeds beneath the level of consciousness before it becomes mediated by language. *Body & Soul* offers a demonstration in action of the distinctive possibilities and virtues of a *carnal sociology* which fully recounts the fact that the social agent is a suffering animal, a being of flesh and blood, nerves and viscera, inhabited by passions and endowed with embodied knowledges and skills – by opposition to the *animal symbolicum* of the neo-Kantian tradition, refurbished by Clifford Geertz (1974) and the followers of interpretive anthropology, on the one hand, and by Herbert Blumer (1966) and the symbolic interactionists, on the other – and that *this is just as true of the sociologist*. This implies that we must bring the body of the sociologist back into play and treat her intelligent organism, not as an obstacle to understanding, as the intellectualism drilled into our folk conception of intellectual practice would have it, but as a vector of knowledge of the social world.

Body & Soul is not an exercise in reflexive anthropology in the sense intended by what is called 'poststructuralist' or 'postmodern' anthropology, for which the return of the analytic gaze is directed either onto the knowing subject in her personal intimacy or onto the text that she delivers to her peers and the circuits of power-knowledge in which it travels, in a contradictory and self-destructive embrace of relativism (Hastrup, 1995; Marcus, 1998). Those forms of reflexivity, narcissistic and discursive, are rather superficial; they certainly constitute a useful moment in a research undertaking by helping to curb the play of the crudest biases (rooted in one's identity and trajectory, affects, rhetorical effects, etc.). But they stop the movement of critique at the very point where it should start, through the constant questioning of the categories and techniques of sociological analysis and of the relationship to the world these presuppose. It is this return onto the *instruments of construction of the object*, as opposed to the subject of objectivation, which is the hallmark of what one may call *epistemic reflexivity* (Bourdieu, 2002; Bourdieu and Wacquant, 1992). And here is another difference with the 'egological' or textual reflexivity of the subjectivist anthropologists: epistemic reflexivity is deployed, not at the end of the project, *ex post*, when it comes to drafting the final research report, but *durante*, at every stage in the investigation. It targets the totality of the most routine research operations, from the selection of the site and the recruitment of informants to the choice of questions to pose or to avoid, as well as the engagement of theoretic schema, methodological tools and display techniques, at the moment when they are implemented.

So *Body & Soul* is a reflexive book in the sense that the very design of the inquiry forced me to constantly reflect on the suitability of the means of investigation to its ends, on the difference between the practical mastery and the theoretical mastery of a practice, on the gap between sensorial infatuation and analytic comprehension, on the hiatus between the visceral and the mental, the *ethos* and the *logos* of pugilism as well as of sociology. Likewise, *Urban Outcasts* (Wacquant, 2008), the companion book of macrosociology which draws up the comparison of the structure and experience of urban relegation in the Black American ghetto and the French urban periphery, is a work of reflexive urban sociology because it ceaselessly interrogates the very categories it puts into question and into play – 'underclass', 'inner city', '*banlieues*', hyper-ghetto, anti-ghetto, precariat – to think the novel configurations of marginality in the city. And because it rests on a clear-cut demarcation between folk categories and analytic categories, which is for me the plinth of reflexivity.

Epistemic reflexivity is all the more urgently needed by ethnographers as everything conspires to invite them to submit to the preconstructions of common sense, lay or scholarly. By methodological duty, they must be attentive to the agents they study and take seriously their 'point of view'. If they do their job well, they also find themselves bound to these agents by affective ties that encourage identification and transference (for an astute analysis of the methodological use of transference in *Body & Soul*, see Manning, 2005). Finally, the public image of ethnography (including, regrettably, in the eyes of other social scientists) likens it to story-telling, diary-writing, if not to epic. Thus, the anthropologist or sociologist who relies on fieldwork must *double the dose of reflexivity*. This is what I tried to demonstrate in 'Scrutinizing the Street' about recent trends and foibles in US urban ethnography (Wacquant, 2002b). The considered target of my critique is not the three books on race and urban poverty that I subject to a meticulous analytic dissection (and still less their authors, who are, here, simply points in academic space, or their political positions, to which I am completely indifferent), but a certain epistemological posture of unreflective surrender to folk apperceptions, to ordinary moralism, to the seductions of official thought and to the rules of academic decorum. This posture is the fount of serious scientific errors, as these errors are systematic and have both ordinary and scholarly common sense on their side.

To enable the reader to experience the thrills of the apprentice boxer and make palpable both the logic of the fieldwork and its end product required adopt-ing a quasi-theatrical mode of writing. How to go from the guts to the intellect, from the comprehension of the flesh to the knowledge of the text? Here is a real problem of concrete epistemology about which we have not sufficiently reflected, and which for a long time seemed to me nearly irresolvable (notwithstanding the varied attempts at and discussions of formal innovation and poetic construction among anthropologists). To restitute the carnal dimension of ordinary existence and the bodily anchoring of the practical knowledge constitutive of pugilism – but also of every practice, even the least 'bodily' in appearance, including sociological analysis – requires indeed a complete overhaul of our way of writing social science. In the case at hand, I had to find a style breaking with the monological, monochro-matic, linear writing of the classic research account from which the ethnographer has withdrawn and elaborate a multifaceted writing, mixing styles and genres so as to capture and convey 'the taste and ache of action' to the reader (Wacquant, 2004a: vii-xii).

Body & Soul is written against subjectivism, against the narcissism and irrational-ism that undergird so-called 'postmodern' literary theory, but that does not mean that we should for that deprive ourselves of the literary techniques and instruments of dramatic exposition that this tradition gives us. That is why the book mixes three types of writing, intertwined with each other, but each given priority in one of the three parts, so that the reader slides smoothly from concept to percept, from analysis to experience. The first part anchors a classic sociological style in an analytic mould that identifies at the outset structures and mechanisms so as to give the reader the tools necessary for explaining and understanding what is going on. The tone of the second part is set by ethnographic writing in the strict sense, that is, a dense depiction of the ways of being, thinking, feeling and acting proper to the milieu under consideration, where one encounters again these mechanisms but in action, through the effects they produce. The experiential moment comes in the third part, in the form of 'sociological novella' that delivers felt action, the lived experience of a subject who also happens to be the analyst.

The weighed combination of these three modalities of writing – the sociological, the ethnographic and the literary – according to proportions that become gradually inverted as the book progresses, aims to enable the reader to feel emotionally and understand rationally the springs and turns of pugilistic action. For this, the text weaves together an analytic lattice, stretches of closely edited field notes, counterpoints composed by portraits of key protagonists and excerpts from interviews, as well as photographs whose role is to foster a synthetic grasp of the dynamic interplay of the factors and forms inventoried in the analysis, to give the reader a chance to 'touch with her own eyes' the beating pulse of pugilism. Here again, everything hangs together: the theory of habitus, the use of apprenticeship as technique of investigation, the place accorded to the sentient body as vector of knowledge, and formal innovation in writing. Indeed, there is no point in carrying out a carnal sociology backed by practical initiation if what it reveals about the sensorimotor magnetism of the universe in question ends up disappearing later in the writing, on the pretext that one must abide by the textual canons dictated by Humean positivism or neo-Kantian cognitivism.

Many social researchers view theory as a set of abstract notions that either float high up in the pure sky of ideas, disconnected from the nitty-gritty of the conduct of inquiry, or constitute responses to the empirical questions that the latter raises, to be discovered in the real world, as in the approach labelled 'grounded theory'. This is a misconstrual of the relationship of theory and research, and ethnography in particular. Whether the investigator is aware of it or not, theory is always driving field inquiry because, as Gaston Bachelard (1971) taught us, 'the vector of knowledge goes from the rational to the real', and not the other way around. And it must of necessity engage observation in order to convert itself into propositions about an empirically existing entity. This applies to habitus, which, like every concept, is not an answer to a research question but an organized manner of asking questions about the social world – in the case recounted here, a methodical plan to vivisect the social fabrication of pugilists in their workaday environment.

Note

1   This is a slightly modified version of 'Habitus as topic and tool: Reflections on becoming a prizefighter', in W. Shaffir, A. Puddephatt and S. Kleinknecht (eds) (2009) *Ethnographies Revisited*, New York: Routledge.

'THREE FUNERALS, TWO WEDDINGS, FOUR BIRTHS AND A BAPTISM': ON THE IMPORTANCE OF EMBODYING SOCIOLOGY

Chris Shilling

Body & Soul (Wacquant, 2004a) is not a conventional product of the sociology of sport and nor does its author, Loïc Wacquant, contextualize it within the major parameters and debates of this sub-discipline. It is, however, an exceptionally important book for anyone interested either in the study of sport or in wider questions concerning what culture is or how cultures get transmitted between people within groups and societies.

Why is *Body & Soul* important? Outside of a few notable exceptions – including Theodore Adorno and Norbert Elias – most influential sociological theorists have neglected sport (Dunning, 1999), yet Wacquant provides us with a fine example of the general insights that can be gained from an in-depth interrogation of sporting activity. In this respect, his carnal ethnography stands as a compelling illustration of how cultures depend for their future upon a process of *embodied pedagogy* resulting in specific forms of habitus conducive to the reproduction of the milieu in which they were formed. It is the wide-ranging sociological relevance of these insights, and the framework from which they are born, that makes *Body & Soul* far more than a specific analysis of the pugilistic habitus. Before I elaborate upon its general significance, however, let me first address the particularities of Wacquant's study.

Wacquant sought to de-exoticize boxing by avoiding sensationalist accounts of the sport and focusing instead, in a manner informed deeply by the work of Pierre Bourdieu, on the relationship between the boxer's habitus and the field that produced it. In doing this, Wacquant (2004a: 98) adopted a methodological approach that he understood as radicalizing the procedures characteristic of conventional ethnographic research in an attempt to erase 'the scholastic distinction between the intentional and the habitual, the rational and the emotional, the corporeal and the mental' by revealing the complexities of 'embodied practical reason'. Manning (2009) refers to the 'consensus model' of ethnographic research as one requiring familiarity with a field in order to gain access to the symbolic meanings used by its inhabitants, and *Body & Soul* certainly shows signs of such closeness with its author having lived with the gym members through life events including three funerals, two weddings, four births and a baptism. Nevertheless, Wacquant's immersion also involved a challenge and a physical wager that went beyond that associated with many conventional ethnographies.

The *challenge* required him to become accepted as the only white member of a boxing gym ('a quintessentially masculine space into which the trespassing of the female sex is tolerated only so long as it remains incidental', Wacquant, 2004a: 50) located in an African-American neighbourhood suffering from urban decay, racial and economic segregation, and problems associated with drugs and gang violence. This was made possible, we are informed, by Wacquant's French nationality granting him a certain exteriority from the specific oppositions characteristic of race relations in America, although he is keen to emphasize that acceptance was granted only because he subjected himself to 'the full rigors of the craft and paid his dues' (Wacquant, 2005a: 448).

The *wager* involved the hope that an experiment on his own embodied self involving (an initially unintended) three years of training in the Woodlawn Boys Club (as well as in other gyms), getting hurt (the only way of becoming able to tolerate the pain of blows 'is to get hit regularly', Wacquant, 2004a: 94), fighting in the Chicago Golden Gloves competition, and experiencing a degree of 'intoxication' from his involvement that resulted in him dreaming of aborting his academic career and turning 'pro' (Wacquant, 2004a: 4), would help him construct a revealing study of the boxer's craft.

Having become immersed in the sentient world of boxing, Wacquant's primary interest was to understand the multi-layered nature of the pugilistic habitus, and to construct a sociology not of but *from* the body (Wacquant, 2005a: 446; see Crossley, 1995). These aims are reflected in the unconventional structure and style of *Body & Soul*, consisting as it does of '3 texts of deliberately disparate statuses and styles, which juxtapose sociological analysis, ethnographic description, and literary evocation'. The last comprises what Wacquant (2004a: 7) refers to as a 'sociological novella', that followed the author's 1990 Golden Gloves fight, while their accumulated impact aims to demonstrate that 'theoretical mastery' of a practice is by itself of limited value if that practice is not 'inscribed within one's bodily schema' (Wacquant, 2004a: 69).

How can a boxing gym become a location for a study of sport that has sociological significance way beyond its own confines? There are I think two major reasons for this. The first concerns the clarity with which this bounded milieu (a milieu that exerts a pervasive pull on its regulars) enables one to see, hear, smell, feel and even taste a culture in action. As Waquant (2004a: 56, 67) expresses it, the gym is a quasi-total institution, requiring a reorganization of one's lifestyle, a form of monastic self-disciplining that bears comparison with religious technologies of selfhood (Foucault, 1990). The clarity of this culture is highlighted further by what appears to be a Simmellian pact of sociability in which members 'do not carry into the club their outside statuses, problems and obligations' that might interrupt the shared focus of their intra-gym interactions (Wacquant, 2004a: 37).

The other main reason for the gym's significance is that its clearly visible 'culture in action' highlights the visceral *processes* involved in the transmission and mediation of ideas and practices. The cultural processes in evidence here are inadequately captured by Parsonian notions of cognitively steered norms, or structuralist/post-structuralist accounts of linguistically determined rules or discourses. The field of body studies has long argued that cultural incorporation, reproduction and change involves physical, sensory and sensual processes (Shilling [1993], 2012; Shilling and Mellor, 1996), and Wacquant's study provides us with a compelling explication of the pedagogic practices, expectations and implicit rules that seek to shape the physical dispositions and capacities, the senses and sensualities, and the beliefs of those who exist within and embrace the practices of this particular culture.

Having drawn attention to some of the main features of Wacquant's study, and their general significance, I now want to highlight several specific reasons why *Body & Soul* is an important work of general social theory. Following my comments in the previous paragraph, the first of these is that it manages to construct a detailed account of carnal socialization. Building on the insights of Mauss and Durkheim, Bourdieu, and a host of body theorists, Wacquant highlights the embodied nature of how cultural incorporation occurs through diverse modes of pedagogic transmission. Woodlawn gym's culture possesses a 'hidden curriculum', and 'internal regulations' apparent in the deportment and demeanor, actions and interactions of the regulars (Wacquant, 2004a: 56). Boxers serve as 'visual models', sometimes to themselves, when shadowboxing in front of a mirror, while the temporal metric of three-minute rounds laid out, policed and internalized by the trainer, and enforced further by the visual surveillance that members extend to each other, exerts a pressure that makes it 'unthinkable to be working out of sync' with others in the gym (Wacquant, 2004a: 114, 116). The cumulative effect of these and associated practices is what Durkheim describes as an intoxicating effervescence in which bodies shaped by the demands and disciplines of a specific culture are steered in a particular direction (Shilling and Mellor, 2011). The result of this effervescence is neither virulent violence nor complete de-individuation, but a control of emotions consistent with a culture forged in relation to the demands of fighting. Different cultures and occupations will seek to organize and reorganize people's senses and sensualities, capacities and dispositions, in different directions, but *Body & Soul* shows us how these questions can be pursued through a theorized ethnography.

The second specific accomplishment of *Body & Soul* is to provide us with not only a general account of these culturally embodied processes, but also a highly detailed, multi-layered and nuanced analysis of a pugilistic habitus developed and internalized. Wacquant's work is a revealing study of the gradual transformation of a novice into a boxer whose schemas, emotions and capacities are deemed ready to engage in a competitive fight; an insight that develops through an engaged and reflexive account of the changes occurring in his *own* dispositions, capacities and desires. From early sparring in which he describes how his 'lungs are about to explode', and his strength deserts him in 'a fog of fatigue, sweat and excitement' ending in exhaustion (Wacquant, 2004a: 66), we follow him on a journey in which injuries including a broken nose are withstood en route to a body schema that is changed gradually 'in and through endless physical drills repeated *ad nauseum*' (Wacquant, 2004a: 69):

> From session to session, my field of vision clears up, expands, and gets re-organized: I manage to shut out external calls on my attention and to better discern the movements of my antagonist, as if my visual faculties were growing as my body gets used to sparring. And, above all, I gradually acquire the specific 'eye' that enables me to guess at my opponent's attacks by reading the first signs of them in his eyes, the orientation of his shoulders, or the position of his hands and elbows.
>
> *(Wacquant, 2004a: 87)*

Wacquant may have been knocked down in the process of narrowly losing his only fight, but we are left with a rich account of the dispositions, exertions, the morning runs, 'the billions of gestures . . . and oh so many punches – thrown, absorbed, taken in and dished out' that result in someone being able to accomplish even this much in the sport (Wacquant, 2004a: 235). As Manning (2009: 774) notes, moreover, even in those occasions where Wacquant's own aspirations and interpretations seem fanciful, what we may well be reading is the internalization of the romanticized aspirations associated with the pugilistic habitus itself. In this case, *Body & Soul* may also be seen as an interesting example of how knowledge is thoroughly embodied or *carnal* (Mellor and Shilling, 1997: 23–5, 56–9, 132–5), with the metaphors and intimations of reality we have connected closely to our experience of being an agent embodied within a particular environment (Johnson, 1987), and with our sense of self tied inextricably to the sensory and sensual awareness we have of seeking to survive and develop in our environment (Damasio, 2010).

The third specific accomplishment of *Body & Soul* to which I want to draw attention involves its contribution to the study of sport and civilizing processes. As Elias and Dunning (1986; see also Dunning, 1999: 55–60) demonstrate, the 'sportization' of boxing can be seen as part of a wider historical modification of the manner in which conflict occurred. Having himself described the boxing gym as 'a small-scale civilizing machine' (Wacquant, 1995a), Wacquant provides us with a detailed account of how boxing involved certain webs of interdependence that engage and gradually modify the affects of its participants. Sparring, for example, is an inter-corporeal, dyadic affair, predicated on a 'principle of reciprocity' that regulates and limits the amount of violence displayed during this facet of training. This dictates that the better boxer not translate his superiority into domination and also that the weaker not take advantage of this control. Losses of temper provide another example of the civilizing potential of boxing: such loss of control is associated with a worsening of technique and consequent physical punishment.

There is, of course, no guarantee that the demands and imperatives of the boxing will be experienced in a manner that reproduces its cultural parameters or its civilizing consequences (there are interesting questions to be asked here about the rise of Mixed Martial Arts and the decline of boxing), and Wacquant details the high turnover of novices who leave the gym after only a few weeks. The culture of boxing exerts itself on those *established* within its confines and it is interesting to note that recruits to Woodlawn gym tend not to be outsiders from the local community. As Wacquant (2004a: 43) notes, they come not from the most disenfranchized sections of the 'ghetto subproletariat' but from segments of its working class 'struggling at the threshold of stable socioeconomic integration'. The gym exists as an island of temporary escape amidst a sea of wider problems, defining itself in and through a relation of 'symbiotic opposition' to the ghetto that surrounds it, while drawing for its members on that masculine culture of physical toughness that pervades its forms.

Body & Soul provides us with a fascinating example of what Crossley (1995) refers to as 'carnal sociology', developing an analysis in which theory and empirical research are intimately entwined. It illustrates the importance of pragmatistically utilizing opportunities that present themselves to one in the field (it was only after 16 months that Wacquant decided to shift from using the gym as a 'window' onto the ghetto to observe the social strategies of the young men in the neighbourhood, to making the craft of boxing a study in its own right). In addition to taking advantage of a situation in which — at least among those he knew — his whiteness was mediated culturally and inter-corporeally through his French nationality, this study also illustrates how life consistently 'gets in the way' of research in a manner which can facilitate, hinder and ultimately compel the completion of a work.

Wacquant's study does not exist in a vacuum. It combines aspects of a long tradition of ethnographic research (containing limited affinities with that classic of body studies *The Hobo* (Anderson [1923], 1961)) with the theoretical influence of Pierre Bourdieu, and is part of a tradition of research in anthropological and sociological work in which the researcher flirts with 'going native'. It also builds on and supplements a still continuing growth in embodying social theory and research that is as vibrant in the study of sport as anywhere else. While I am sure that other interesting ethnographies could have been constructed from the perspectives of other members of the Woodlawn Boys club, the one provided to us by *Body & Soul* will long survive as a stimulus to the sociological imagination both inside and outside the sub-discipline of sport. It is a fine study, and one that repays reading and re-reading for anyone undertaking ethnographically informed research.

4

MISCHIEF MANAGED: TICKET SCALPING, RESEARCH ETHICS AND INVOLVED DETACHMENT

Michael Atkinson

In 1995 I approached Peter Donnelly at McMaster University about the possibility of conducting an ethnographic study of ticket 'scalpers' (men and women who illegally sell tickets above their 'face value' for sports events, concerts, plays/musicals and festivals). I thought he would reject my request outright. As a Master's student in the Department of Sociology at McMaster, I found considerable allure in sociology's tradition of ethnographically studying groups on the margins of social respectability. I knew several ticket scalpers in Canada, and possessed a little background knowledge about their subculture. To my astonishment, Peter encouraged me without a pause. Over the next two years, I spent several hundred hours ethnographically immersed in ticket scalping scenes in Toronto, Ontario, as the bedrock of my Master's thesis. I reflect on this study fondly on a regular basis, for a million and one reasons. From time to time, I wonder whether or not I would be able to conduct a similar study today. Regrettably, I think not.

Much transpired in Canadian universities during the 1990s with respect to research ethics and their administration by institutional/research ethics boards (REBs). Canadian sociologist Will van den Hoonaard (2001, 2002) has written about the relative moral panic about 'proper' ethics protocols for the (largely qualitative) social sciences in the late 1990s. Will argues, in part, that REBs often do not understand the mandate of qualitative sociology and, coupled with forces and trends outside of the university (an increasingly litigious society, the rise in audit cultures demanding university accountability and research productivity, the proliferation of technological tools for monitoring and surveilling people such as mobile phone cameras and voice recorders), a ubiquitous scrutiny of qualitative research efforts has followed. It is not impossible, *per se*, to conduct qualitative research in Canada, but the act is certainly more constrained, restricted, evaluated, screened, monitored and discouraged than ever before. I have conducted 11 qualitative projects with ethnographic elements to/in them, and each ethics proposal becomes lengthier and lengthier. My projects are progressively less risky along a number of lines, involving more people in the social mainstream (well, at least on the fringes of the mainstream), and on topics far less intriguing to me, if I am to be honest, than those like ticket scalping. I consider myself lucky to have conducted the scalping study before a pan-institutional 'cotton wool' sensitivity about research subjects and practices spun into fruition. The metaphor springing to my mind regarding the timing of the ticket scalping study is inspired from the great scene in the first Indiana Jones film (when I was young, I saw *Indiana Jones: Raiders of the Lost Ark* in the cinema, and immediately decided upon a career path into academia!), where Indy rolls under a slowly dropping stone wall (grabbing his trademark hat before the door slams to the earth) and barely avoids being pulverized. I'd never make it safely under that wall today.

Today, we all stand on the other side of the stone barricade. It is securely entrenched into the research ground. I recently attended the Canadian Sociology Association's 2012 annual meeting. The conference organizers invited me to speak on a panel focused on the institutional challenges facing qualitative researchers. I spoke at length (probably too lengthy for some) about the relative lack of sociology (and sociology of sport) students interested in pursuing ethnographic modes of research in their work. During the question and answer period of the talk, several of the graduate students in attendance shared stories with me about how they were once enthralled with ethnographic work, but were systematically discouraged from undertaking such ethically problematic modes of inquiry by their supervisors or REB representatives in their respective schools. These stories are neither isolated nor uncommon in the social sciences in Canada. For at least two generations now, students of the social sciences have received little in the way of encouragement into ethnography, in large part because of the supposed ethical impossibilities, risks or dangers in the method. Warnings and discouragement of this sort are typically offered by researchers with little to no experience in fieldwork, understanding of ethnographic processes, or sense of how people in the so-called 'real world' are not nearly as powerless, gullible, emotionally vulnerable or easily duped as we present them in ethics policy and practice.

In this chapter, I revisit a series of ethical surprises, negotiations, dilemmas and realities I encountered during my ticket scalping research. Any of these would, today, turn the average REB member's hair grey with worry, fright or anxiety. Nearly two decades ago (I even hate writing that, as I am now immediately aware of my age), REB members were more liberal in their orientation toward research ethics and believed more strongly in the average researcher's ability to temper professional ethics with personal morality, insight, compassion, empathy and, dare I say, flat out intelligence in the research process. Through the discussion, I highlight how ethical decision-making can be neither templated strictly by naïve governing policies in Canada such as the *Tri-Council Policy Statement: Ethical Conduct on Research Involving Humans* (the veritable Bible in the country delineating all ethical research practices), nor gleaned from mass-produced and discipline standardized research methods textbooks. Here, I argue that researchers (and, in this instance, ethnographic researchers) should be granted considerable agency for grounded, ethical decision-making with people whilst engaged in the field. The research process is invariably and inevitably enhanced for both participants and subjects within this framework of decision-making in context. My stories about ethical decision-making practices with scalpers are further contextualized against, or perhaps within, sociologist Norbert Elias's seminal discussions of the role of involvement-detachment in the research process.

What's the big deal with ethics, anyway?

Research that involves human subjects or participants raises unique and complex ethical, legal, social and political issues. This goes almost without saying. From my institutional experience, there are three objectives in research ethics. The first and broadest objective is to protect human participants from being 'harmed' in the research process. The second objective is to ensure that research is conducted in a way that actually serves the interests of individuals, groups and/or society as a whole (this, while a lofty and idealistic goal, is difficult to achieve). Finally, the third objective is to examine specific research activities and projects for their ethical soundness, looking at issues such as the management of risk, protection of participant confidentiality and the process of informed consent.

Every study undertaken in a Canadian university by a student or professor must pass ethics review by at least one (but normally two or three) ethics review committee. In many cases, members review protocols outside of their fields of expertise, disciplines and, for all intents and purposes, life experiences. The most important issue arising in the ethical review of scientific research involving human participants is risk of harm. Notions of risk and harm in human participant research have evolved from a biomedical tradition, having been borne out of atrocities such as medical experimentation carried out by Nazi physicians in the Second World War and the Tuskegee Syphilis Study, alongside tragic events such as the Sonoma State Radiation experiments and the experimental use of thalidomide in the 1950s and 1960s in North America. However there have also been ethically questionable research endeavours in the social sciences and humanities, such as sociologist Laud Humphreys' ethnographic study (*Tearoom Trade*), psychologist Philip Zimbardo's Stanford Prison experiment and social psychologist Stanley Milgram's experiments on obedience to authority.

Today, many research projects in sport, exercise and health are what we would classify as involving 'minimal risk' of harm – usually meaning that by participating in the study, research subjects face no greater personal risks that those they encounter in their everyday lives. This is the gold standard of all academic research. In Canada, research ethics in universities, and the principles of what constitutes minimal risk, are generally outlined by the *Tri-Council Policy Statement: Ethical Conduct on Research Involving Humans* developed by the Canadian Institute of Health Research (CIHR), the Natural Sciences and Engineering Research Council (NSERC), and the Social Sciences and Humanities Research Council (SSHRC).

Such codes of research ethics exist to protect, fundamentally, the rights of subjects and to ensure they are not exploited for the sake of scientific inquiry or the pursuit of academic knowledge. Fair enough! These codes contain core ideas, or principles, to guide how researchers treat people in the research process. For example, the principle of *voluntary participation* requires that people not be coerced into participating in research. Closely related to the notion of voluntary participation is the requirement of *informed consent*. Essentially, this means that prospective research participants must be fully informed about the procedures and risks involved in research and must give their consent to participate. There are two standards applied in order to help protect the privacy of research participants. Almost all research guarantees the participants' *confidentiality* – they are assured that identifying information will not be made available to anyone who is not directly involved in the study. The stricter standard is the principle of *anonymity*, which essentially means that the participant will remain anonymous throughout the study – even to the researchers themselves (whenever this is possible, but the principle is most easily achieved in experimental research).

Other ethical principles promoted within particular policy documents in governmental and non-governmental agencies include: honesty (i.e. in reporting data, results, methods and procedures); objectivity (i.e. strive to avoid bias in research design, data analysis, data interpretation, peer review, personnel decisions, grant writing, expert testimony and other aspects of research where objectivity is expected or required); disclosure of stakeholder relationships (i.e. disclose personal or financial interests that may affect research); integrity and carefulness (i.e. avoid careless errors and negligence, carefully and critically examine your own work and the work of your peers); openness (i.e. share data, results, ideas, tools, resources); respect for intellectual property (i.e. honour patents, copyrights and other forms of intellectual property, do not use unpublished data, methods, or results without permission); responsible mentoring (i.e. help to educate, mentor and advise students through research studies); social responsibility (i.e. strive to promote social good and prevent or mitigate social harms through research, public education and advocacy); and animal care (i.e. show respect and care for animals when using them in research). Given the above, I think it's best practice to consult a solicitor before even entertaining any fashion of ethnographic research project.

Rolling hard and hanging out

From the very first day in the field with the ticket scalpers, I felt like former FBI agent Joseph Pistone (aka 'Donnie Brasco') going undercover to investigate the New York City mafia. Well, at least in my mind I was Donnie Brasco. There is a certain thrill with conducting research on 'criminally problematic' groups like scalpers, and a sense of connection with legendary ethnographers of the past like Clifford Shaw, Ned Polsky, William Whyte, Henry Leisure and Paul Willis. I first met a ticket scalper at the age of 17. Well, that's only half true. I first met the scalper in question at the age of three; but he was not a scalper at that time. One of my cousins, on my mother's side, starting scalping in his early twenties whilst living in the city of Montreal. He specialized in acquiring and selling tickets for Montreal Canadiens ice hockey games, but also dabbled in rock concert tickets on the side. I first learned my cousin James had become a scalper when my father employed his services for a Canadiens playoff match we had set our hearts on seeing. Seven years later, I drew on his status as an internationally known scalper to launch my study into the subculture in Toronto.

I had seen scalpers (or ticket touts as they are referred to elsewhere in the world) dozens and dozens of times at concerts, games and events in my youth. The lack of formal policing directed toward ticket scalping always amazed me. These guys sold and purchased tickets, illegally, in broad daylight with little displayed fear of reprisal. They are a taken-for-granted, almost forgotten, aspect of the urban entertainment scene, and I wanted to study their inner workings, everyday experiences, and perspectives on the street hustle. Why? Well, before starting the Master's programme at McMaster, I studied sociology at the University of Waterloo under the dyed-in-wool ethnographer and symbolic interactionist, Bob Prus. Bob is a Chicago-style ethnography enthusiast, with a series of brilliant ethnographies on criminal subcultures under his belt, including the hotel prostitution community and card hustlers. Bob inspired me to pursue a Master's thesis on ticket scalping. Among other lessons, Bob taught me to envision groups of so-called social deviants as case studies for learning about the generic social processes/features of life. The point of ethnography was not to romanticize a deviant life world, to become its champion, or expose its morally corrupt nature. The goal, Bob told me, was to study the group in order to ask core sociological questions about how people live with one another in groups, how social life is organized, how behaviour is approved or castigated, how roles and statuses are meted out in life, and how the world makes sense to us only in social context.

Now, the issue is that REBs used to understand the mandate of sociology along the above lines. But as Paul Hollander convincingly argued some time ago in 'Saving sociology?' (1999), academic scepticism and fear abounds regarding pervasive ideological trends in contemporary sociology on both sides of the Atlantic. The decisively leftist, interventionist and increasingly public directions of contemporary sociology (wherein the sociological craft and enterprise serves the political ideologies, agendas and life practices of its practitioners) makes members of university REBs rather concerned, to say the least. As a result, REBs in Canada and elsewhere question the scientific objectivity of the knowledge-gathering process in sociology. To this end, ethnographers not only face questions regarding the ethical bases of their research efforts, but also questions regarding the very mandate of the work. I cannot help but think back to my ethics review application at McMaster University in 1995 for my scalping study. A process that encompassed less than a month then, might take more than a year now.

In what follows, I look back at some of the major ethical issues and ethical negotiations I made during the scalping study. Most of these relate to the daily give and take during ethnography of being simultaneously involved and detached.

Brief reflections on becoming involved

Any introductory research methods textbook warns of the methodological dilemmas inherent whilst 'doing' ethnography. Embedded in the Canadian Tri-Council policy statement is, to be sure, more than a bit of scepticism and caution regarding the performance of ethnography. I vividly remember lessons from under-graduate and graduate courses on ethnography in which we reviewed the major debates including how to secure entrée, finding social roles in the field, being safe while conducting research, protecting participants from harm, the risks of covert versus overt research, and maintaining personal integrity through the research practice. We learned the spectrum of membership involvement as outlined by Raymond L. Gold (1958), and discussed classic ethnographic strategies for meeting people, becoming friendly, recording data, and producing realist accounts of human cultures. Throughout all of these discussions, emphasis fell on the importance of learning culture, as ethically as possible, in the ethnographic interchange; that is, to see the world through the eyes and life experiences of those under investigation, and the corresponding 'best' (read *ethical*) practices of engagement.

Well into my doctoral research on tattooing in Canada, I picked up a copy of Elias's 1956 article in the *British Journal of Sociology,* titled 'Problems of involvement and detachment'. This article made me rethink why and how ethical practices were required in the field as part of doing ethnography. To summarise a complex and weaving narrative on the sociology of knowledge in Elias's work, he argues that ideological involvement in the world is a precondition of our existence. We cannot help but see life subjectively, as from the time we are born, we learn, live and think through the lenses of the cultures we both inherit and reproduce. Thus, we are by nature *involved*. The ethnographic mode of inquiry is, almost by definition, the attempt to become involved in others' collective involvements so that we may learn their worldviews/practices in the process of refining sociological conceptuali-zations of the world; what Elias (1956, 1987) refers to as the process of pursuing more *reality-congruent* or *object-adequate* sociological readings of life. Pursuing involvement is not, however, where research ethics becomes problematic. The art of ethnography is far more complicated when universities, and the researchers com-prising them, fully believe that whilst we might become involved to know social life in more reality-congruent ways, we must do so with a full measure of detachment. For me, this is when ethical issues largely arise for an ethnographer.

Elias (1987) strongly argued that in order to avoid falling into a pit of cultural relativism and hyper-subjectivity through the research act (i.e. by only seeing the world through the eyes of the people we study in the field), academics must conduct conscious 'detours via detachment'. Elias meant that some degree of distance, objectivity or detachment from our research (and research participants) is vital for a researcher committed to the process of seeing sociological events and processes in the field. Elias's (1956, 1987) point, also made by others who have raised the 'value freedom' issue in research (see Sugden, 2012), is not that researchers must re-frain from becoming involved with subjects in messy ways (i.e. socially, emotionally, cognitively or others), but that sound sociological knowledge stems from our abilities to step back and observe the constitutive ingredients in the cultural soups in which we plunge ourselves.

I briefly raise Elias's emphasis on walking the involvement/detachment line in academic research as, from my perspective (one developed from conducting ethnographies for nearly two decades and working on REB panels in several universities), REBs are far more comfortable with a pendulum swing toward full detachment in the research process. Involvement means intervening into people's lives, and into the varied material and ethereal spaces they inhabit. Involvement means interruption of people's lives, an opening of their unpredictable and uncontrollable perspectives and experiences, and thus carries with it the risk of 'harm' to them. Thus, serious detachment is favoured in most, if not all, contexts of social research. Whereas Elias championed detachment as the twin to involvement, REBs now mandate detachment (thinly hidden in discourses and policies of minimal risk – which more likely means 'minimal involvement') as *the prime directive*. In order to be more ethical with, respectful toward and cautious among research participants, our involvements with them must be more symbolic rather than material. Our knowledge of the world, it may be argued, becomes similarly symbolic and less reality-congruent over time.

I have sat at my office computer at least a dozen times in the past five or six years with the intention of writing a 'thank you' letter to the McMaster REB for allowing me to conduct my research on ticket scalping in the mid-1990s. If I thought the letter would be received for its true, that is sarcastic and ironic, tone, I would have mailed it ages ago. I would laud the REB of the time for focusing on the sociological content of my research rather than the potential ethical risks of 'involvement' it posed. Whilst REBs do not serve an official scholarly review role within Canadian universities, research projects were formerly assessed in relation to the involvement/detachment required to address legitimate sociological interests and curiosities. If the academic task at hand could be well articulated, linked to a sociological tradition, couched in relevant literature and justified within extant research ethics policies, permission to conduct research would be normally granted.

My ticket scalping research fell into a massive volume of literature on surreptitious street behaviour catalogued in the sociology of deviance. I articulated the study as an exploratory venture into the lives of street scalpers as a vehicle for understanding how and why some forms of street 'crime' come to be considered as tolerable deviance (Stebbins, 1996) in a country like Canada. I described my interest in ethnography, that my cousin agreed to be my sponsor, how I would interview scalpers about their life histories in the trade, and that I would likely not be able to secure 'formal' informed consent from the group members (strange, but guys like scalpers tend to avoid signing any documents attesting to their involvement in criminal behaviour). With both pessimism and trepidation, I submitted the research application to the REB at McMaster and awaited the verdict. I am still shocked by the relative ease and speed of approval. I had the official institutional approval to be involved with ticket scalpers.

But being approved to be involved and actually being involved interactively, on the street, in the thick of daily life, is another matter entirely. Becoming involved with people is always fraught with ethical, moral and interpersonal dilemmas. This is the nature of social life, and ethnographic research is not immune to these problems. Ironically, ethics protocols and policies do not cover many of the most important ethical issues which, I think, ethnographers face. To begin, these include what happens when you do not like or have ideological/interpersonal confront-ations with people, and what happens when people simply do not want you around their social group. OK, so here is where the backstories on being 'ethical' in the research process commence.

The first few days of the ethnography on scalping were terrifying. My cousin came down to Toronto from Montreal to meet with me, and take me to see a core group of about seven ticket scalpers who worked Toronto Maple Leafs' and Blue Jays' games. I started the ethnography in the winter of 1996 in front of the Maple Leaf Gardens, and so early days were spent hanging around the stadium with them watching and keeping my mouth shut, a classic 'observer-as-participant' role according to Gold (1956). My cousin had spent a few weeks prior convincing them to let me be around for research purposes, on condition that I would not disrupt them in any way shape or form (and of course, that I was not an undercover police officer). Because I did not know them and they did not know me, I com-pletely understood. For the first four months of research, I stood anywhere from 10–15 metres away from them watching. I paced up and down the pavement, went for the occasional hot dog or drink, and tried my best to be invisible. At times, they would say a word or two of hello, or ask me how things were going. I could take no notes whilst there, I asked no questions, and generally acted like someone new in a group. As one might imagine, I learned very little about the group's culture, but volumes about the social structure of the street hustle.

A naïve person might assume I would immediately love all of these guys, and they in turn would love me. Such is never the case in any social group. I could tell that two or three did not trust me, and one in particular, named Chris, went out of his way to tell me he thought I was 'bullshit', claiming that if I really wanted to do something good, I would 'fuck off and let [them] doing their own thing'. My cousin, who hung around for the first month of my study, assured me the guy in question is just normally abusive to people. So what do we do when confronted with 'jerks' in the field? To the best of my knowledge, there is no ethical statement or policy, or code detailing how to behave when there is a clash in social tectonics between people. Fundamentally, I think this is because ethics policies are not reality congruent with how social life actually unfolds. Intuition, experience and my cousin's own advice told me to stand up to him, politely confront him about his hostility, and refuse to be pushed around. Basic sociological advice. People test new members of a group in a variety of ways, and responding to these tests in contextually appropriate ways can make sound ethical sense. Why? Simply because the most direct, uncomfortable and potentially harmful course of action (according to ethics policy statements) might be the least disruptive to the group in the short and long terms. So, after receiving a jibe from Chris one day about being a poser, I responded with, 'Can you tell me, for the love of fuck, why I should give a shit about your opinion, my man?' Chris immediately stiffened his back, shot me a curious look, and sort of smirked. Two of the other guys were right there on the street corner with us and laughed. While I fretted internally, all three simply turned on their heels and got back to work. Chris never said another word to me until late one cold evening about a month later.

The latter months of the winter in 1996 were exceptionally moderate, and I found myself wearing only light winter jackets to my street observations of the scalpers. While standing with them on a Saturday night in late March of 1996, the weather turned quickly and the evening became bitterly cold. I was freezing in my lightweight jacket, but in a group of hyper-masculine street vendors, I could not excuse myself from the evening due to a wardrobe issue! Instead, I stood there trembling for about an hour and a half before the Maple Leafs' hockey game, until Chris came over and simply said, 'Hey, idiot, come with me for a minute'. From time to time there are definitional moments in an ethnography. I had to decide right there and then what to do with the request. On the one hand, Chris might have carried a grudge about my last comments to him and sought retribution. A refusal could signal a further lack of deference to him, and might exacerbate his anger. It would also illustrate a comfort in being close to the group, but still interactively detached from them. On the other hand, going with him might inch me closer to involvement with the group, and further symbolize my refusal to be bullied. So, without skipping a beat, I said, 'Yeah, alright'.

He led me to a small alleyway beside the Gardens, pointed to the west side of the alley, and said 'Go fucking stand over there, shithead'. By the time I reached the point of destination, a huge relief washed over me. Chris had directed me to an exhaust vent from the Gardens that shot out warm air. 'Stand there for a bit, Mike, and come back when you not just about ready to die.' It was the first time he ever called me by name. He then took a small packet of cocaine from his inside coat pocket. He laid the product out on a garbage can lid, snorted it, and immediately turned to me, saying nothing. What an uncomfortable space. He looked for a reaction from me, and I supplied him with, 'You know, it's on nights like this when I think these losers [the Maple Leafs] should only play afternoon games'. He laughed and then walked out of the alley, I stood there for about ten minutes to thaw, and went right back to work. From literally the next day on, Chris took me under his wing and we were practically inseparable in the research process. We keep in contact to this day, and he was the one who helped me ingratiate myself interactively into the group.

The methodological point of the above vignette is quite simple. Group life is interactionally tough, and negotiating the politics of group involvement is never easy. I hated Chris for his constant mockery and the barriers he subtly raised regarding my involvement. Confronting people is such an everyday part of life, and a central component in being genuine with people. I had to be respectfully confrontational in varying degrees to gain their trust and respect; this is a core code of practice in their group. Playing nice, staying cool and detached or shrinking into the background would have been methodological suicide – disrupting them more in the process. Hard guys like other hard guys. Period. I was by no means 'street hard' since I am a relatively tall but muscularly streamlined academic, but neither was I a pushover. We had to explore being uncomfortable and causing degrees of emotional harm with one another in order to establish a 'cool' interactive dynamic. Andy Hathaway and I (Hathaway and Atkinson, 2003) later wrote about confrontational research methodologies as vital in the ethnographic process. Just about every year, one research ethics board member or another from a university in North America writes to me, chastising me at length about inherent dangers in being aggressive with people in the field. After receiving these less than collegial notes, I am reminded of Chris, who told me late in 1996 that, 'I started being okay with you when you kind of told me to go get fucked. I can't respect and sort of trust a guy who snivels at someone's feet like a dog.' To be engaged with people like Chris, the ethics, morals and street codes creating 'minimal risk' in his life often stand in stark opposition to those outlined in research ethics policy statements. In other words, I had to become slightly detached from textbook 'ethics' in order to pursue their essence fully.

Problems of being involved with (and detached from) scalpers

By late 1996, I burned my original plan of attack for research with the scalpers. I found myself shifting toward a participant-as-observer, if not full participant, role with them. I actually scalped tickets on occasion, but mostly helped them communicate with one another during busy nights (they tend to, despite appearance, work in crews), stood in line at ticket offices to buy tickets for them, or spent time on the phone with preferred customers of theirs marketing upcoming events to them. I could feel myself losing degrees of academic detachment at times, whilst at others my relative detachment became apparent. For example, despite their open and flexible daily schedules, I still had classes to attend, tutorials to lead, and other university obligations to uphold. I had other friends and family outside of the business. And at times, we discussed how I would one day need to write a thesis about them, defend it, and then move on to pursue doctoral research somewhere else and on another subject. These are sobering realities in the ethnographic field.

Notwithstanding the above, I have never found that ideological involvement and detachment is as arduous as methods textbooks portray. To be honest, it is easy to develop friendships with people in the field, take their side on issues from time to time, and fancy oneself as a member of a rogue social group. During the study, I found myself burning the candle at both ends, staying out late with them in bars and restaurants after scalping sessions, eating and drinking too much and putting on weight, neglecting other friendships, and depleting my bank account to less than comfortable ends. All of the above are normally represented as the stereotypical personal risks of involvement with others. But many ethical dilemmas pertain to thinking too much like a researcher rather than as a member of the social group under study; that is, detouring too consistently and widely into the role of detached observer.

Across ethnographies I have conducted, I have learned that one of the most enduring and generic features of group life is that new members of a social conglomerate are often too eager to demonstrate an understanding of the group, its central activities, or ideologies as a means of illustrating commitment. Yet status is rarely conferred upon people for these displays. Ethnographers may become exceedingly keen to demonstrate understanding by speaking like a researcher to others via 'informed' question asking. Asking people questions in the course of interaction can be terribly annoying to people, and can seem contextually out of place when it occurs. Further still, hurriedly asking questions in the race for data on issues one thinks one understands can be catastrophic. For example, the term 'weight' came up quite a bit in conversations I overheard or in which I participated with the scalpers. Given the context and form of the conversations, I decoded the term as a subcultural slang for tickets. So, one day whilst in a hotel room with an internationally famous scalper who was visiting Toronto (whom I was beyond keen to impress), I asked him if he moved a lot of weight each year. He grabbed me by the shirt collar, pinned me against a wall, and asked why the hell I would want to know about that at all. Terrified and confused, I reminded him as quickly as possible that my study was about ticket distribution through street networking and so I wanted to know if he sold a lot of tickets. 'Then why would you ever fucking ask me about cocaine?' he said. Such a rookie, detached, overzealous mistake for someone who had been in the field for a year! What might be perceived to be a rush to display one's insider knowledge is inaccurate here. I should have thought as an insider, as someone on the inside would never be so brash or eager to please. He calmed down after I apologised for the language misunderstanding. He let me go and laughed his head off at me for about ten minutes. He said, 'I guess that's how much a university teaches you, Mike'. Pursuing academic detachment can be wise, but when rushed or undertaken to impress people in the field, detours via involvement might be better ethical advice.

I found myself at a downtown Toronto police station in the winter of 1997 with a group of nine scalpers in what is, in all likelihood, the most exciting research night of my life. A Toronto city councillor initiated a brief moral panic about ticket scalpers (i.e. as violent, drug-taking, predatory felons) that winter, prompting police to sporadically crack down on the street sale of tickets (mainly in front of Maple Leaf Gardens). One night, four police vans showed up about an hour prior to the start of a game, and the police (who practically knew all of the scalpers by name) ushered about 25 of them into the vans. Scalping carried with it a maximum fine of (CDN)$5,000 at the time as a minor misdemeanour in the city. When a policeman approached the scalping crew, I had to make a decision. I could bail out of there with haste, use my university/researcher status as a get-out-of-jail card, or attempt to negotiate this quite regular event in the career of a scalper with both insider knowledge and a detached sensibility. So, I negotiated. I followed the lead of guys in the crew like Chris and his best friend Steve. I showed the police respect, said 'Okay, officer' and followed them into the van. The scalpers were amazed I followed them, and we spent the better part of the night in a police cell laughing about the money they would lose that evening. Elation came over me at the end of the 'lockup' when I realised not one of them had asked me about how this might affect me as a student or researcher. They no longer cared. I cannot help but think that refusing to spend an uncomfortable, but neither dangerous nor upsetting, night in the proverbial 'steel hotel' might have re-underlined my other social status as a detached/immune researcher. It felt natural to go downtown with them as an insider, but I also wanted insight, as a detached observer, on a normal aspect of their lives as scalpers.

I think my research on ticket scalping might have suffered had I ignored the importance of being involved with others in the ticket distribution process in Canada. Whilst not an ethical issue *per se*, I found that interviewing members of the legal distribution system in Canada (i.e. sports promoters, members of ticket distribution companies like Ticketmaster, and others) was especially important. Additionally, in taking yet another involved detour into detachment, by interviewing people on the other side of the ticket scalping process (clients, police officers and Crown prosecutors) I became simultaneously more involved in the process, but detached to a degree from the core group of scalpers. The potential problems associated with social and ideological over-alignment with the scalpers were partially deflected by attending to the constructions of ticket scalping realities to others. In doing so, I learned much more about how scalpers come to frame the activity as a brand of Robin Hoodism within the sport and entertainment industries (Atkinson, 2000). Whilst I was worried, at first, that the scalpers might envision my conversations with others with either jealousy (almost as, 'Why are you taking the emphasis off me?') or fear ('Are you going to tell them about us and what we do every day?'), most of the scalpers begged me to regale them with inside information about what these groups know, think and feel about scalping. As a result, a whole new set of ethical issues arose. Amazingly, because so much of the interaction between everyone in the ticket scalping figuration tends to be surface level, brief and fleeting, they scarcely come to know one another. I told them what I could without breaching confidentiality and anonymity assurances. The lads in the group appreciated my research from an entirely different perspective, somewhat valuing my ability to be detached.

Conclusions: Reflections on finally detaching from 'the boys'

Amongst the biggest misconceptions in REB culture in Canada and elsewhere is the degree to which administrators perceive that our research subjects are as worried about ethical conduct in research as researchers themselves. My experience with research subjects, even those on the social margins, is that they find our degree of ethical i-dotting and t-crossing quite amusing and unnecessary. I never presented an informed consent sheet to a ticket scalper, for fear of either being beaten up or distrusted forever. Fieldwork is about finding one's normality in a social group or the settings they haunt; and sometimes, the institutional props and devices we attempt to blindly inset into these spaces do more damage than benefit. At best, the formal informed consent process can be somewhat bizarre and unusual for participants whilst, at its worst, it reminds people like my scalping friends that they are separate, unequal, and ultimately in need of protection from their social superiors. The latter, of course, is never good during an ethnography, and may just in fact precipitate one's premature departure from the field.

Still, departing the field is in most cases a reality. The massive literature on ethnography instructs that at one point or another we will eventually fully detach from our subjects. Our research subjects, like my ticket scalping friends, are always aware of this fact. Whilst some projects last years, and leave social, emotional and ideological imprints on our lives, there is almost always one great detour via detachment awaiting every project. In the autumn of 1996, I rode a Toronto streetcar with a scalper friend of mine named Karl. We were heading to Karl's house to drop off some medicine for his wife, who was suffering from a rare cancer. Karl had been a scalper (among other street 'professions') for nearly 20 years at the time of my study, and knew everything there is to know about the game. A heavy-set man with a soft but intimidating voice, Karl came to be one of my chief informants in the research. I ran errands for him, helped him sell tickets at times, and visited his house at least a dozen times for dinner. Almost out of the blue, he leaned over and said to me:

> You know, you've been trying to get to know [scalpers] for the last year, but we've also been trying to get to know you too. I think we all forget that. I like you, Mike, and the guys like you, because you've never judged us or shit. I don't know what will happen next. It seems kind of weird that your job is to write about my life, and to become friends with a guy like me. I never thought someone like you [a university student] would want to learn about the crap I do every day. But it's like watching Sylvia [his wife] go away. It's not the same, I know you know that, but what I mean is that when you have a sort of finish line to a friendship, that's hard to swallow. It'd be easier if you just said fuck you guys, or something, and we could hate you for being a prick and not being around anymore.

We talked about the strange nature of ethnography, got off the streetcar at his stop, and never broached the subject again. Just before I left Ontario for Calgary to pursue my doctoral studies, the scalpers threw a party for me at a downtown Toronto pseudo-Irish pub where I'd first met a lot of the guys. Karl was noticeably absent that evening. I tried emailing him a few times after I left town for good, but he never responded. Whenever I think about him and some of the scalpers I've not seen for 15 years, I think maybe someone should have made me sign an informed consent sheet detailing the problems of detachment.

Research ethics manuals and protocols also fail to teach us how our friends in the field are likely the best 'covert' researchers around. They size you up, make personal assessments, talk about you to others, form opinions without your awareness, and always hold back important 'truths' from you at times. Karl taught me this in the final weeks of my research. Real ethical decisions about how involved, detached, overt, covert, explicit and secretive people are in the field together (as we are in *any context of social interchange*) are made by people like my scalping friends as a normal course of interaction. In the case of my scalping ethnography, they, better than I, knew how and when to 'let me in' as a means of managing what we like to call the inherent 'risk' in and through the research process. I did not have to explain this to them on a form, or through a well-worn set of institutional policies. I think REBs and others preoccupied with ethics by the book forget how complex and nuanced the give-and-take of involvement/detachment is for people, and how our subjects know far more deeply than us how to socially, emotionally and psychologically protect themselves. How could a group of men like ticket scalpers, who carefully manage their identities, relationships and livelihoods every day, be either surprised or threatened by someone like me? A scalper named George once said to me, 'Mike, do you ever think you could fucking know something about me that I didn't want you to know? Really?' We spend so much time thinking about how to safely watch and interact with 'subjects' that we forget that they are watching, monitoring, managing us, making their own conscious choices about how much involvement and detachment they will allow us to experience. A progressive turn in REB mantra and practice might commence from the basic appreciation of agents' abilities to know more about what constitutes 'minimal harm' than researchers.

Finally, students, colleagues, friends and family members incessantly press me to tell stories about scalpers not on the public record. To be sure, scalpers' lives are richly layered by a range of nefarious activities I never reported; nor will I ever report. I cannot imagine anyone would be surprised to learn how tickets are not their only street trade, that many have perfected the art of breaking social laws, and their social circle is not the softest or most gentlemanly at times. But I've selectively edited my narrative about ticket scalpers over time not because they are my friends, because I hide behind ethics canons of anonymity and confidentiality, because the grifting and rounding nature of their lives does not fit with some preconceived theoretical picture I aim to paint, or because I might meet with retribution from 'the boys'. I choose not to articulate the nooks and crannies of their street hustling pursuits as, to me, the most important ethical question any ethnographer faces is the only one that matters at all; just because I can tell something, should I? Is the only goal of my venture into the empirical world knowledge acquisition and exposé, and at what cost does reporting knowledge (even when gained 'ethically') come for all involved? When I consider these questions, I remember how I was permitted to be mischievous as a researcher with a group of mischievous men by an institutional REB that, at the time, found good cause to allow people to manage their collective mischief together. I miss that trust in our universities, and the ways in which I used to be able to manage ethical knowledge production with people like Chris, Karl, George and my other scalping friends.

THE UPS AND DOWNS OF HANGING OUT WITH TICKET SCALPERS: REFLECTIONS ON DOING ETHNOGRAPHIC RESEARCH

Kath Woodward

Mike Atkinson is someone who not only does ethnography, he is also someone who brings ethnography to life in distinctive and productive ways, not least by going to some of the places other ethnographies have not yet reached. His work is in the tradition of the Chicago School and brings the innovative and creative approaches of qualitative work within that tradition to the sociology of sport in original ways. Atkinson has engaged with a wide range of aspects of the sociology of sport, including those on the margins, from body modification (Atkinson, 2003) to criminal activities (Atkinson and Young, 2008). His work is part of a movement in the sociology of sport which shifts the cultural and social spotlight from women's to men's bodies. Sport research often attracts participant observation, with particular emphasis on participation, but Atkinson's critical approach pushes forward the knowledge and insights that can be generated by qualitative research because his questioning and reflective analyses challenge assumptions, not least because he is operating in fields that are either sub-cultural or transgressive. His work always engages directly with what might otherwise be taken for granted and pass unchallenged. His research has made methodological interventions which have developed the scope of ethnography as well as entering under-researched fields within sport, not least involving those activities which operate on the margins of legality and legitimacy. One of the aspects of methodology which is particularly important in Atkinson's work is his acknowledgement of his own position as the researcher and the complex ways in which the researcher occupies a situation which is both inside and outside the field of research. His reflections on the experience of research on scalping (what would be called ticket touting in the UK) earlier in his career in the chapter in this volume demonstrate with integrity and honesty the possibilities and the pitfalls of participant observation, but most especially the strengths of getting inside the field. Ethnography can be disruptive and can throw up as many questions as it seems to settle, which is a very good reason for doing it.

Atkinson's work makes a major contribution to the way in which we understand and do ethnography, not only by producing valuable insights into the social worlds which are both central to sport and yet on its margins, but also by highlighting some of the troubles and difficulties of ethnography. Despite of the explosion of bureaucratic regimes of measurement, surveillance and quantification which mark the lives of all of us in higher education, not least in the conduct of our research activities, ethnographic methodologies present challenges which can be very productive. Fortunately we are still able to benefit from the critical analysis of ethnographers whose reflections on their work create opportunities as well as guidance for new researchers. Things have changed but, by revisiting the research on ticket scalping, it is possible to suggest some practical solutions as well as a few regrets about the expansion of regulatory mechanisms. There are also enduring qualities to ethnography and this work is a celebration of its strengths. This work also highlights what is at the heart of the craft of ethnography in sociology: the point is to ask sociological questions about social worlds, not to make value judgements or interventions. By asking these questions, ethnographic work like Atkinson's can be seen to generate new questions and creative ideas, methodologically, conceptually and theoretically, as his later work, for example, more directly addressing masculinities, demonstrates.

Nonetheless there has to be an acknowledgement of the situations and values of participants in the research process, including the researcher. What Elias described (1956) as the problems of involvement and detachment are central to the craft and practice of ethnography, as Atkinson says. The tensions play out in different ways in particular contexts. There are spatial and temporal particularities in the practices and requirements of regulatory bodies within the academy and these ideas travel in different ways. For example, there have been productive alliances across disciplines, including social psychology and the psycho-social, and especially in feminist and gender studies, which have emphasised the value of qualitative research, including auto/ethnography. Recent developments have, however, reinstated quantitative methods, albeit in new and exciting forms, including digital ethnographies of data analysis and critiques of big data which acknowledge the situated researcher in the research process. Nothing can quite get into the social world, its affects and emotions and the power axes which intersect in everyday spaces, quite like ethnography in its diverse forms.

There is also some slippage in the literature between qualitative and quantitative approaches and objective and subjective, especially in debates about ethnography in the context of tensions between inside and outside (Woodward, 2008). As Atkinson shows so powerfully, there is a whole range of ways of being inside the field of research, little of which is related to objectivity in relation to subjectivity. In my own experience of researching men's boxing, I have been inside as a fan and someone who admires the excitement as well as fears the dangers of boxing but, unlike most male researchers in this field, definitely not as a participant – in the ring or in the gym (Woodward 2006). Being sympathetic and relating in some way to the people you are working with is the only way to get inside and most researchers find out pretty quickly the points at which their positioning as a researcher might become jeopardised. Gold's continuum from observer to participant is sometimes challenged, for example in the case of Loïc Wacquant (2004) going off the scale as a totally immersed participant, albeit an observing one.

Gold's continuum has its uses in the classroom and lecture theatre but as Atkinson's work and his reflections, especially on his early experience, show, the actual research experience is often more disruptive than part of a continuum. The researcher may move from one end to the other on the same day (and even end up in a cell as he did on the occasion recounted here in his research into the social world of scalpers), but not without considerable research benefits.

Some of the expansion of apparatuses of monitoring and surveillance can be allied to the recent growth of a culture of litigation, when even before letting any of us embark on a research project, the university has to protect itself against the risks of any breach of ethical guidelines with the ensuing and ever more likely threat of legal action. However, as Atkinson's work demonstrates so well, there is often only a limited fit between the policy documents, including the ethics compliance forms on the one hand and the experience of being in the field on the other, especially when we are immersed in the process of research. The other aspect of this, which Atkinson's chapter in this volume demonstrates, is the sequential process whereby in order to obtain ethics clearance researchers have to anticipate some of what cannot be anticipated. This is not only an issue for the early career researcher; ethnography *per se* means dealing with the unexpected. The experience of those who have been there, however, offers really helpful routes through negotiating some of the more unexpected aspects of the research process. Central principles emerge however. Atkinson's work most importantly highlights a central principle which really matters, which is respect for those among whom the ethnographer is mixing and who allow this participation in their world, and what is inevitably some degree of intimacy. As Atkinson shows, we also have to respect the anxieties and insecurities of those who are the subjects of our research.

Once the researcher enters the ethnographic field there are many of the everyday tensions of human relationships which may or may not be specifically informed by the actions and processes of conducting research, although the researcher has to remain attentive to this aspect of outsider status. Response to the unexpected has to be tactical, although in the immediacy of the moment it is not always the case that the inexperienced researcher will find help in the ethics guidelines because, as Atkinson suggests, ethics policies are not quite in keeping with the unfolding of everyday life. Detachment is itself a tactic and a very useful one and there are moments when, however immersed the ethnographer is in the field, there has to be some drawing back, either methodologically through a reassertion of the purpose of the research, or more personally there has to be a distancing of the social worlds the researcher and the subjects of the research occupy; everyone has to acknowledge their own situatedness in this collaborative process.

We are all human, however, and notably in ethnographies of sub-cultures and cultural practices and social worlds which are outside the mainstream, the researcher still shares other points of connection as well as disconnection, especially in relation to gendered identity, which has been central to my own work. Although sport is a field so dominated by the binary logic of sex gender (Woodward, 2012), with its separate competitions and insistence upon only two sexes, the authenticity of which can be ascertained by gender verification tests, in the research process masculinity so often goes unstated and unmarked (Woodward, 2008; Woodward and Woodward, 2009, 2012). The sex gender of male researchers is as important for them and in exploring the relationship of the researcher to the field of research in the production of knowledge about social worlds as it is for women. Gendered, like racialized and ethnicized, identities often pass unrecorded however.

In sport, sex gender matters, but people have particular investment in gendered identities, which cross boundaries between everyday experience and more public visible representations of gender, for example in the sports celebrities who dominate media spaces. Investment in and identification with sex gender demonstrate the interconnections between public and private arenas and different social worlds, which ethnographic research can explore. Masculinities, especially the kind of hegemonic masculinity which is so often enacted in sport, can feel threatened in different ways, so that researchers have to consider their own situation. This applies to us all, although in sport as in many other fields, if less directly and visibly, the assumed normativity of masculinity has often suggested that it is only women who are marked by gender (Woodward and Woodward, 2009). A direct engagement with the matter of sex gender and sexuality is also one of the advantages of ethnographic approaches and illustrates the importance of researchers reflecting upon the expectations and anxieties of the subjects of research as well as their own concerns about accessing and entering the field.

Atkinson's work offers some excellent illustrations of the interrelationship between the researcher and the subjects of research in the context of the social and cultural production of gender identities. He describes the way in which he is able to command respect by in a sense fighting back, by buying into the same codes of masculinity to which the scalpers adhere. This is clearly the right strategy for the moment, not that it would probably be what we would advise our doctoral (or undergraduate) students to do now, being mindful of the guidelines, but it does demonstrate how the researcher has to play to the points of connection with the people in their field of research. Research is a practical process of strategic and pragmatic response in the context of everyday encounters, even if the social worlds we are researching are very far removed from those we usually inhabit. As a relative outsider in men's boxing, I have had to adopt less pugilistic, but nonetheless gender specific, tactics in order to gain the confidence of the men I worked with. In my own work, especially in the early days, adopting the non-threatening persona of a mother proved to be a particularly effective strategy at the time when women, other than members of the trainer's family, were not admitted to the gym. Another time, I stressed my media credentials as someone who had made television programmes about the sport. Boxing is a social world which receives and even welcomes some media intrusion, especially in the coverage of the sport's successes, although the guys in the gym were a bit more puzzled at my interest in the everyday routines rather than interviews with some of the celebrities. The general point is that ethnographers have to be responsive in the field and to know what matters in this social world. Much of this intelligence can only be gathered by engagement and even immersion in that social world.

As Atkinson shows so well, ethnography is an iterative process; one does not only have to gain the confidence of the subjects of one's research in order to gain access to the field, but there is a constant to and fro of exchanges and encounters, often with unpredictable outcomes. Ethnography is dialogic in the ways it is carried out but the advantages of engaging in the pragmatic responsiveness that is required can be enormous. Atkinson's work demonstrates the need to listen and to respond within the research situation in ways that highlight what matters about ethnographic research, which survives in ever more productive forms whatever the constraints of bureaucratic surveillance mechanisms and shows so well that the people we need to listen to are those who have been there and done it. Experienced ethnographers are also able to warn those who are new to the craft that our role is to explore and give voice to those whose worlds we are researching and not to make judgements. We are collaborating in the production of knowledge.

5

BODYBUILDING, DRUGS AND RISK: REFLECTIONS ON AN ETHNOGRAPHIC STUDY

Lee F. Monaghan

A visit to a needle-exchange facility

Gavin, my training partner and key ethnographic contact, accompanied me to Pumping Iron Gym for one of our regular morning workouts.[1] However, I first had to visit the local health authority needle-exchange facility, which was situated close to the gym. My research on drug use among bodybuilders, which Gavin knew about and supported, incorporated an element of time-sampling at needle-exchanges and a Well Steroid User Clinic (Williamson *et al.*, 1993). As part of a harm-reduction approach to illicit drug-taking, these agencies provide sterile injecting equipment in order to promote safer injecting practices and to check the spread of HIV. Hence, the facility I was visiting represented a *potential* site for contacting steroid-using bodybuilders, outside of those gyms I was surveying across South Wales.

In making the detour I wanted to obtain confirmation from the drugs outreach worker that I could spend the afternoon there. I gave Gavin the option of going to the gym ahead of me because I knew bodybuilders often have reservations about visiting needle-exchanges (many prefer to obtain clean injecting equipment from their steroid dealer). Gyms represent the bodybuilders' 'natural habitat' and I thought Gavin might prefer more familiar surroundings. However, he decided to accompany me. As a practising 'ethnopharmacologist' (Korkia and Stimson 1993: 122), Gavin wanted some needles and syringes for an imminent 'chemistry experiment' (Bloor *et al.*, 1998). He told me he was planning a nine-week 'cycle' (course of anabolic steroids), which included a shot of 'Deca' (Deca Durabolin) administered intramuscularly every five days. He thus required an adequate supply of 'blues' – a type of needle which is larger than the orange coloured insulin needles favoured by other types of drug injector, so-called 'junkies' who take 'street drugs' such as heroin.

The needle-exchange facility was housed inside an anonymous-looking building, accessible via an intercom. Once inside I asked the receptionist for the drugs outreach worker. I was told he was currently with a service user but we were welcome to wait for him. We agreed and were shown to the waiting room, which was unoccupied. The room contained wall-to-wall health education posters and several rows of chairs. The smell of disinfectant permeated the air. It reminded me of a general practitioner's surgery, or a hospital waiting room. I sat opposite Gavin and surmised from his body language that he felt anxious:

Lee: You look a little uneasy. I know a lot of bodybuilders don't like coming to places like this.

Gavin: Can you blame them?

Lee: Is it because they think they'll be seen as druggies?

Gavin: Yes. Don't get me wrong, places like this do a necessary and important job, especially in the times we live in with AIDS. Saying that, my mate at Olympia Gym won't go to a place like this. He asks me to get his needles for him. It's just the idea that people will think you're some kind of drug addict. Personally, I'm not that bothered. I have enough confidence in myself to know what I am and so I'll come to a place like this. If other people think I'm a drug addict then that's their problem. I know I'm not so I don't worry about it.

From steroids and violence to the negotiation of identities

The above ethnography provides a taste of the research that I undertook in South Wales between 1994 and 1996. The research was part of an Economic and Social Research Council (ESRC) funded project on the supposed links between bodybuilding, steroids and violence. While working on the 'Steroids and Violence Project' (SVP) I also registered as a Ph.D. candidate, combining my paid research with a qualitative investigation into drug-using bodybuilders' negotiation of potentially deviant identities. As noted with respect to Gavin, who had been pumping iron for 20 years, bodybuilders normalise the instrumental use of steroids. Also, despite injecting drugs, bodybuilders rejected the 'druggie' label and tended to avoid faci-lities that catered to opiate injectors and others taking illegal 'street drugs' (see also Lenehan, 1994). My research sought to make sense of bodybuilders' understandings, risk practices and construction of identities amidst broader social censure and stigmatization.

I subsequently obtained a doctorate from Cardiff University and an edited version of the thesis was published as a monograph (Monaghan, 2001a; see also Bloor *et al.*, 1998; Dobash *et al.*, 1999; Monaghan, 1999a, 2001b, 2001c, 2002; Monaghan *et al.*, 2000). Themes explored in these writings range from bodybuilders' justifications for illicit steroid use to the value of researching the body in everyday life. Amidst unflattering depictions of bodybuilders as inadequate 'muscle heads' who are uncontrollably violent and 'in crisis', the research provided an empirically grounded insight into (chemical) bodybuilding as understood by members themselves. In short, I took seriously the ethnographer's precept of entering the 'subjective world' of social actors and seeing the world from their viewpoint. That, of course, necessitated intensive fieldwork over a prolonged period (ethnography should ideally be undertaken for at least 12 months). Through immersion I developed good rapport with many bodybuilders and was able to learn about and then re-present their social reality in all its richness and complexity to an outside audience. As per Robert E. Park's injunction to students at the Chicago School of Sociology in the early twentieth century, this meant 'getting the seat of one's pants dirty in real research' rather than 'grubbing around' in the library. Such an undertaking can be very challenging, especially when researching groups labelled 'deviant' (Becker, 1963).

Bodybuilding became more visible and acceptable during the 1980s fitness boom, though a residue of public disrespect still hovered over the subculture (Klein, 1993). One of my interviewees, a gym owner, believed the public viewed bodybuilding 'like bondage almost! You know, it's like something that's done, sort of, you know what I mean? Out of the way!' (cited in Monaghan, 1999b: 76). During the early 1990s, the media were also constructing bodybuilders as 'folk devils' or 'dangerous individuals' who not only risked their own health through 'steroid abuse' but also, more disturbingly, threatened others through uncontrollable outbursts of aggressive violence. So-called ''roid-rage' allegedly culminates in domestic violence, assault, homicide and near homicide. Yet the medical and behavioural science literature on 'steroid psychosis' was equivocal at best, suggesting a need to undertake research among people who took, or associated with others who took, these drugs for non-medical purposes. This was the central aim of the SVP (Dobash *et al.*, 1999), while my doctoral study sought to explore bodybuilders' use of various physique enhancing drugs and their construction of 'appropriate' bodies and identities. In total, 67 interviews were undertaken with a range of bodybuilders and weight-trainers plus 16 months of fieldwork in gyms (though I continued exercising in gyms after this period and I still regularly lift weights given my personal interest in maintaining an active lifestyle).

Biography and biology: accessing the world of drug-using bodybuilders

Ethnography depends on social access which, in turn, depends on building rapport and trust with members of a given collectivity. Access is thus an ongoing practical accomplishment and the fieldworker should anticipate problems along the way. Indeed, it is not unusual for ethnographers to be mistaken for tax inspectors, spies, or some other intrusive outsider, rendering fieldwork challenging and sometimes impossible (Hammersley and Atkinson, 1995). Access may be especially difficult in the context of illicit drug-taking. As explained by Becker (1963), who undertook participant observation among marijuana-smoking jazz musicians, illicit drug users often erect barriers against those 'outside' of their subculture. And, in relation to my substantive topic, other researchers reported problems accessing steroid users' understandings in the field (Pates and Barry, 1996). An early contact, Dan, whom

I met in a 'hard core' bodybuilding gym in South Wales, also told me that others had tried to gain access and failed. Dan recounted how a university student visited the gym and, when the student asked if he could interview steroid users, 'the lads told him to fuck off'.

I have previously discussed how I accessed bodybuilding subculture, citing interview extracts and field notes where many contacts viewed me as a fellow participant (Monaghan, 1999b). I will not reproduce that discussion here, though I will make some contextual comments about my biography and biology or, rather, my embodied dispositions and the social meanings ascribed to my physical body. I will then describe a case of mistaken identity where it was rumoured I was a journalist interested in sensationalizing the subject of bodybuilding, steroids and violence. This discussion will, in turn, provide a useful point of departure for the latter part of this chapter where I reflect upon how I addressed my Ph.D. examiners' concerns and their request to revise the thesis. Their main concern related to my supposed 'bodybuilder identity'. Paradoxically, whereas my examiners had reservations about how my 'insider' status impacted the study, some bodybuilders had suspicions that I was an 'intrusive outsider' rather than being too close to their group.

How an ethnographer is viewed and received by members of a studied collectivity is not incidental. Ethnographic data are actively generated as the fieldworker interacts with group members and establishes relationships over time. Moreover, such processes are embodied with the fieldworker's body serving as the primary research instrument (Monaghan, 2006). My biography, which had visible bodily effects in terms of my physical size, shape, weight and composition, provided me with a form of capital that was useful during this research. I had a history of sports participation (mainly boxing) from early childhood. I also regularly lifted weights for two and a half years before moving from Manchester to South Wales in 1994, aged 22. Hence, I was fairly muscular and relatively lean before commencing my postgraduate research. Because of my physicality people often imputed the 'bodybuilder' identity to me, as in the case of a journalist from the *Manchester Evening News* (*MEN*) who, in 1993, reported on my undergraduate sociology dissertation, which explored the meanings of steroid use.[2]

The *MEN* article was, on balance, positive insofar as it conveyed the non-judgemental stance that I adopted and the situated rationality of steroid use among bodybuilders. However, contrary to the headline used by the *MEN* – 'Bodybuilder gives weight to new idea on steroids' – I did not call myself a 'bodybuilder'. And I have always been ambivalent about that social identity, not least given disparaging cultural stereotypes where it is assumed all bodybuilders abuse steroids. Furthermore, I have never entered a physique competition and I did not have the type of steroid-enhanced body that would win championships (body fat levels below three per cent, for example). Nonetheless, when I was in my early twenties I realized from various people's reactions that I had enough 'muscle mass' to 'pass' as a bodybuilder, or at least I was seen as a gym enthusiast who was committed to developing his physique. When I relocated to South Wales I also tended to pass in gyms because of my field role and 'presentation of self' (Goffman, 1959). I regularly lifted (reasonably heavy) weights, I hung around gym counters talking to members while drinking protein shakes, and I adopted the bodybuilders' symbolic style, i.e. I wore the baggy trousers, XXXL label sweaters and vests that were fashionable in gyms at the time. Furthermore, some contacts immediately assumed I was a steroid user. This normative subcultural identity was imputed to me not only because of my muscularity and self-presentation but also because I had acne and acne scarring, notably on my shoulders. My acne, which flared up during puberty, was the natural consequence of my own overactive hormones rather than a side-effect of synthetic testosterone. Bodybuilders typically assumed otherwise, which was not necessarily a bad thing. For example, the first time I trained in one gym, a young employee immediately initiated conversation by saying 'I recognize those scars' before openly talking about his steroid-assisted bodybuilding and other ethnopharmacological practices.

In short my biography plus biology, which shaped my physicality and 'habitus' (embodied dispositions) (Bourdieu, 1977), were advantageous from an ethnographic viewpoint. My habitus, in turn, allowed me to deepen my immersion in the bodybuilding life-world when this effectively became my full-time job in South Wales. It was through ethnographic immersion and befriending men like Gavin, a 'locator' who made proper introductions (see also Stewart-Clevidence and Goldstein, 1996: 36), that I became well acquainted with a network of bodybuilders, gym owners, steroid dealers and others close to the subculture. In practice, this aspect of the research entailed interacting with group members in various contexts, including occasional nights out at bars and clubs, sunbathing in the local park, meeting in homes, chatting in the supermarket, attending bodybuilding competitions and seminars. Productive field relations were also established and maintained over time because I expressed a non-judgemental attitude when discussion turned to steroids and steroid-accessory drugs, or when I observed drug-related practices. On one occasion, relatively early in the research, I also agreed to a gym owner's request to obtain a large box of sterile injecting equipment from one of the health authority needle-exchange facilities. He knew I was visiting these facilities and, in the interests of good field relations and harm minimization, I agreed to his request.

Before discussing difficulties associated with my research and how I negotiated these, I will stress that I do not believe ethnographers must 'go native' in order to learn about a culture. As explained elsewhere (Monaghan, 1999b: 78–9), I am critical of 'insider myths' which claim that only members are capable of doing valid research (see also Merton, 1972); indeed, it is often sufficient to adopt a field role that *meshes* with one's contacts (McKeganey and Bloor, 1991). Furthermore, the idea of becoming 'one of them' in the context of bodybuilding subculture is naïve insofar as there are 'many of them'. And bodybuilders are heterogeneous even in their orientation to the one thing that unites them, 'creating the perfect body' (Monaghan, 2001a). In that respect I agree with other qualitative researchers who contest the 'insider/outsider' categorization, such as Kim (2012), a Korean woman who researched South Korean women's lives in the UK. However, when frequenting gyms I was fortunately fit, healthy and motivated enough to be able to embrace the physical demands of participant observational research. I immersed myself in the bodybuilding life-world and I relished the opportunity to undertake a study that overlapped with my personal 'body project' (Shilling, 2003). Because I was unencumbered by the demands of family life at the time and those administrative and teaching requirements associated with more senior academic posts, I also sometimes lifted weights twice a day (what body-builders call 'double-split routines') in different gyms. Besides adding muscle to my frame, such immersion enabled me to survey multiple sites on a time-sampling basis and broaden my range of ethnographic contacts. In short, I adopted an 'active membership role' (Adler and Adler, 1987) where the ethnographer moves away from the marginally involved role of the traditional participant observer. Consequently I was seen by many of my contacts to be committed to the demanding bodybuilding lifestyle, albeit within limits. And, as fieldwork progressed, I easily recruited interviewees from gyms, with one contact remarking 'it is like talking to one of their own when they're talking to you' whereas 'an outsider, they would mess people like that around' (cited in Monaghan, 1999b: 80). In this context it is worth noting that other contact strategies (for example posters in needle-exchange facilities and a well steroid user clinic plus an advert in a British bodybuilding magazine) were not particularly successful. Efforts to hold a focus group at the end of the study also failed, though this was due to my reliance on a gym owner, Rex, who 'messed me around' after he offered to organize the session on his premises. Rex co-owned Olympia gym, and there was a lingering suspicion about my 'true' identity and intentions at that site.

'Don't talk to him, he's from the papers': Lingering suspicions at Olympia gym

Social access, irrespective of one's actual or assumed 'qualifications' for undertaking a specific study, can never be taken for granted. Access is a consequential social process comprising dynamic relations, contingencies and demands that are also external to face-to-face encounters but which bear upon them. I reflexively learnt about this first-hand early during my fieldwork in South Wales. While I immediately 'hit it off' with many local bodybuilders and I became well integrated into their subculture, I learnt six weeks into the project that some bodybuilders viewed me with suspicion. The words 'don't talk to him, he's from the papers' circulated at a local physique competition that I attended as an observer hoping to initiate fieldwork contacts. This rumour and warning emerged with reference to a newspaper article featured in the *South Wales Echo* (*SWE*) (31 May 1994).

Russell Dobash, one of the SVP grant holders, contacted the *SWE* shortly after the study commenced. Contacting the media was understandable given the ESRC's expectation that grant holders should widely publicise their funded research. Because my previous engagement with the media was positive, I was also favourably (perhaps naively) inclined to meeting a journalist and I deferred to my senior supervisor, who acted as the leading authority for the journalist writing the article. However, the article was problematic. The most obvious problem was the sensationalist and misleading title: 'Why Do Steroids Pack a Punch?' The article also contained speculative comments about the potential significance of male unemployment in post-industrial South Wales. Aside from the unproven implication that steroids cause violence, with our research allegedly seeking to explain this violence among those who are not 'clean' (polluted, dirty), the article implied that bodybuilders were out-of-work men in search of a secure masculine identity. The 'masculinity in crisis' thesis was something of a cliché in relation to male bodybuilding (Klein, 1993) and I subsequently critiqued that thesis on empirical and theoretical grounds (Monaghan, 2001a).

Of course, when it came to accessing the drug-using bodybuilders' world and negotiating barriers, it did not really matter whether the locals had actually read the *SWE* article. In the human world there can be plenty of smoke without fire, with rumours quickly spreading and morphing on the basis of nothing substantive. However, the article did not help matters. I knew that if bodybuilders had read it they would have been justifiably frosty towards the study and, by extension, me. After all, there was a broader media moral panic about ''roid-rage' which constructed bodybuilding as a collection of atavistic types. In such a context, bodybuilders tended to avoid journalists, or any other intrusive outsider who would have likely misrecognized their world and simply criticized it. And if I was one of these outsiders then, as with Dan's comment about a student hoping to interview steroid users, I could hardly be surprised if I received the 'cold shoulder' or was basically told to 'go away'.

At the local bodybuilding competition, my intention was to 'hang around' as an observer and strike up conversations with spectators, organizers, judges and competitors. During the event I talked with the organizer, Carwyn, who told me about the rumour. Fortunately, I had previously contacted Carwyn by letter because I wanted formally to introduce myself to a potential gatekeeper, and the organizer of a physique competition was an obvious choice. (As it subsequently transpired, he was well respected by the local population and he had kudos as a former professional bodybuilding judge who personally knew icons such as Arnold Schwarzenegger.) My letter to Carwyn included a copy of the *MEN* article, which usefully conveyed my approach to bodybuilding and steroids. In Carwyn's eyes I was 'safe' and he was happy to help me with my studies, including negating, as far as possible, rumours about my 'true' identity and intentions.

While I never let the early rumours deter me and I pressed on with the fieldwork, Carwyn informed me nine months after the physique competition that some members of one gym I frequented, Olympia, remained suspicious. Carwyn attributed this to my research interest in supposed steroid-violence associations plus broader negative media attention which, in his words, had taken the issue 'out of context'. While it is unrealistic to expect total acceptance in any large group, many bodybuilders from Olympia and elsewhere were nonetheless open and they granted me access to their world in order to make sense of it. On an objective note, more interviewees were recruited from Olympia gym than any other site. Of those respondents (n=44) who exercised in bodybuilding gyms (as opposed to leisure centres, for example), 34 per cent (n=15) exercised at Olympia. Rex's and *some* other members' lingering suspicions never scuppered my research. However, their ongoing reticence illustrated how some bodybuilders remained sensitive to (real or imagined) outside negativity, especially regarding putative steroid-violence connections. This also perhaps explains why Rex 'messed me around' after I talked to him about organizing a focus group.

Becoming qualified: Reflexivity, advocacy and academic credibility

Ethnography is not only a process but also a product (Hammersley and Atkinson, 1995). The product includes the dissertation, journal articles, chapters in edited collections and the ethnographic monograph. Difficulties may therefore arise at various stages of one's study, including after the fieldwork has formally ended and the ethnography is written up for a larger audience. Indeed, whilst participant observational research necessitates reflexive engagement with and attentiveness to field relations as one learns from 'the natives', as academics we are also members of another peculiar tribe. This tribe similarly comprises particular rites of passage and barriers that need to be carefully understood and negotiated. I began this paper with an ethnographic excerpt, recorded early in the research; in this section I will discuss the outcome of and my response to my *viva-voce* examination at the end of the research. This exam was, without exaggeration, much more difficult than getting drug-using bodybuilders to talk with me about their ethnopharmacological practices.

I submitted my thesis in 1997. As part of the examination process I had to sit a *viva-voce* which, in my case, lasted three hours and left me with a pounding headache. I remember leaving the examination feeling far more exhausted than if I had done a double-split routine in the gym. The outcome of the *viva* was acceptance of the thesis subject to the satisfactory completion of several important revisions. The main stipulation was that I had to rewrite my methodology chapter and offer a more reflexive piece on how my 'bodybuilder identity' impacted the research. As explained above, I never explicitly called myself a bodybuilder but I was generally viewed as a muscle enthusiast and I capitalized upon that social identity for the purposes of getting in and getting on with the research. Lingering suspicions at Olympia gym notwithstanding, being seen as a bodybuilder often facilitated social access and data generation in a 'closed access' group. However, my examiners were suspicious that I was too much of an 'insider'. And if I was an 'insider', how might that have affected the dissertation? What were the disadvantages associated with my social identity? While I agree with Kim's (2012) recent assertion that the 'insider/outsider' dichotomy is too crude given the complex, multi-faceted and dynamic nature of field relationships and identities, I had to address adequately my examiners' concerns in order to obtain the Ph.D.

I was reflexive throughout the research process, systematically recording my observations, thoughts, feelings, plans and analytical memo in a field diary imme-diately after each field trip. Hence I addressed my examiners' concerns by revisiting my field diary and discussing various issues contained therein. Given exigencies of space, I will focus here on one particular issue tied to 'insider' identity: the problem of 'advocacy' or the possibility of being cast into an 'intellectually disabling' (Bloor, 1997: 222) role where systematic analysis is abandoned in favour of other concerns, such as presenting 'one's group' in a positive light to outside audiences. When revising my dissertation I addressed additional concerns, such as the possibility of 'over familiarity' and steps taken to explicate members' tacit, routinized understandings. However, I will reflexively address the issue of advocacy here, given its broader methodological relevance and implications for academic credibility.

Within the academic literature, notably anthropology, there is debate about advocacy, with some contributors arguing that ethnographers are ethically obliged to promote the interests of 'their people' (Kellett, 2009). Similarly, feminist researchers are intellectually and emotionally committed to promoting women's interests, while key contributors to interactionist sociology unashamedly favour 'the underdog' (see Bloor and Wood, 2006). While such concerns are pressing in relation to particular oppressed groups and politicized issues, such as the topic of infant mortality and chronic hunger (Scheper-Hughes, 1995), I also recognise that calls to 'take sides' may result in a type of research that is hamstrung by 'a prior commitment to a revealed truth' (Silverman, 2001; cited in Bloor and Wood, 2006: 186). I also recognized that, at least for my examiners, there was a potential source of bias in my work where I was simply seen to be on 'the bodybuilders' side', rather than engaging in the programmatic task of generating reliable, trustworthy data and subjecting these data to a rigorous analysis.

My own view regarding advocacy is that ethnographers are often juggling various, sometimes contradictory, demands and the perceived need to adopt a partisan role is emergent, context specific and dependent. Power, oppression and exploitation certainly render some groups more vulnerable than others, with the researcher justifiably adopting an overtly politicized and morally engaged stance in certain settings in an effort to effect positive change. Given the distorting operations of power in society, I certainly have sympathy for underdog and critical sociology. As discussed in my more recent writings on the obesity debate, I would also eschew 'judgemental relativism' in the interests of social justice and emancipatory paradigms (Bhaskar, 1989; cited in Monaghan, 2013). However, my aim in my postgraduate study was fairly modest: I was undertaking an explicitly phenomenological and thus interpretivist piece of empirical research. My priority was to understand a largely unexplored life-world rather than change the world. This undertaking was, to some extent, shaped by my sample as well as epistemological concerns. Despite the 'crisis' rhetoric surrounding male bodybuilders and the vulnerabilities associated with particular configurations of masculinity, most men I met in commercial gyms were materially secure and relatively privileged (certainly when viewed in a global context). Granted, many post-industrial South Wales communities have continued to suffer the corrosive consequences of neoliberal globalization, though there was no evidence from my research that bodybuilding was a knee-jerk response to such forces. There was, in fact, much disconfirming evidence, with other commentators making similar observations elsewhere in the

UK (see Monaghan, 2001a). Furthermore, my bodybuilding contacts, unlike impoverished Brazilian women in Scheper-Hughes' (1995) research, did not explicitly ask me to engage in politically engaged advocacy on their behalf.

Even so, it should be clear from what has been described above that I was not coldly detached from the cultural setting and the people co-constituting it. During my research, notably while interviewing, I also knew partisanship was sometimes tacitly expected, i.e. where the goal was to avoid lending any credence whatsoever to outsiders' objections. It was when I breached this tacit understanding that I also became acutely aware that some contacts implicitly positioned me as somebody who should protect bodybuilders' public image and interests. For example, researching bodybuilding ethnopharmacology was relatively unproblematic (experienced steroid users were only too happy to explain the intricacies of their drug-related knowledge), but asking questions about the putative ''roid-rage' phenomenon was sometimes fraught. This difficulty emerged given the implication that bodybuilders are dangerous individuals, rather than responsible and sophisticated risk managers. And because I regularly lifted weights and was ecologically close to this outwardly peaceful group, I presumably had no need to ask questions about alleged steroid-violence associations nor ask my contacts 'to get involved with that line of thinking' (to quote Gavin, during an interview). Yet as an employed university researcher, working with senior academics who had expertise in studying violence, I was professionally obliged to ask about this issue albeit while informing respondents that they did not have to answer any of my questions and that they were free to withdraw from the study should they so wish. In short, there were potential and actual tensions during my research insofar as I had systematically to investigate something which, in many bodybuilders' minds, did not warrant serious attention lest it lent credibility to societal stereotypes, myths and misunderstandings. My ambivalence about such positioning and questioning, as part of a mixed methods study, is captured in my field diary:

> In asking questions about violence I sometimes feel uneasy. I'm sensitive to the idea that I'm seen as a naïve outsider – even though this is an anthropologically valuable role – who believes claims that steroids cause violence. I sometimes think that my contacts believe I should know better. This was evidenced today after I interviewed Carwyn using the interview schedule in the backroom of Olympia Gym. Whilst at the gym counter, Rex and Carwyn exchanged words in front of me. They remarked that there's violence everywhere in society and asked rhetorically: 'Is everyone on steroids then?' Rex then said to me: 'You train. You know what people think. So, why do you have to do interviews?'

Irrespective of my own involvement in gym culture and the 'indigenous' image many bodybuilders had of me, as a researcher I could not assume that I simply knew what they thought. If I did make this assumption, academics could justifiably criticize me for being self-righteous (Silverman, 1993). Hence, and in ensuring the credibility of my research, I had to breach the role of the partisan by asking sometimes awkward questions during fieldwork and, more systematically, when using an interview schedule.

Contradicting in-group expectations, as seen at Olympia gym, was not risk free. Field relations sometimes became strained and a personal feeling of discomfort ensued when broaching sensitive topics. Gavin, my key ethnographic contact to whom I was enormously indebted, forcefully expressed his dissatisfaction when I piloted the interview schedule with him. He bluntly rejected the set questions on steroids and violence. Even though I sought carefully to locate violence within social contexts, he retorted: 'I'm not going to be lured into trying to isolate [my mood and actions] to when I'm bodybuilding and just when I'm on steroids and say I immediately turn into some sort of raving psychopath.' For the purposes of maintaining rapport and ongoing field relations, I therefore had little choice but to assume an advocacy role during particular encounters. The reasoning for such a move, which I reiterated in my revised Ph.D. thesis, is echoed in the anthropological literature. For Hastrup and Elsass (1990: 301): 'the rationale for advocacy is never ethnographic [but] it should be stressed that in particular cases advocacy is no option but an implicit requirement of the social relationship established between the anthropologist and the local people'. Arguably, my research on bodybuilding as a 'demonized drug subculture' represented one of these 'particular cases', with the need for advocacy emerging as a product of circumstance rather than scholarly plan. Whatever impact this had on the validity of the *information* obtained (and the difficulties engendered when conducting particular types of analysis), as Hammersley and Atkinson (1995) explain, insiders' accounts provide evidence of members' *perspectives* or moral forms.

When broaching and exploring sensitive issues, I attempted to minimize problems associated with my perceived 'allegiance' to bodybuilding and the implication that 'I should know better' than ask certain questions. In practice, this meant that I flagged my academic concern with theoretical issues rather than the political goal of simply 'getting the story straight' (Glaser and Strauss, 1967: 15). I offered disclaimers and I carefully preceded questions on potentially sensitive topics with reference to the larger context within which the research was embedded. For example, I told contacts that the university research team I worked with would be unable to write anything worthwhile on violence for an outside audience (e.g. the broader research community, policy makers and clinicians) unless I asked questions about this. After all, given the significance of violence in the moral recasting of steroid use, readers might simply reject the study if the so-called ''roid-rage' phenomenon was overlooked.

During research I also placed myself in a familiar but 'marginal' role, albeit with a conscious realization that I walked a tightrope and risked being cast as an intrusive outsider. During interviews I sometimes said: 'I could be compared to one of those anthropologists you may have seen on TV, who seeks to understand exotic tribes and who then conveys what they have learnt to an outside audience'. Yet, this did not completely negate tacit expectations that I should present drug-using bodybuilders in a positive light. There was much outside negativity which *they* reflected on as part of their situated identity work. When I explained the study's aims to contacts I also stressed that the research sought to transmit *their* understandings to people outside of their group. In undertaking an ethnographic study my contacts' views were paramount; though, at the same time, I knew I had to try to cultivate a sense of 'detachment' during questioning and analysis in line with my more formal theoretical concerns. Despite Rex's objections, noted above, audio-recorded depth interviews were extremely useful in that respect. Interviewing allowed me to take 'time out' from the more immediate work-oriented gym environment and it reinforced my identity as an academic researcher who had a 'special motive' for asking various questions. When using this *complementary* research strategy, I presented alternative ideas and interpretations to my interviewees for the purposes of activating and recording their understandings. This was invaluable when systematically exploring bodybuilders' justifications for steroid use, for example, since accounts are not usually voiced in settings where such action is taken for granted (Monaghan, 2002).

Even so, in remaining reflexive I did ask myself whether I over-identified with bodybuilders, succumbing to the dangers of over-rapport and a concomitant unwillingness and inability to distance myself from members' accounts. Whilst fieldwork has been described as a subjectivist methodology, employing subjective means to study subjective phenomena (Adler and Adler, 1987), qualitative researchers must maintain those twin perspectives derived from being an academic and a participant in the studied collectivity. Epistemological concerns and the credibility of my research, which needed to be formally credited if I had any hope of obtaining a foothold on the slippery academic ladder, were never far from my mind. Whilst the 'bodybuilder identity' imputed to me was, as explained above, a form of capital that facilitated my research, I recognized that academics may have accused me of simply obtaining and presenting materials that celebrated bodybuilding. I defended my thesis against that possible charge with two main responses.

First, following classic writing in the sociology of knowledge on the tendencies of 'insiders' to glorify 'their' social group, especially during periods of conflict (Merton 1972), I explicitly acknowledged that readers might be more inclined to trust research produced by somebody whom they considered to be an 'outsider'. However, regardless of my status as a *relative* insider or outsider (what are, in effect, contingent social identities), my thesis was explicitly and unashamedly focused on bodybuilders' shared ability to glorify their group in a largely condemnatory world. Offering an 'ideal typical' (Weber, 1949) analysis, I therefore accentuated particular viewpoints for the purposes of capturing the relevant traits that enabled members to view themselves in a 'steady moral light' (Goffman, 1959). As a sociologist, I avoided relating bodybuilding to my own personal and subjective idea of what it ought to be. Rather, particular kinds of evidence and observations were selected for the purposes of understanding how members were able to reject outside negativity and maintain *a positive sense of self*. The collective self-glorification I reported, observed in some measure among all groups (Merton, 1972), was thus relevant in my study *of* bodybuilding. These data furthered empirical knowledge of how bodybuilders constructed 'extraordinary' bodies and identities according to their definition of the situation. As Weber (1949) explains, there is a distinction between a judgement of value and a reference to values, and I was focused on explicating bodybuilders' values.

Second, my sociological concerns extended beyond merely understanding bodybuilders' perceived moral worth – their negotiation of a positive self-image, as it were. In aiming to contribute formally to academic knowledge (e.g. in relation to the sociology of the body and risk) I used a 'multi-perspective' lens (Adler and Adler, 1987) to explore the stratified world of bodybuilding and develop theory. In furthering this aim I recruited a range of respondents – including 'marginal members' (such as weight-trainers) and 'negative' or 'deviant cases' (Bloor, 1978) – thereby minimizing the possibility that I would over-identify with particular factions. As Glaser and Strauss (1967) note, such strategies are important when developing substantive and formal theory. These measures enabled me to offer an empirically grounded theory of how bodybuilders acquire, for example, an ethnophysiological appreciation of 'excessive' muscularity (Monaghan, 2001a, 2001c). This theory, in turn, was related to my analysis of ethnopharmacological knowledge. Such knowledge includes bodybuilders' subcultural construction and management of drug-related risks and the *social distribution* of that knowledge, i.e. how ethnopharmacological expertise was a variable product of bodybuilding careers, social location and relative experience (Monaghan, 2001a).

Conclusion: Closeness and cautionary tales

Ethnography, to reiterate, does not necessitate being or becoming a native. Nonetheless, immersing oneself in a group over a prolonged period is requisite when generating rich ethnographic knowledge. To paraphrase Goffman (1989), my research entailed subjecting myself, my body and my personality to the everyday contingencies to which group members were subject, so that I was close to them while they responded to their life circumstances. As a researcher on the SVP and a doctoral candidate, my work entailed learning about, re-presenting and analysing the world of (drug-using) bodybuilders. It was only by getting close to bodybuilders that I was able to generate grounded, in-depth understandings of their subculture and, in the process, be in a position to advance formal sociological theory. Yet, as discussed above, I encountered difficulties, ranging from some members' suspicions that I was an 'intrusive outsider' to my examiners' belief that I was too much of an 'insider' who needed to reflect more on his social identity. However, I recognized and addressed such concerns both during and after my fieldwork, as would any reflexive ethnographer. In so doing I eventually presented a credible and credited study on a meaningful social domain that had largely remained unexplored or misunderstood by other academics and drug researchers.

Finally, I will offer some comments on media coverage, engagement and consequences. The problems reported early during the South Wales research emerged in a moralized context where the media had amplified negative images of bodybuilders as violent steroid abusers. Additionally, following media engagement and coverage of the SVP, I had to come to grips with the rumour that I was 'from the papers' (which could be interpreted as me being a journalist interested in sensationalizing the so-called ''roid-rage' phenomenon). Yet, prior coverage in a Manchester newspaper also served as an 'ice breaker' when I initiated contact with a gatekeeper in South Wales. The media, in that respect, constituted a double-edged sword. Based on these experiences I remain mindful that potential benefits associated with media engagement must be considered alongside possible risks. Such risks may be accentuated when researching sensitive topics and stigmatized groups. Hence, when engaging the media it is important that our eyes remain wide open and we realize that we can never fully anticipate the consequences, for good or ill. This is a lesson that I took from the bodybuilding research and it has retained relevance when I subsequently explored other 'troublesome' topics that are misrecognized by researchers and the media alike.

Acknowledgements

The SVP was funded by the ESRC (grant number: L210252008) and supervised by Michael (Mick) Bloor, Russell E. Dobash and Rebecca P. Dobash. Mick was especially supportive in his role as my Ph.D. supervisor at Cardiff University between 1994 and 1997. Other people, notably my anonymous fieldwork contacts, were crucial to the research and are acknowledged in my monograph (Monaghan, 2001a).

Notes

1   All names of individuals and gyms are pseudonyms.
2   I initiated the *MEN* article at the end of my undergraduate studies because I was interested in pursuing the research for a Ph.D. and I reasoned that publicity would further legitimise my work in the eyes of possible funders, collaborators and potential field contacts.

RAISING THE BAR IN BODYBUILDING RESEARCH: A COMMENTARY ON *BODYBUILDING, DRUGS AND RISK* BY LEE F. MONAGHAN

Martin Roderick

From early in my academic career I have regularly found the content of academic books and articles on the (il)licit use of drugs by athletes unsatisfying to read. Most academic, but in particular social science, studies rely heavily on a variety of secondary sources in order to develop their arguments and explain the motives of athletes and the contexts in which decisions are made about the use of drugs to enhance performance. This theorizing is frustratingly detached from an understanding of the thoughts and feelings of those people who acquire and ingest or inject the drugs. Athletes who take illicit performance enhancers are undoubtedly a hard-to-reach group, and the unavoidable stigmatizing of those 'caught' and publicly shamed renders this issue a sensitive one on which to undertake empirical research. Yet I would concur with Monaghan's comment that most studies of *the body*, including those concerned with risk taking, lack the empirical detail to test analytical insights. Even today, studies of drug use by athletes appear to eschew an empirically grounded approach concerned with human embodiment; for this reason, Monaghan's text emerges as classic research among studies of drugs and risk in the context of sport because of its phenomenological approach, which captures in brilliant detail the attempts by bodybuilders to sculpt and construct their bodies with chemical assistance. I acknowledge, however, that Monaghan's participants are different from athletes in what might be loosely termed conventional or official sports, since among Monaghan's research participants their drug use is seen as essentially unproblematic, and their conduct remains for the most part unregulated by bodybuilding organizations; in bodybuilding, drug use is accepted and legitimized. Even so, beyond this subculture, drug (ab)use in bodybuilding remains widely condemned and stereotypical images of irresponsible risk-takers are widely reproduced.

I came across Monaghan's study by chance in 2001, two years before I submitted my own Ph.D. thesis (Roderick, 2003). It proved to be an invaluable source of ideas in terms of the presentation of a rich and wide-ranging set of qualitative data, and the manner in which each chapter builds to expose a meticulous picture of the lives of a specific group of body-trainers. In short, I found his work to be engaging, insightful, theoretically informed and well written; for me it set a benchmark of sociological rigour and research craft to which I could aspire in my own examination of the careers of professional footballers (Roderick, 2003, 2006). What I found most interesting though was the manner in which the writing connected to and developed mainstream ideas associated with embodiment and risk as much as it offered a micro perspective on a clandestine subcultural activity. Monaghan's work thus reached beyond and engaged conceptually with a range of literatures, and importantly added to knowledge related to the interconnections between science, technology and the body. This short commentary for the most part is written in praise of this book and Monaghan's accomplished approach to interpretive research. There are three main points on which I want to expand briefly.

First, like all excellent ethnographies, Monaghan presents a thorough and sustained examination of bodybuilders' lives and provides thick descriptions of the processes through which they gain an understanding of physique-enhancement in this sport: the *art* of bodybuilding. As readers, we too are taken on a journey by Monaghan and, like all neophytes in this activity, we progressively gain a distant but meaningful appreciation of the use of scientific wisdom in this process of creating 'the perfect body': bodybuilders' ethnopharmacological knowledge. Monaghan examines the fashion in which bodybuilders appropriate their nuanced comprehension of not only their use of drugs – what to take, how often to repeat dosages etc – but also how these work in combination with training and recuperation schedules and diet and nutritional supplementation. We acquire some appreciation of how bodybuilders conceive of necessary personal characteristics such as sacrifice, self-control and dedication as part of their regime to construct the ideal body – muscular, symmetrical and low-fat – so sought and admired within bodybuilding culture. Central to this book – and among Monaghan's key contributions – is his erudite sociological analysis of the complex means through which bodybuilders become familiar with the 'scientific' expertise to build their perfect bodies, a social process undertaken entirely beyond the sphere of activity of formal medical and exercise physiology practitioners.

Second, this study offers a sophisticated challenge to what, in this context of high-level sport, is understood to be the established, expert knowledge of physique enhancement. As the study unfolds, we acquire as readers a striking sense of the symmetry between the construction of ethnographic knowledge established by Monaghan in this research field, and the style of (ethno)scientific knowledge-production constructed by the bodybuilders themselves – the development of steroid-taking 'lay' insight beyond recognized authorities is superbly articulated. Yet, even though a pre-given ethnopharmacological stock of knowledge represents a guide to action within this subculture, Monaghan makes clear that bodybuilders' understandings result decisively from their own accumulated experimentation and experience; standard intelligence makes clear that drug regimes which work for one may have alternative physiological effects for others. In fact, the customary *investigational* dimension of their bodybuilding trajectories stood out for me in two senses: (i) I was struck by the manner in which innovative and highly individualized trialling with chemical interactions with the body is legitimized; and (ii) how this form of experimental risk-taking with steroids, so routinely undertaken, offers an indication – and perhaps a cautionary note – of the mode of quasi-scientific search for information which may occur in other sports in which physique (and physiological) enhancement is paramount.

Third, although Monaghan's bodybuilders are represented by him as co-operative subcultural actors who 'build' expertise by integrating individually and collectively acquired pharmacological understandings – thoughtfully reflecting on personal physiological reactions to drug regimes – there is for me a foreboding backcloth to this study which remains underplayed. The depth and richness of Monaghan's research and the eloquence of his writing makes it too easy for readers to succumb to normalizing vocabularies tied to, and rationales of, drugs use, to see their world with all its validation of experimentation and sacrifice through their eyes, yet marginalizing unwittingly some of the ways in which athletes' bodies are at risk. Similar in kind to interpretive research that exists on other elite athletes (track-and-field athletes, gridiron footballers, gymnasts), Monaghan largely avoids an analysis of problems which may accrue for those who are injured, or who fall ill, and are (temporarily) disengaged from bodybuilding *action,* preferring to prioritize such risks as needle exchange, steroid abuse and violence. That said, I wonder whether his analytical focus may reflect a common habitus – possibly embodied unintentionally by Monaghan – which eschews forward thinking, rarely considering critically the cumulative human costs of a life spent perfecting a hyper-muscular body.

Monaghan integrates into his analysis the notion of 'risk boundaries', meaning the limits beyond which bodybuilders should not venture, that relate to the use of specific drugs and culturally improper behaviour. Long-term risks to health are rarely considered in terms of such limits but are instead conceived of in quite specific ways. The following two revealing quotes taken from interviews are indicative of Monaghan's evidence:

John: I do not think about it in years to come. You know? 'How long am I going to live?' Or 'When I'm 40 am I going to be in a wheelchair or something?' But like, it's what I want now, no matter what I want when I'm 40-odd like. It's what I want now.

(Monaghan, 2001a: 117)

Bill: When you use steroids [to the extent necessary to win competitions] you really have to weigh up the pros and cons, and you might be shortening your life. You might cause problems in later life [...] A sensible person would weigh up the pros and cons and I've often – in my 'I don't give a fuck' time type of attitude, I would think I have sort of justified it all by saying that I would rather be a meteor and flash brightly through the sky than be a twinkling star for seventy years and do nothing which is a bit – dramatic, isn't it?

(Monaghan, 2001a: 117)

Information-seeking bodybuilders, it seems, keep to the periphery of their thoughts the long-term physical and spiritual effects of persistent chemical self-experimentation and lifestyle constraints; rather, as Monaghan infers, their myopic ideological approach to bodybuilding as an 'ennobling and self-realising project' largely silences any misgivings they may harbour towards their (self-accredited) 'controlled' and 'regulated' drug taking.

Monaghan's work provoked in me two further thoughts, undoubtedly as an outcome of my own sociological worldview. The first is that I felt a wider sense of the lives of bodybuilders beyond the gym would have added to our comprehension of this sporting culture and bodybuilding habitus. I wanted to discover more about their families, the nature of the relations they maintain at 'work', and the way they fill the time between gym sessions. Secondly – and perhaps beyond the scope of his research questions – I wondered throughout why we did not find out more about the networks of people who constitute the drug supply chain. Given the variety and combinations of chemicals used by bodybuilders, we never learn how these steroids are acquired by bodybuilders and who makes them available (and at what personal risk?) However, these are undoubtedly studies for others to take forward. These minor frustrations apart, it would be unfitting of me not to conclude by re-acknowledging the breadth of Monaghan's ethnographic contribution. In sum, very few studies of 'sport' ever offer this kind of detail and insight. Only ethnographers who submit to their craft can construct such an engaging analysis; there is little doubt that Monaghan immersed himself, body and soul, in this research field, and the outcome of his persistence and ethnographic acumen is an academic monograph which exhibits exemplary sociological rigour. This is classic research which has not yet received the recognition among sport scholars that I feel it richly deserves.

6

HOME AND AWAY REVISITED – WARTS AND ALL

Scott Fleming

Introduction

'*Home and Away': Sport and South Asian Male Youth*[1] was published in 1995 (Fleming, 1995). It was based on my Ph.D. study that began in 1987 at the Chelsea School, University of Brighton, and was finally completed in 1992 (Fleming, 1992a). Supervised by Alan Tomlinson and Teddy Brett, the project was conducted in collaboration with the Greater London and South East Regional Sports Council, and was a study of sport, leisure and youthful South Asian masculinities. It was based on a typological analysis and highlighted cultural heterogeneity and the impact of racism, as well as addressing implications for policy in sports development and physical education (PE). A period of fieldwork was spent in North London between April 1988 and April 1989 at a large multicultural secondary school, at local sports clubs and local authority 'playschemes'. I wrote about the rationale and much of the operational detail of doing ethnographic research in the thesis itself (Fleming, 1992a) and in *Home and Away* (Fleming, 1995). I have also attempted to illuminate some of the complexities of an ethnographer's role conflict linked to what has since become for me an enduring commitment to research ethics (Fleming, 1997).

The experience of being a postgraduate research student was a rich and rewarding academic training in empirical sociology. I presented work at conferences and I was fortunate (not to mention flattered) to have a chapter published in what I still regard as one of the landmark contributions about sport and ethnicity (Jarvie, 1991). My description of a small-scale piece of empirical work was not groundbreaking, but it *was* different.[2] I had also been invited to offer a manuscript from the thesis for publication.[3] All of this positive reinforcement for the work, and hence of me as a researcher, was reassuring, but my confidence was a bit fragile, at least privately. I heard that a senior figure in the sociology of sport and leisure in the UK had described me as a 'self-styled "race" expert', which I did not regard as a compliment.

When *Home and Away* was published it was well received by reviewers. In a review essay on three books published in 1995 and 1996 which included *Home and Away*, Tara Magdalinski (1997: 312) wrote:

> It is refreshing to see a researcher recognize the inter-relatedness of identities, instead of trying to understand influences on identity as distinct and non-interactional. Instead of depicting Pakistani boys monolithically (e.g. as 'Pakistani' or 'Islamic'), Fleming looks at the interactive effects of masculinity, religion and nationality.

The conceptual basis of this intersectionality[4] was not something that I had set out to emphasize. My point of departure was simple – the lives of these young people were complex. Having spent a prolonged period amongst many of them in different situations, I did feel that I had something to say.

The period of my Ph.D. studentship also coincided with some significant life events. I got married, the first of our children was born, I secured my first full-time post in higher education, and suffered from a bout of pneumonia – in part linked, I suspect, to my obsessive and unhealthy early morning studying habits.

Almost 25 years after the start of the fieldwork for *Home and Away*, the invitation to contribute to this volume is an opportunity to re-engage reflexively with that hugely influential period of my development – or, more accurately, my memories of it – and to share the 'messiness' of doing ethnography. This chapter draws upon *Home and Away* itself, the Ph.D. thesis and my fieldnote diary. It has five substantive sections about aspects of my personal background, the contextual framework, gaining acceptance, what to discard, and what to include. I then conclude with some summary remarks.

History and biography

The origins of *Home and Away* were a product of my own personal history and political biography (Mills, 1959),[5] the discovery of an academic sub-discipline that 'chimed' with that background, and an interest in the minutiae of everyday life. Born in the 1960s, I was brought up in Kidderminster – at the time a predominantly mono-cultural, medium-sized town in the West Midlands (England) with a history of carpet manufacturing. My family had strong working-class sensibilities. My father was heavily involved in socialist politics locally and was a trades union activist and campaigner. My first recollection of exposure to 'race relations' was hearing him critique Enoch Powell's infamous 'Rivers of Blood' speech,[6] and doing so with unusual anger. My mother moved to Birmingham from a farming community in northwest Ireland in the 1940s. Her brand of left-wing politics was shaped by the anti-Irishness to which she was subjected during the post-war years, and in particular the backlash against Irish communities in parts of England following the Birmingham pub bombings in 1974.[7]

As a child I was not particularly engaged by children's television of the early 1970s, and (rather embarrassingly) became absorbed by the early evening television serial drama 'Crossroads'. The micropolitics of social life enthralled me, and I liked the unfolding interdependence of the lives of the characters. Some years later as a teenager I started attending the home games of West Bromwich Albion, a professional football team in the West Midlands, then managed by Ron Atkinson. At a time when there were still relatively few high-profile black players, Albion had three in a very successful team. But it was not this that struck me most, rather it was the journeys to the ground – as I explained in the Preface to *Home and Away* (Fleming, 1995: ix):

> Travelling to the ground in order to avoid the heavy traffic leaving the motorway, the coach took a route through the inner-city streets of Sandwell. On nearing the drop-off point there was a particular road that the passengers on the coach would use to predict the result of the game. Down this road, when the coach passed a white person, a cheer would go up – a goal 'for'; when the coach passed a South Asian, there was a loud 'boo' – a goal 'against'. Why?

In my early teenage years, I kept a diary. It contained little about me, and much more about what was going on around me. It was neither as elegantly written nor as interesting as the pieces of his 'memoirs' that John Sugden (1997) has shared about his experience as a voluntary worker in Sudan, but it was the start of what later became a capacity to write extensive fieldnotes as an ethnographer. During a 'gap year' I worked as a lifeguard in a Swiss hotel. Time at work passed very slowly and, again like Sugden, I wrote letters. For me, letter writing became an exercise in finding something to say to relieve my boredom. I thought hard about what might be interesting to others. It was not easy, but as it turned out these attempts to see the strange in the familiar (Berger, 1963) were also valuable training as an ethnographer.

I left school with an undistinguished academic record. Having spent my final school years preoccupied with delusions of adequacy as a fast bowler in cricket and having devoted more time to scrummaging and lineout practice in rugby than I had to examination preparation, it was suggested by my biology teacher that I consider Sport Studies. I applied for and was offered a place on an undergraduate programme that was delivered jointly by Newcastle and Sunderland Polytechnics. The multi-disciplinarity and applied nature of the course appealed to me and I metamorphosed into a diligent student. I was captivated by the sociology strand and after graduating took this interest into my training as a PE teacher at Loughborough University. One of our assessed pieces of coursework was an essay about a curriculum issue linked to our main subject, and I chose to write about multicultural education, young Muslims and PE.

This brief and very selective set of anecdotes might be thought a *post-hoc* rationalization of my interest in 'race relations', sport and leisure, interpreted with 20:20 hindsight. It is also possible, though, that my commitment to these broad themes was inspired by at least some of these experiences, and some of my skills as a researcher were cultivated quite by chance.

Background and context

I enrolled at the Chelsea School at a time when the research culture was still maturing. There were only a few research students and the administration of research degrees was managed through the Faculty of Health. At the outset I was unclear exactly what direction my proposed research would take, but a link with the Sports Council enabled a focus to emerge. Sport policy had focused on 'target groups' (Sports Council, 1979, 1982), and minority ethnic groups were among them, but in the main the attempts to engage the South Asian communities in sport and physical activity had been unsuccessful. The research problem was therefore framed around developing a better understanding of the role of sport and leisure in South Asian cultures.

For the first few months as a research student I attended classes in multicultural and anti-racist education. I was profoundly influenced by the tutor, Mike Cole, and his work (Cole, 1986a; 1986b), and also by the work of Robert Miles (1982), A. Sivanandan (1976, 1982) and Paul Gilroy (1987). I read material that was new to me in the sociology of sport and leisure (e.g. Hargreaves, 1986; Roberts, 1983; Scraton, 1987; Sugden, 1987; Tomlinson, 1986; Whannel, 1983) as well as ethnographies in the sociology of education (Ball, 1981; Corrigan, 1979; Lacey, 1970; Willis, 1977). I was drawn to descriptions of research that emphasized methodological flexibility (Willis, 1978), and particularly to Hammersley and Atkinson's (1983: 2) summary:

> The ethnographer participates, overtly or covertly, in people's daily lives for an extended period of time, watching what happens, listening to what is said, asking questions; in fact collecting whatever data are available to throw light on the issues with which he or she is concerned.

Before too long I felt able to prepare a research proposal for an exploratory study that was basically a school-based ethnography of South Asian male youth. My training and experience as a teacher and coach of different sports provided me with a role and a 'bargaining position' to try to negotiate access. All I needed was a school.

My contact at the Sports Council was able to broker a meeting with the PE Advisor for Northbridge,[8] and together the three of us discussed a number of schools and the local sports clubs that would enrich the data collection. Parkview School was their suggestion but the final choice was left to me. I did some preliminary reconnaissance of the borough on foot and agreed with them. This was just as well because I did feel under an obligation to act on their recommendations. Importantly too, Parkview School satisfied my own concerns about the logistics of transport – it was reasonably close to an Underground station. All of this took a little less than a month, it was late March 1988 and I was keen to start the fieldwork at the beginning of the summer term. There then followed a frustrating hiatus. The PE Advisor's role as gate-keeper was crucial to securing access, but he did not reply to my letter confirming my intentions, numerous phone calls were unsuccessful, and messages were unanswered. I felt as though the clock was ticking and I was powerless to resolve the uncertainty. In late April we spoke again, he confirmed that he had arranged a meeting for me with the Deputy Head in charge of Placements and Students, and within only a few days I met with her, with the Head of PE, and with the manager of a local sports centre.

Whilst all this had been going on, my formal proposal to undertake a research degree was being scrutinized by quality management committees at school, faculty and university level. By the time it was eventually approved it had been through 11 iterations – though in truth there were only three significantly different versions. The major stumbling block seemed to be the absence of some quantitative indicators of sports participation as part of the overall research design. At first I tried to argue that these data would not address the research problem satisfactorily, but I was not persuasive. Capitulating to the path of least resistance I reluctantly included a questionnaire survey, realizing that the ethnography could, as Janet Finch (1986: 183) put it, 'be smuggled in under cover of something more respectable'.

In *Home and Away* I reported the key questions that needed answers:

> What were the actual patterns of sports participation? Were the formal indicators for sports participation applicable to South Asians? What other sorts of sports participation might South Asians have been engaged in? What was the wider picture of South Asian leisure lifestyles? Did South Asians want to be involved in more sport? If so, what was required in terms of provision? And what, if any, were the barriers to them?
>
> *(Fleming, 1995: 2)*

In fact, these reflected more the objectives of the Ph.D. study than what *Home and Away* finally became.

Gaining acceptance

During the period of the fieldwork Parkview School catered for around 1,000 pupils. The demographic profile of the school reflected the ethnic diversity of its catchment area and there were significant groups of families that originated in sub-Saharan Africa, the Caribbean, central southern Europe, and the Indian sub-continent. The school was situated in Northbridge, one of London's inner-city boroughs and I tried to describe the environment thus:

> At the heart of Northbridge, the Elm Park ward is a sprawling residential estate. A large proportion of the terraced houses and multi-storey tenement

blocks were once, or are still council-owned, and there are a few owner-occupied semi-detached houses ... At the centre of the estate, [are] the playing fields and parkland that surround the two-storey buildings of Parkview School. The immediate scene is a mixture of breezeblock and red brick, fenced playgrounds and grassy verges, open spaces and quiet corners. Around the school there is evidence of use and of the users: an ice-cream van in the car park, discarded cigarette-ends behind the bike sheds, wire fences distorted from being climbed over or scrambled under, and ubiquitous graffiti tags.

(Adapted from Fleming, 1995: 68–9)

Travelling to Parkview School involved a train, the Underground and a 15-minute walk taking about an hour and three-quarters. But there was much more to gaining acceptance than merely getting to the school.

I began the fieldwork on 26 April 1988. The first fortnight was an odd mixture of being treated either as a student on 'work experience' or as a school inspector evaluating pedagogic practice. Teachers would offer what I'm sure they thought were helpful observations during PE lessons, but they were evidently unclear about my role and trying too hard to volunteer information that they thought would be useful to me. My first note on the first day was a comment from a member of the PE Department: 'Watch how they pick the teams – any evidence of racism here?' And later: 'Asians are more respectful and much nicer to work with.' After a while the working relationships stabilized when I started to get involved in some teaching. In terms of the 'host-guest' relationship that I wrote about later (Fleming, 1997), the bargaining position that I had established in the preliminary meetings was now paying dividends. I was *de facto* an additional member of the department who could share the workload with them. I began to get treated more like a colleague and there was an important symbolic moment when I was included on the departmental clothing order.

The role that I established always felt like a balance of maintaining the goodwill of my new colleagues (by 'mucking in') and taking the opportunities that presented themselves to gather the data that I thought I needed. I was much more interested in talking to the South Asian teenagers than I was in delivering, for example, a basketball lesson to the General Certificate of Secondary Education (GCSE) group. Yet for a while at least, confusion remained amongst some of the Parkview pupils about my role, and I was described to a colleague in the PE department as 'the tall geezer that's here to make sure we react proper!'

Alongside the fieldwork at Parkview School I also visited a number of sports clubs in Northbridge. On my first day I spotted a poster on a school noticeboard advertising a local boxing club.[9] Acting on impulse I went along and introduced myself to the Head Coach, Stan. I explained that I was a researcher investigating sport, 'race relations' and experiences of racism. It was a naïve blunder – but an open and honest one – and it caused alarm. Understandably, Stan went on the defensive immediately confirming that, 'One of my best boys is coloured [*sic*]'.

Despite the reservations that I only fully understood much later, in the spirit of the wording of the poster, 'All Welcome', I was told that I could attend future sessions. I returned the following week and noted my first impression that, 'they weren't over-welcoming'. The week after that there was an 'Open Boxing Show' at a cabaret club on Canvey Island. I made my own way there and there seemed to be some surprise that I'd made the effort. I chatted to the boxers after their bouts and towards the end of the evening Stan approached me. His was a familiar but sincere story:

> I set up the club to give local kids a chance to get off the streets. Some of the kids, especially the poorer ones, were in trouble with the Old Bill [police], and were very keen. I wanted to pick up the strays and I got a load of real diamonds. You've got to be disciplined in this game. You need determination 'cos you can't hide.

It was clear that he was unsure, even suspicious of me. 'Are you in favour of boxing then?' he asked. 'Perhaps in a couple of weeks you'll tell me what you've concluded.' Almost a month later he was still curious: 'Who are you answerable to? What's it all for? What do you get out of it?' I kept visiting the club until the end of August. By then I had become accepted (I think) – I was entrusted with glovework drills with younger boxers, I was the butt of some good-natured jokes about being a teacher, and I was included in the hyper-masculine 'banter' of the gym about dodgy deals, villains doing time, sexual conquests, and encounters with nightclub 'bouncers'.

I was not, however, gathering data about South Asian youth. In an area where a large proportion of the community originated from the Indian sub-continent, they were conspicuous by their absence. But I was learning about research and presentation of self in the researcher role. I was writing detailed fieldnotes that have served no purpose (until now) except to rehearse the skills of data capture. I wrote in microscopic detail about the structure, content and organization of the coaching sessions, the spatial arrangement of the venue, and the licensing arrangements for competitive boxers. I had intended at the time that this might form the basis of an article on the 'ethos' of amateur boxing, but nothing ever came of it.

Importantly, too, I was also keen not to be thought of as a 'user' who discarded research participants as soon as they had fulfilled their usefulness.[10] I later discovered that the club had been the subject of an article in a Sunday newspaper a few months before my arrival. I was told it had suggested that boxing should be banned. I had no idea, and I don't think that I could have found out, except by chance. As a researcher, you don't know what you don't know.[11]

Elsewhere my contact at the Sports Council had paved the way for my visits to other clubs (athletics, badminton, cricket, swimming, table tennis, weight training). My interviews with the small number of South Asian youngsters were arranged, conducted, analyzed and did not reveal anything particularly interesting. I was made to feel both welcome and important. The only other lead that I pursued independently of the Sports Council was at a second swimming club because I had been told during an interview at school that there were two South Asian swimmers.

Sensitized (even chastened) by my experience at the boxing club, I was more cautious about approaching this club. I sent a letter of introduction to the club Secretary and an appointment to visit the club was arranged on the phone.

I described the hostility I encountered on my arrival in *Home and Away*:

> I was introduced to the club coach but he was busy. A few minutes later he returned and demanded to know precisely what I was doing. I explained in the briefest and most general way, and he seemed placated. He even suggested that if there was anything I needed to know I only had to ask . . . At the end of the session I asked him if I could arrange a chat with the South Asian swimmer [Dinesh], to which he replied: 'I'll ask him, and you won't talk to him unless I'm there.' I was taken aback by the aggressive tone he adopted, and that I was clearly perceived as a threat . . . I explained what I wanted to talk about, and he made it clear that I was not to talk about anything other than swimming: 'And if you do talk about anything else, I'll punch yer lights out.'
>
> The threats of violence did not particularly alarm me . . . but the tone for the interaction was set . . . It was perhaps an unsurprising reaction to my interest in the club, particularly when the coach's view of research of this kind was placed in some sort of context:
>
> 'I think it's people like you, on their soap-boxes, who spout on about it that cause all the trouble. Kids come here, and whether they're black or white, no-one cares. It's only when attention's drawn to it that there's a problem. I went through Higher Education, so I know.'
>
> At the time my emotions went through a range that included despondency, frustration, anger and amusement. It all took place at a relatively advanced point in the fieldwork and there was insufficient time to gain acceptance in the ways that I had been able to previously.
>
> *(Fleming, 1995: 56)*

Having arranged the interview and parted on reasonably amicable terms, I reflected in my fieldnotes:

> I had hoped to ask about how sport fitted into his lifestyle, what he did, what he enjoyed, what he didn't and so on. But these are apparently off limits. I feel that my hands are tied in terms of the questions I can ask and I'm already skeptical about the quality of the data I can collect. However having gone this far I'm determined to see it through. This was by far my worst experience of doing research. It feels like an attack on me and my integrity. I am furious.
>
> *(18 January 1989)*

I interviewed Dinesh the following week, as much out of bloody-mindedness as anything else. He was chaperoned by the club Secretary and was articulate but not particularly forthcoming. The interview was brief and as soon as I turned off the tape recorder he got to his feet and strode purposefully out of the room.

These experiences highlighted some important themes. First, managing the disclosure of information about me and the project was context sensitive in a way that I didn't appreciate until after mistakes had been made. Greater accuracy at the outset might have prevented some of the ambiguity about my role at Parkview School, yet the danger of causing alarm by revealing the nature of a project that was inevitably perceived to be sensitive was also exposed at Northbridge Boxing Club. Second, being a member of the PE department whilst being a researcher at Parkview School created some role conflict (Fleming, 1997), and there were tensions between the professionalism of being a ('sort of') teacher and the importance of building rapport and trust with key informants for the research (see Fleming, 1995: 58–9). Third, the Sports Council, and my contact with it, fulfilled 'gate-keeper' functions. In most instances 'doors were opened' and the research facilitated, but there were few South Asian youngsters involved in these clubs and there was little return on the effort involved. As an ethnographer pursuing hunches and occasionally acting independently, I would have welcomed Sports Council support at the second swimming club. Yet I sensed (without ever addressing the question directly) that the same support would have resulted in even more suspicion at Northbridge Boxing Club – a fear of institutional surveillance with the authority of a quango.[12]

What to discard?

In the final preparation of *Home and Away* some of the key decisions concerned what should be included and what should not. From the Ph.D. study there had already been a commitment to a questionnaire survey of participation amongst South Asian males and the findings were included in the thesis. I felt that I had an obligation to gather data in this way and I began by considering the possibility of using a psychometric inventory to explore the link between the mechanisms of physical activity participation and psychological benefits that accrue from it, especially those associated with enhanced self-esteem. The idea was derived from a very superficial understanding of exercise psychology, but did seem an interesting avenue to explore. I wrote a paper explaining the theoretical basis of Robert Sonstroem's (1978) Psychological Model for Physical Activity Participation and tried to persuade myself that, as part of the ethnography, the Physical Estimation and Attraction Scale (PEAS) would help to unlock the research problem. Halfway through the 4,000-word paper my supervisor, Alan Tomlinson, noted in the margin 'You must think through the relation of these sorts of data, so gathered, to your ethnographic fieldwork data'. He was right and I had not. Towards the end of the paper there was a section noting the limitations of the model and its inability to predict exercise adherence. The conclusion was a weak and unconvincing attempt to explain how the proposal to include a survey using the PEAS would add value to the project.

In truth, by the time the paper had been written what had initially seemed like a good idea had evaporated into a waste of time. I had attempted to argue a case and found that the planks for the argument were simply not up to the job. Before offering a timely reminder about ethnographers not importing conceptual frameworks that might influence the social behaviour they were investigating, Alan began his concluding comments positively: 'Generally, you've worked out how you've nothing to lose.' But he was wrong about that, there was plenty to lose – not least the opportunity cost of exploring that particular 'dead end'. I had become temporarily absorbed by empirical expediency and had lost sight of the epistemological platform for the entire project. We had arranged a tutorial to discuss the paper: it did not last long. The PEAS was discarded without further ado.

Nevertheless, I still felt obliged to gather some quantitative data and pursued a more conventional line of enquiry. I designed a survey instrument predicated on certain tentative hypotheses that emerged from the literature and extant policy documents: young South Asians were under-represented in sport; they participated in a limited range of activities; there were clear preferences for some sports rather than others; they encountered barriers to participation not experienced by other groups; and they were not a homogeneous group. I attempted to gather as much data as I could in order to shed light on the research problem. But the 'You and Sport' questionnaire was created using primitive word-processing software[13] and was large and 'clunky'. It filled six sides of A4 paper and invited respondents to indicate their attitudes to 25 specific sports/physical activities on Likert scales. There was an attempt to gauge levels of participation, awareness of venues to participate, involvement in out-of-school clubs, barriers to participation, and demographic details. It was piloted and refined in the usual ways and then administered.

My role in the PE department provided me with some opportunities to get pupils to complete the questionnaire and it soon became clear that asking participants to give up their 'free time' at break or after school to complete this task was not going to be successful. I explained the approach that I eventually adopted in the thesis:

> Most of the pupils at Parkview School seemed to enjoy PE, or at the very least found it a welcome diversion from pen-pushing in the classroom. Not surprisingly they were unimpressed to discover that their time for doing PE was being eroded at the expense of work that they perceived to be akin to 'school-work' ... The coping strategy was to attempt to use non-PE time for the questionnaire, which in turn necessitated the cooperation of other members of Parkview staff. In the event, and in spite of the pressures that the teachers were working under, all of those who were approached were very helpful. Moreover, the way that PE was seen as 'precious' worked positively in the non-PE situation as respondents seemed to be enthused by the content of the questionnaire.
>
> There were two points of contact: English, and Personal and Social Education (PSE). The questionnaire was introduced under the auspices of developing 'communication skills' in English, and as both a form-filling exercise and a means of conceptualizing sport as leisure in PSE. In both instances the different sets of respondents almost always reacted positively to something that was perceived to be more interesting than what they would otherwise have been doing. One respondent whose English lesson had been

disturbed remarked: 'I'd rather be doing that thing about sport than shitty poetry.'

(Fleming, 1992a: 381–2)

I had anticipated that the questionnaire would take between 15 and 25 minutes to complete. As it turned out, it took some respondents up to 35 minutes. Part of the difficulty was that many pupils had problems with basic literacy; I was told as many as 80 per cent had a reading age two years behind their chronological age – but this was unconfirmed. Of those who were able to complete the questionnaire there were some who were deliberately troublesome:

> Marjorie Saunders allowed me to do the questionnaire with her 4th year group. She was present throughout and seems to have no rapport with the group. They only did what she asked begrudgingly and they made their irritation audible and obvious. Jayant and I had spoken previously and he had been cooperative and frank – an ideal interviewee. In this different environment he was the opposite – awkward, obnoxious and objectionable.
>
> In front of an audience he adopted an anti-authority mode of behavior – which included his responses to me. Later when we met in the corridor we shared a joke and he apologised for the way he'd behaved: 'I was a pain in the arse, wasn't I? But you gotta do it, 'aven't you?' I asked him if he'd complete the questionnaire again, properly this time.[14] After checking to make sure no-one was around he agreed and took a copy. He returned it the next day.

(Fleming, 1992a: 385)

The reality of attempting to undertake a survey in the school was fraught with other difficulties too. The respondents were a 'captive audience' but there were a number of reasons that accounted for a response rate of only 75 per cent overall – a burst water pipe resulting in closure for a day, 'red-nose' day [charitable fundraising] activities, negotiated timetables and truancy. The findings were unremarkable and I dutifully sought those results that showed statistical significance. I spent time interpreting and analyzing these data and began to offer commentary, but I constantly returned to the fieldnotes and interview transcripts to provide explanation.

The questionnaire did provide some contextual background. For example, South Asian families were disproportionately over-represented in lower socio-economic class groups. Crude analyses of South Asian groups did not accommodate the heterogeneity of South Asian cultures adequately, and there were more similarities than differences in the reported participation patterns between ethnic groups. Perhaps the clearest findings were linked to the barriers to participation. In contrast to their non-Asian peers, significantly more of the young South Asians at Parkview School reported their perceptions of 'not having time' ($p < 0.01$), 'parental/guardian disapproval' ($p < 0.01$) and 'feeling unsafe' ($p < 0.01$).

In the end, though, the statistical evidence did not seem to me to add anything of value to *Home and Away*. It was the richer, deeper observation and interview data that I trusted more. The analysis of the questionnaire findings felt formulaic and tedious, and I was working to a 'page budget' for the manuscript. I decided not to include any of it.

There are two general points here. First, as an ethnographer I had the opportunities to chase leads which I thought could be fruitful. Indeed to deny those opportunities would have stifled one of the principal strengths of an ethnographic research design. Some of the leads that I chased were fruitless, but this was seldom (if ever) knowable prior to the chase. Crucially, though, as an ethnographer I found myself being carried away by what seemed superficially to be a purposeful way forward. Attempting to provide a robust rationale – in this instance in writing – was the 'acid test', and it was unsuccessful. Many of my fieldwork decisions were made hastily because they had to be, but matters of research design required more careful thought and consideration. Second, the extensive questionnaire survey that was conducted was very time consuming. Reassuringly, it did not reveal anything unexpected, which begs the question 'Was it worth doing?' In this instance, the answer is probably a cautious 'Yes'; but it added nothing original to the body of knowledge and would, I think, have been a distraction from the substantive arguments contained within *Home and Away*.

The wheat and the chaff

The fieldwork for the study yielded a very large volume of data – approximately 350 pages of fieldnotes, 400 pages of interview transcripts, and 376 questionnaire responses each with over 100 items. A large proportion of what was gathered did not feature in the final draft of *Home and Away* and one of the challenges for an ethnographer is to decide what to include. There were three principles that guided the decision-making: relevance, importance and interest.

The year-long period of data collection was characterized by three distinct phases that coincided roughly with the three school terms. Broadly the first phase was about building relationships with the key actors and informants who enabled me to address the research problem. I attempted to write about anything and everything, but it turned out to be mostly something of nothing. At the end of the term I was beginning to get concerned that I was not getting anywhere. The second phase began with a real sense of purpose about gathering relevant data. The interviews began and the progress was almost immediate. Those with whom I had managed to cultivate a rapport were helpful and candid, and my anxieties began to ease – though I did note frequently my feelings of frustration when arranged interviews did not occur as planned. The final phase was concerned additionally with the questionnaire survey. After my last day at Parkview School I noted: 'As I left the school for the last time I felt a huge weight lifted from me and a sense of genuine relief. The role [of teacher] has enabled me to gain the sort of in-depth information that I would not have been able to obtain in a shorter period of time. It's still too early to see what's been achieved.'

By this time the analytical process had already begun and I was beginning to make sense of the data. In the end, most of the material that I gathered in the first term was not relevant, but I didn't know that until a very advanced stage. Importantly, the irrelevant fieldnotes that I recorded were also comforting (because I had something to show for time spent in the field) and cathartic (because I could vent my spleen).

Having filtered the relevant data, particular pieces of evidence were then identified as also being important. I remember vividly the sense of excitement of knowing (or at least thinking) that I'd got something useful. Some were incidents and episodes that were described to me in interviews. Others, like Rashid's story, I had observed:

> Rashid seems to be picked on a lot. Today he had some new trainers, but these were not a recognised brand name ... They were similar in appearance to cheap 'market-bought' trainers and had been designed to look like the 'Adidas' brand – but with two stripes instead of three ... He was humiliated in front of the whole PE group whilst getting changed:

> *John:* [to the rest of the group] 'Who's got some new trainers then? They look like Adidas, but they've only got two stripes' [laughs].
> *Rashid:* [indignantly] 'They're just as good' [laughter from everyone].
> *John:* 'How much were they then?'
> *Rashid:* [with pride] '£14' [laughter from the rest].
> *John:* [sarcastically] '£14. Fuckin' 'ell, they must be good then' [laughter from everyone].

Days later I spoke to Rashid about his experience:

> Rashid again bullied by his peers, but he is reluctant to admit it when we talk, and he won't name names. His loyalty to a group in which he is unpopular, and even ostracised, is fascinating. Sadly for him, his unwillingness to 'grass up' his classmates does not seem to endear him to them. If anything, the opposite may be true: he is sneered at and held in contempt because of his failure to do anything about his situation.
>
> *(Fleming, 1995: 76–7)*

Having identified the data that were both relevant and important, the third criterion was that they should also be interesting. This is perhaps more a matter of judgement than the other two, but it provided an analytical 'rule of thumb'. For example, on the policy-related matter of multi-cultural dance in the PE curriculum, Jayant was especially outspoken:

> All that Asian dancin' and that, it's OK, but most kids here think it's a load of shit. Can you imagine if Joel 'n' Anton [African-Caribbeans] had to do it,

they'd really take the piss out of us [South Asians]. If you wanna teach us dance, teach us 'moonwalking' an' that.

(Fleming, 1995: 103)[15]

And Dinesh was equally forthright about the way that he had confronted racist abuse when it had been directed at him:

Now and then when I go down the park to play football, they [people at the park] say things like 'Get back to your own country "Paki", What are you doing here? Your lot can't play football.' At the time you just swear back: 'Fuck off! You don't know what you're talking about.' Or sometimes I just lose my temper and say 'OK, if you want to fight, let's fight now'. Sometimes they back off, but sometimes they start fighting; I've had lots of fights. I used to get called a lot – a couple of years ago, but not so much now.

(Fleming, 1995: 92)

The material included in *Home and Away* was often typical of broad patterns of behaviour rather than unusual events. For every example chosen there were others that would have made the point – though in my judgement they would not have made it as clearly. This is partly a rebuttal to the criticism directed at ethnographic research that it is too haphazard and due more to serendipity than systematic enquiry. Simply, if an ethnographer spends enough time in the field, most of the routine day-to-day events will be encountered sooner or later. Rather than the critical incidents with which, for example, investigative journalists are often concerned, the sociological ethnographer's priorities emphasize ordinary everyday life (Sugden, 2005).

Concluding comments

The fieldwork that informed *Home and Away* was a combination of a sustained period at Parkview School, a series of ethnographic visits at different sports clubs and paid work at school holiday 'playschemes'. The contribution of the last of these to the overall analysis is reflected in the attention devoted to it earlier in the chapter – that is to say, hardly anything at all. The time spent at the sports clubs was more valuable, but mainly in terms of finding out about the nature of the ethnographic endeavour. In addition to seeing at first hand the influence of an institutional 'gatekeeper', there were important lessons learnt about self presentation as a researcher. The main empirical basis of *Home and Away* was, overwhelmingly, from the year-long, school-based research.

Before all of that, though, there was my own history and biography as well as the preparatory work before entering the field. I may be guilty of 'cherry picking' anecdotes from my childhood and adolescence to help explain my interest and commitment to the project but they were, nonetheless, vivid memories. They still are. More than anything, however, the grounding in anti-racist education was the cornerstone of the project. I therefore entered the field with an open mind (I hope), but not an empty head (I'm sure).

The apprenticeship as an ethnographer was physically tiring, emotionally draining but ultimately very rewarding. There is a suggestion that ethnographers should leave only footprints, but this was really only ever an aspiration for me. The prolonged period of engagement in the field inevitably meant that relationships were built and managing the withdrawal from those relationships was an important part of my attempt not to 'muddy the waters' for future researchers. Insofar as I impacted on the lives of those with whom I interacted during the fieldwork, I hope that I did not cause harm – I am not aware that I did.

As I left Parkview School for the last time I met the Head Teacher for the first time. He commented that I had made a good impression during my time there, and that there was a fixed-term contract available to cover for a member of the PE department who was taking a 12-month sabbatical. He enquired whether or not I might be interested. I was not, but it was nice to be asked.

Acknowledgements

I am indebted, above all, to Alan Tomlinson whose supervisory support and guidance I appreciate even more now than I did at the time. I am also grateful to Graham McFee whose influence on my experience as a research student was much more profound than I had realized, and to the editors of this volume who invited me to take a stroll down Memory Lane and who offered some eminently sensible suggestions on a previous draft.

Notes

1 Hereafter, '*Home and Away*'.
2 In a review of the collection in *Sport, Education and Society,* Faulkner (1996: 123) concluded: 'Taken individually [...], each reading in this collection is well-written, interesting and makes a contribution to the literature. Fleming provides an excellent overview of his study of young Asians in Britain and their perceptions of sport and their participation in it.'
3 The original invitation to publish a version of the thesis came not from Avebury Press, the final publisher of *Home and Away*. The delay in getting it to print was a combination of a decision to close the original publishing house which took time to confirm, and the requirement to prepare the manuscript in a 'camera ready' format. By the time *Home and Away* was published, some of the data were already seven years old.
4 For a recent conceptual exploration of intersectionality in leisure studies, see Watson and Scraton (2013).
5 For a further elaboration of the link between intellectual biography and the sociological enterprise, see Brewer's (2005) account of Mills's vision of sociology.
6 Enoch Powell was the Conservative Member of Parliament for Wolverhampton South West from 1950 to 1974. A classics scholar, he was a powerful and persuasive orator. He made the 'Rivers of Blood' speech in 1968. Essentially a warning against what he considered the economic and other consequences of unchecked immigration, it was controversial, provocative and condemned by many at the time as racist – see Heffer (1988).

7 The Birmingham pub bombings occurred in Birmingham in 1974. 21 people were killed and 182 injured in explosions at two city centre pubs. The Provisional IRA was blamed, though it denied responsibility – see Mullin (1990).

8 Like all descriptors linked to places and people, Northbridge and Parkview School are pseudonyms.

9 Before embarking on the fieldwork I had been encouraged to read Gorn's (1986) excellent book, *The Manly Art – Bare-Knuckle Prize Fighting in America*, and I wrote a review of it. I also became familiar with Sugden's (1987) account of boxing sub-cultures. Perhaps boxing was more prominent in my thinking than it needed to be.

10 See Tomlinson's (1997) depiction of 'flattery and betrayal' for a further illustration and elaboration of how this perception can arise.

11 For a careful illustration of the kinds of known (or unknown) and knowable (or unknowable) information that exist, see Horne (2007).

12 The Sports Council is more accurately described as a 'non-departmental public body'. I am grateful to my colleague Nicola Bolton for drawing my attention to this distinction.

13 At the time Amstrad word processors were a cheap alternative to old-fashioned PCs. They were reasonably intuitive but had very limited functionality and compatibility. Importantly though, they were affordable – even for a research student on a tight budget.

14 Jayant had defaced the original questionnaire and I was able to identify it and extract it from the data set.

15 I later used this evidence as part of an overall argument challenging the tokenistic basis of multi-cultural dance – see Fleming (1992b).

A REFLECTION ON THE IMPACT OF *HOME AND AWAY*

Karl Spracklen

When I go to re-read Scott Fleming's 1995 book '*Home and Away': Sport and South Asian Male Youth* in my university library, the first thing I notice about the copy I find is that this is a book that has been well used by students of Leeds Metropolitan University over many years. I know I am one lecturer here who still includes the book on reading lists and who still tells dissertation students interested in sport, 'race' and racism, or ethnographies of sport and education, to take this book out and read it wisely. No one has yet written a critical ethnography of sport and the intersectionalities of identity that has surpassed it. This is probably partly because the book was published at a time when publishers were still keen to publish books based on Ph.D. theses – since the late 1990s, it has been unusual to see ethnographic research in sociology of sport of the depth, richness and quality that only comes from a sustained Ph.D. study published in book form; and these days students who do cash in their theses for the title of 'Doctor' are encouraged to carve up their work into smaller journal articles. But another reason for the sustained importance and relevance of the book is its uniqueness of content: what we get from Fleming is the messy reality of doing ethnography with young people, navigating through the gatekeepers and the ethical problems, and providing a full and honest appraisal of the process. The book is an inspiration to those of us who want to provide similar 'thick' accounts of the multiplicity of practices and people in sport and leisure, and the complexities and tensions of power and structures that work like cobwebs between the people and organizations in our research.

My first introduction to Fleming's work was the chapter he wrote (Fleming, 1991) in Grant Jarvie's *Sport, Racism and Ethnicity* (Jarvie, 1991). I had started my own Ph.D. in 1993 and was grappling with the same problems Fleming faced: how do you do a critical ethnography in an organization that constructs and reproduces so many of the social inequalities of modernity? I was motivated by an exploration of class and gender in rugby (league and union) but I soon realised in my own fieldwork that issues of 'race' and racism were central to my analysis. In the days before the internet became a standard tool of academic research, I had to rely on word-of-mouth, library catalogues, the newsletters of various learned societies and bound copies of journals to work out who else was doing similar qualitative, ethnographic work on sport and identity. My supervisory team soon put the details of Jarvie's book my way, and I bought my own copy. I was taken by Fleming's chapter because of the clarity and honesty of his writing, and the fact that he was actually producing qualitative, empirical data grounded in his thesis. I was also impressed by his politics and his understanding of the fallacy of essentializing racial identities. When he published a paper on the latter in the journal *Leisure Studies* (Fleming, 1994), it became the work that helped me make sense of my own critical use of 'race' and my understanding of racism in sport and leisure – that paper informed my Ph.D., the research I did with the Rugby Football League on the nature and extent of racism in their sport (Long *et al.* 1997), and the research I have done more recently on sport science and racial science (Spracklen, 2008).

'Home and Away' came out just too late for me to use it in my Ph.D. By the time I became aware of it my Ph.D. was almost finished and I was not about to throw my writing plan off schedule by threading in reflections on and reactions to another key text. At the time I thought it was sound practice to impose a cut-off point on my bibliography. On reflection, I realize now that I did not want to read it because I had reached that point in the writing process where I was scared of reading anything that would raise doubts about my own ability as a researcher and a sociologist of sport and leisure. But I was teaching research methods and I used the book to teach students about ethics, access, participant observation, reflection and analysis. Unlike the standard ethnographic works by Geertz (1975) and Whyte (1993) and so on, 'Home and Away' gave my leisure studies students something they could relate to and understand. They all knew about schools and physical education and school sport, and they all knew about the social tensions of this country. Anyone who wanted to do research in a school setting about 'race' and masculinity, and sport and leisure now had a guide and critical friend.

I left academia for seven years between 1997 and 2004, but I maintained a connection with it through doing research and guest lecturing at universities. I started work for the Commission for Racial Equality on their Sporting Equals project (jointly funded by Sport England), trying to put into practice some of the social and political implications from the work of Fleming and other sociologists of sport such as Ben Carrington and Grant Jarvie. 'Home and Away' was a useful resource and recommendation whenever any policy-maker in a governing body of sport, or in an Active Sports Partnership, wanted to know what research was 'out there' that demonstrated there were issues interconnecting sport and prejudice. People who worked in sport were obviously too busy to actually read the full thing, but the book (along with the important collection of work by Carrington and McDonald (2001), which again included a contribution from Fleming (2001)) was an important test of the quality of the social research that stood up to the sceptical gaze. The length of time Scott spent in the field, the reach of his ethnographic gaze, and the judiciousness of his conclusions were all 'proof' of the social and political problems that existed (and still exist today).

When I returned to sociology of sport and leisure I found Fleming's book was still relevant, and still in use among my colleagues and students. Fleming's work appeals to sociologists of education and physical education who wish to look at inequality in school settings using the same tools of participant observation and interaction. It also appeals to sociologists of sport and leisure who look to undertake critical ethnographies of 'race' and gender in sports settings. His work is not a step-by-step guidebook for doing ethnographies on racism in sport, to use one example, but it does help researchers ask the right questions: What is my role as a researcher and a participant? What should I challenge and let go? What is my responsibility as a critical friend and advocate? How do I capture the complexities of the identity work I see? How do I give my participants a voice while protecting their anonymity? How do I balance the need to promote social justice with the needs of a given research project? Academics have a strong position of power in any research project – in Fleming's book we see how we can use that for the good, for the benefit of society, rather than just for our own careers. His book also gives ethnographers the philosophical and methodological rigour to defend ethnography from its critics; this is research that has solid epistemological and ontological foundations, which can give us an understanding and analysis of an issue that is as strong as any other method in the social sciences.

There are, of course, many things that have changed since Fleming did his field-work. In the book, he sends letters to potential gatekeepers and waits with rising impatience for their reply. These days, the use of email for all formal communications makes it far easier to identify people who can help us do our research (and quicker for them to reply, positively or negatively), and we no longer have to spend months chasing correspondence. Email and other electronic and social media make it easy for us to discuss projects with partners, collaborators and potential participants, so that many of the misunderstandings he mentions are less likely to happen in the planning stage. The other major change is the instrumentalization of research ethics in universities, which means far more rigour and attention is now given to the undertaking of research projects. Fleming's own fieldwork is ethical, and the book clearly describes the ethical questions he asked himself as he planned and did the fieldwork. But it would be more difficult for him to do the same kind of project in today's climate of caution and fear over risk when it comes to research ethics policies. It is not uncommon for research with young people to be classified as 'high risk' and subject to full scrutiny by ethics committees, which leads researchers and postgraduates to decide to avoid such research, and researchers who do go ahead with such work to be pushed to cover every possible issue before they get approval from the committees (schools also have their own policies covering child protection that make it far more difficult for outside researchers to get clearance to do work in those places). This is fine for experiments with clearly defined protocols, but more difficult for ethnographies where many of the issues cannot be anticipated in advance of the fieldwork and where the boundaries of the project may be ill-defined. Ethnography itself has become a method that some ethics committees view with suspicion, because it is difficult to know how full informed consent can be given (and sometimes full disclosure of the research might not be possible).

Fleming is now thinking about these issues and writing about them (a keynote he did at the 2011 Leisure Studies Association conference was called, provocatively, 'Revisiting, Deconstructing (and perhaps re-inventing) Links between Methods and Ethics in (some) Leisure Research' (see Fleming, 2011)), but research ethics policies and processes in higher education still seem to follow the medical model designed for clinical tests and experiments because they do need to be completely transparent and rigorous when it comes to design and informed consent. Any postgraduate wanting to follow in Fleming's footsteps has to plan in far more detail about how they protect the safety of young people, how they get informed consent and from whom they get it, what information is made available, how anonymity and confidentiality are built in, and how to minimize risk to participants, partners, gatekeepers and themselves. It is a difficult task, but not impossible. And my advice to that postgraduate student would still be: read Scott Fleming's book, and look how he did it, and then think about how you would do it.

7

METHODOLOGICAL ISSUES IN RESEARCHING PHYSICAL ACTIVITY IN LATER LIFE

Elizabeth C.J. Pike

Introduction

This chapter will examine the methodological issues which emerged when researching the lived experiences of sport and physical activity in later life. In particular, I will focus on issues of epistemology, the influence of sociological theory on methodology, defining 'age' and sampling procedures, practicalities of the multi-method approach, and inter-personal relationships in the research encounter. However, before I examine these specific topics, I will briefly explain how I became interested in studying ageing and the role of physical activity in later life. The reason for this personal information is by way of 'positioning myself' in the research process. There is a widely accepted tradition of writing the researcher into the research, in order to make visible and transparent the relationship between the researcher and the researched. The argument is that research by humans with humans involves complex personal relationships that should be acknowledged, not least by way of countering the power relationships that may be experienced in the research encounter (see Coffey, 2003).

As a sociology of sport student, I was struck by the widespread discourse that 'sporting activities' in their various manifestations are inherently healthy (both physically and morally), and have the capacity to prevent deviant behaviour and build positively valued characteristics (see Sport England, 2000). There has been substantial research to test such claims and it informs us that, even if athletes are temporarily distracted by sport and learn positive social behaviours on the athletic field, very often this does not influence how they behave in other areas of their life (Coakley and Pike, 2009; Griffin, 1998). Furthermore, it is possible that sports may be morally neutral, or even provide a context and environment for deviancy and negative social values (Nichols, 2007; Ramella, 2004). As Smith and Waddington (2004) have argued elsewhere, it is important to avoid adopting a one-dimensional view of sport as an unambiguously wholesome activity, and consider a more balanced perspective (see also Dunning and Waddington, 2003; Smith *et al.*, 2004).

As I read more widely, I became particularly interested in the injurious risk-taking behaviours of many athletes at all levels of participation, a trend which is both widespread and also challenges the perception of sport as inherently healthy. This topic became the focus of my doctoral thesis in which I examined the risk, pain and injury experiences of female rowers through an extensive period of ethnographic research (see Pike, 2000). The study of injury risk became an investigation into 'damaged bodies' in sport more widely. While injury in sport is generally avoidable (even if this means not doing particular sports), and most are treatable and reversible, I started to question what happens if sporting bodies are damaged in ways that are unavoidable and irreversible. It was at this point that I began to try to better understand the ageing sporting body, as the ageing process is one that cannot be avoided or reversed. When researching sport-related injuries, I had some shared experiences with the participants in my study: I had competed in the same sports, I had been injured myself, and I shared aspects of their biography. In what follows, I will explain the challenges faced as I sought to understand the experiences of an ageing population. While this research was, in many ways, a development of my studies of injury, it involved, in contrast to the earlier work, interactions with people with whom I had limited shared ground as I was at least 20 years younger than my research participants and so could not share their lived experiences of their ageing bodies. During the course of this chapter I will explain how this influenced my research methodology. I will return to the issue of inter-personal relationships in research at the end of the chapter.

'Knowing' the ageing sports participants

Social gerontology and studies of exercise and ageing have been criticized for their tendency to be dominated by an objectivist approach to research, which suggests that it is possible to claim knowledge through tangible evidence, and generally draws on positivist, quantitative and survey-style approaches in order to provide statistical information which serves as proof of knowledge (Grant and O'Brien Cousins, 2001; Markula *et al.*, 2001). Such research attempts to systematically place older people in distinctive categories according to, for example, age and lifestyle. In this way, objectivist research may tell us that more people aged 50–55 play football than do people aged 80–85, while there are more participants in lawn bowls aged over 70 than under 60. While this information may be useful, it is argued that it 'is not particularly good at explaining what it is like to become and be old' (Blaikie, 1999: 169). In particular, Nimrod (2007) suggests that while the concept of 'successful ageing' has received considerable attention in recent years, there is no agreed interpretation of what this means. Furthermore, people experience the ageing process in such diverse ways that it is not possible to have a 'one size fits all' explanation (Nilsson *et al.*, 2000; Thompson, 1992).

As a result of this critique, rather than attempting to simply 'measure' aspects of the ageing experience, I was keen to give a voice to the study participants in order to understand their interpretation of their own ageing and the role of physical activity in their lives. This is indicative of a more subjectivist epistemology which claims that knowledge is subjective and based on personal experience. This approach relies on people telling their own stories, and these are accepted as knowledge of how that person views their own social world. It was particularly important to do this with older people who engaged in intensive sporting activities, as these are people who are 'atypical' in challenging traditional age-appropriate expectations of behaviour and bodily usage (see Tulle 2008a, 2008b, 2008c). I wanted to hear their stories in their own words in order to gain an in-depth understanding of a group whose voices have not been widely heard, and whose experiences may inform future policy and practice in making appropriate provisions for older people's physical activity. My own research has, therefore, adopted a multi-method sub-jectivist approach drawing on participant observation, semi-structured interviews, written stories and semiology. My studies of physical activity in later life have included hearing the stories of those who are international athletes, keen recreat-ional participants, and those for whom physical activity is an unpleasant necessity for health reasons. Some of these participants spent time speaking with me, some wrote their stories for me, and others I observed while participating in physical activities alongside them. I also examined policy documents related to physical activity in later life from a number of different countries. And I have read many fictional representations of ageing in order to understand what contribution fiction might make to our understanding of the ageing process. I will explain each of these methods in this chapter, following an explanation of the sociological theory which informed my approach to the research, and the sampling procedures I adopted.

The influence of sociological theory on methodology

The methods that I chose to use in my research have been informed by the work of Goffman, a sociologist whose work is mostly associated with the traditions of symbolic interactionism. Goffman has been labelled as 'the consummate sociologist' (see Birrell and Donnelly 2004: 49), someone who was always observing and writing notes on human behaviour, whether mid-way through a dinner party or at the scene of a traffic accident. Goffman believed that sociology was not just something to be read about but is something that should be 'done' through observ-ing and interacting with everyday life. He was interested almost exclusively in the subtle nuances and minutiae of human speech and activities that underpin human interaction and which he termed 'face work' (Goffman, 1967). This influenced my own research and, in particular, the decision to spend time with, and talk to, the participants in my studies (see Pike 2010, 2011a, 2012).

This approach to my research also addressed the critique of objectivist method-ology stated earlier. This is particularly important in studies of ageing because the longer a person lives, the greater the array of life experiences they are likely to have had, making older populations increasingly heterogeneous and less easy to categorize in a way that is meaningful (see Nilsson *et al.*, 2000; Pike, 2012; Thompson, 1992). Therefore, it was important to me to identify the variety of experience of ageing. Instead, I sought to understand individual differences and, in particular, to examine the meaning and significance of people's physical activity experiences in later life (Langley and Knight, 1999; Roper *et al.*, 2003).

Defining 'age' and sampling procedures

Undertaking this research raised a number of dilemmas when deciding who to include in the study. For example, when considering sampling procedures, it became necessary to define at what point is a person defined as 'old' and, indeed, does this categorization in itself perpetuate negative classification systems and stereotypes. There is a variety of ways by which researchers can decide who to involve in their research studies. Some researchers choose to adopt 'random sampling' procedures, whereby participants may be engaged in the research process by ensuring that every member of a population has an equal chance of being chosen for the project (for example, drawing names from a hat). Others use more purposive sampling, whereby participants are deliberately selected due to the relevance to the research study of their biography or experiences.

With respect to the selection of participants in my research, I wanted to hear the voices of people who were in later life but it was important to recognize the varied experiences of the chronological ageing process. As Nilsson *et al.* (2000) explain, chronological age tells us very little about a person's experience of being or feeling 'old' and, while some older people report feeling old, many claim that they do not. As a result, when selecting people to tell their life stories, I did not feel that it was appropriate or relevant to define people as 'old' once they reach a particular age. Instead, I used a particular life event, that of retirement, as a marker of a definitive stage in the life course (see Pike, 2010, 2012). As Nimrod (2007) notes, retirement represents a transition from middle to old age and is an invention of modern societies. While the legislation regarding retirement differs across nations, and has recently been amended in the UK, where my research was based, the participants had all experienced the requirement to retire from paid employment at the age of 60 for women and 65 for men, and so all the study participants were at least 60 years of age.

A further reason for choosing retirement as the basis for selecting research participants is that it is widely accepted as a life stage which is significant in its impact on lifestyle, access to regular social networks, physical activity and mental stimulation. In order to access the study participants, I made contact with people who were known to me and who regularly took part in exercise classes including Masters swimming clubs and a Scottish dancing group, and so would be able to share their experiences of maintaining physical activity into later life as a positive lifestyle choice. I was also introduced to others who had been referred to an exercise programme for particular health benefits (specifically cardiac rehabilitation and diabetes). Finally, I reached some people through a process of snowball sampling, whereby additional people are contacted who are known to the researcher or other participants. While this latter process is useful in extending the reach of the study beyond those with whom I had direct contact, it does mean that the research is likely to draw on the experiences of similar people who are networked through shared life experiences. I attempted to broaden the stories I heard by accessing people through various avenues as described, but it is important to acknowledge that my research did not use random sampling methods, and that the participants in the study were purposively sampled for the stories that they might tell. In particular, the study was dependent on people volunteering to tell their stories. Only two people whom I approached declined to be involved, largely because they did not want to be involved in a study about ageing as they felt it would label them as 'old'. These stories would have been interesting to hear on this very basis, but are necessarily excluded from my research, thus limiting the breadth of information that can be presented.

The multi-method approach

Earlier, I explained how I had chosen to adopt a multi-method approach to my research, informed by subjectivist epistemology and drawing on participant observation, semi-structured interviews, written stories and semiology. I will now explain each of these methods in turn to highlight the benefits and complexities of using the multi-method approach.

The participant observation was undertaken over a period of two years by participating in Masters swimming training sessions (see Pike, 2010, 2012). Access to the group was easy as I was already a Masters swimmer training in a different age category, and so I could simply move into different lanes to be with different people. This is not uncommon practice as swimmers often change lanes depending on the sessions that are being run, whether people are injured or feeling tired and so on, minimizing any effect that I may have had on people's behaviour. At times, I also observed sessions from the side while indicating that I needed to rest, in order to attend to the activities uninterrupted by my own exercise. The purpose of the participant observation was to provide a context for the research, and to personally experience the sport and social relations in the clubs from a range of perspectives (Tulle, 2008b) in the way advocated by Goffman. In addition, I was able to introduce to people my interest in their experiences of ageing while we trained together, and in this way I developed contacts for the interviews.

Unstructured conversational interviews (Amis, 2006) enabled the collection of some biographical data about the study participants such as their age and family life, their lived experiences of physical activity and the changing role of exercise in participants' lives as they aged, their relations with others, and their (in)active bodies. The choice of conversational interviews as a methodological tool enables the researcher to 'give back' to the researched, not only by listening and reassuring those who are socially marginalized (in this case by age) that they are worthy of attention, but also by giving visibility to them, making the private public, and offering the potential for socio-political change (Denzin, 1989; Elbaz, 1990; Gitlin, 1990; Plummer, 1983). During the course of the interviews, several people mentioned to me that they appreciated someone taking an interest in their stories, and that speaking to me about their experiences had increased their awareness of their own lifestyles and may influence their own behaviour. Some felt that they were now inspired to 'be more active' (77-year-old woman). However, for others this was an unhappy experience, with one 71-year-old woman stating: 'I am in tears now thinking about the things I can't do anymore.' This illustrates the messiness of doing research: my intention was to hear and share personal stories in order to better understand and inform future practice. While I largely achieved my research aim, it was only a positive experience for some of the participants, and was negative for others. This became particularly problematic as I then needed to withdraw from the research environment and participants in order to write up my findings. Many researchers experience the end of research studies as challenging, often feeling guilt that they no longer appear interested in their participants once data have been collected (Coffey, 2003). I was careful to ensure that they knew how to contact me if they wished to communicate further, and personally corresponded when there was further contact, in order to avoid any abrupt ending to the research.

Some study participants were also prepared to write down their experiences in addition to face-to-face contact. I offered this by way of an alternative method of data collection, in case some people found it easier to write down their stories or wished to take time to reflect and provide further information following face-to-face contact. Others who were not available for interviews due to geographical distance were provided with a questionnaire which, after some initial biographical data, simply encouraged them to write freely about their experiences of the ageing process, how they felt about their bodies as they grew older, and the role that physical activity had played throughout their lives (see Pike, 2010).

The interviews lasted from 30 to 120 minutes, were recorded on a dictaphone and transcribed, while the written documents varied in length and detail according to the preferences of the study participants. Both the interviews and written documents were coded by systematic thematic analysis, which is used in order to build a comparative picture across the different stories (Plummer, 1983). All research studies need to be able to prove that the researcher's interpretation of the data is credible: in other words, that it accurately reflects the lived experiences of the study participants, and that it is likely that someone else interpreting the same information would reach a similar conclusion. In my studies, I employed member checks (Merriam, 1988; Stake, 1995). This involved cross-checking the themes identified with some of the study participants, offering them the opportunity to comment on the interpretation of data. In the case of these studies, participants confirmed that the themes I had identified were consistent with their own experiences, and so no changes needed to be made. However, such checks recognize that there are many possible readings of such vignettes and so help to authenticate the interpretations (see Pike, 2010, 2012).

In addition to my research in which I engaged directly with older people, I have also undertaken studies of written documentation. This has involved an analysis of policy documents, reports and media articles that promote the perceived benefits of physical activity in later life, as well as fictional representations of ageing (see Pike, 2011a, 2013). I felt it was important to understand the ways in which ageing is socially constructed by policy makers who are framing the ageing experience and making lifestyle recommendations for later life, as well as by those who represent older people in popular culture and so may influence perceptions of the ageing process. This written documentation provided a useful framework for the interviews and observations, and in some cases provided a talking point during the interviews (e.g. asking people what they thought of policy recommendations, or whether they had read particular pieces of fiction). Engaging in this multi-method approach provided me with a more rounded understanding of a life stage that I have not yet experienced.

The policy documents were chosen by searching for English-language documents published in the first decade of the twenty-first century. Relevant documents were identified by using the International Sociological Association's table of countries (http://www.isa-sociology.org/) and searching for the relevant government agency in each country with lead responsibility for their older population and for the sport/exercise/activity agendas. Each English-language policy document found that related to these agendas was downloaded from the appropriate website. In addition, an internet keyword search was undertaken using the terms 'active ageing', 'older people', 'sport', and 'exercise' in order to uncover other reports and media articles. In each case, where documents referred to other sources (similar to the process of snowballing mentioned above), these were also acquired in the original and analyzed. This generated a reasonably comprehensive sample of documents (see Pike, 2011a).

As part of my desire to understand the process of ageing, I was influenced to undertake research into fictional representations of ageing by a reading of the work of Hepworth (2000). He has highlighted the potential of fictional representations of ageing as an important gerontological resource for understanding, and illustrating, the ageing process (see also Zeilig, 1997). My approach to uncovering fictional sources was similar to the sampling of policy documents. I undertook a keyword search of terms such as 'age', 'old', 'leisure', and 'activity' in novels, poetry, song lyrics, plays and films, and this enabled a snowball effect as some cross-referenced to others and these were then also acquired in the original (when available in English) and analyzed. Further sources were enabled by recommendations from scholars familiar with the research. The chosen sources have ageing and/or older people as central themes or characters. My analysis took the form of identifying any words that indicated a particular representation of ageing (as 'positive' or 'negative'), along with words that described an emotional response to the ageing process.

This analysis of the written documents adopted a semiotic approach in order to interpret the messages in these documents and to explore how the audience might be positioned, with particular consideration being given to the ways in which older members of the population were constructed. The definition of semiotics as a science is contested, since there are no agreed theoretical assumptions, models or methodologies underpinning it (Chandler, 2007). The approach taken in my research was derived from Saussure's (1983) structuralist methodological tradition, which searches for the meanings beneath the surface features of signs such as written or verbal language (Barthes, 1967). At a superficial level, the concept may be understood through *denotation*, or the literal meaning of the sign (e.g. what the word 'old' means according to a dictionary definition). My studies of the policy documents and fictional representations of ageing were more interested in the *connotation* or social construction of the sign, where the reader is positioned within a socio-cultural or ideological view of what it is about ageing that is being signified.

As Kennedy (2001) has suggested, since there is no clear methodology for semiotics, any assertions of what might constitute a sign could be considered to be an act of interpretation and selection. It is, therefore, important to produce an accurate description of the original text to provide a first-order analysis of the signifying elements presented. The messages uncovered in the reports, media sources and fictional texts were then cross-referenced against research findings from sociological studies of physical activity and ageing (e.g. Dionigi, 2006, 2010; Dionigi and O'Flynn, 2007; Grant and Kluge, 2007; Phoenix and Grant, 2009; Roper et al., 2003; Tulle 2008a, 2008b, 2008c). The key findings from the semiotic analysis relate to the ways in which ageing is overwhelmingly presented as something negative and a social problem, and that people should be encouraged to engage in anti-ageing practices. While these written documents frame much of the experience of older people, they do not reflect the breadth of the experience of ageing which, for many, can be far more positive than is suggested in many policy reports and fictional documents. Adopting this multi-method approach highlighted for me the complexity and widely varied experiences of the ageing process, which may not have been so apparent if I had collected data by only one method.

Inter-personal relationships in the research encounter

Earlier, I outlined the importance of positioning the researcher in the research process. Goffman (1961) described situations where two or more people engage in a single mutual activity (such as an interview) as a form of focused interaction, or an encounter. Effective encounters require the participants to have a shared investment in the process and to engage in a variety of informal codes of etiquette (how close to sit, allowing each other to speak, making eye contact, and so on). When the encounter is deliberately set up for the purpose of research data collection, the inter-personal dynamics are crucial to the effectiveness of the research process.

A particular factor when undertaking research into physical activity in later life was my position as a researcher who was at least 20 years younger than the participants in the study. This presented me with a dilemma: how could I as a researcher interact with, and make sense of the lived experiences of, people with whom I did not share a common lifespan or biography? The challenges of researching outside of one's biography, whether age, gender, ethnicity, or other personal characteristics, have been discussed elsewhere (e.g. Bartholomew, 2012; Bhopal, 2001; Scraton *et al,*, 2005; Simmonds, 2011). There have long been debates regarding whether only women can fully understand women, and how being female dealing with social constructions of femininity impacts on lifestyle choices (e.g. Hill Collins, 1990). In discussions of research into minority ethnic communities, Bhopal (2001) has argued that those from the dominant culture who are outside the minority community may not fully understand all of the cultural nuances of the minority group. Similarly Scraton et al. (2005) suggest that there may have been power imbalances in their research between the privileged group of white British researchers investigating the experiences of black and minority ethnic groups in sport. In their study, they call for greater reflexivity by researchers to acknowledge such relationships. In my own research, as a middle-aged, white, female, I did not share the biography of the study participants, who were both male and female, at least 20 years older than me, and from varied ethnic groups. This can prove to be methodologically advantageous, as I could ask people to explain to me their experiences of being from a different social group, given my lack of personal experience. At the same time, I sought to find common ground to reduce some differences, for example as a woman when speaking with other females, as an athlete, or by discussing my own experiences of a body that no longer performed as well as when I was younger.

Of course, there is no obvious solution to this issue. To claim that only older researchers should undertake research into ageing implies that all older people have similar experiences of ageing and so inappropriately homogenizes the ageing process. For example, we each have fragmented identities, and studies of ageing need to also consider gender, ethnicity, social class, disability and different age categories. Furthermore, such a suggestion would discriminate against capable younger researchers. There is also the possibility that an older researcher may be too close to the subject matter and unable to be sufficiently objective in their interpretations. Wray and Bartholomew (2010) conclude that the key issue is whether the interpretation of findings and conclusions would be different had the study been conducted by an 'outsider' rather than an 'insider'. In my own research, while there were times when I felt that some study participants believed me to be too young to fully understand their stories, on the whole they were very eager to explain to me what I was likely to face as I approached their own ages, and this enhanced the data collection.

One final dilemma that I encountered while undertaking this research was the need for heightened sensitivity to age-related health issues and the sense of impending mortality experienced by many in the studies. Most of the participants in my research experienced ill-health and disabling conditions which they attributed to age. To ask them to discuss their experiences of physical activity as they negotiated their ageing bodies was sometimes a distressing or depressing experience, as they recounted how much fitter and more able they had been as younger people, as illustrated by the woman who was 'in tears' whose story I recounted earlier. Furthermore, during the course of my research, one of the participants in my study passed away. He had been a keen participant in my research, sending me anecdotes and paper cuttings of his achievements and the value of Masters swimming in his life. After one competition, at which he achieved a personal best time in his race, he collapsed in the showers on pool side, and the medical crew were unable to revive him. On each occasion that I read his words from our research encounters, I have to remember that he is no longer living. Although these experiences reinforced the need to capture and make more visible the stories of older people, it also illustrates the 'messiness' of the research process. Unlike controlled scientific experiments, as sociologists we deal with the largely uncontrolled complexities of human experiences, lives, and sometimes deaths (Ferguson and Thomas-MacLean, 2009). While research methods texts can suggest that the research process is quite straightforward, this is rarely the case when dealing with human participants. And when these participants are in poor health, suffering pain, and even dying, this creates additional dilemmas for the researcher to consider, including their own sense of responsibility for, and emotional attachment to, the people whose lives they wish to represent. Although my own research studies have been published and allowed the voices and experiences of some older people to be shared in ways that I hope will inform future practice and provision for physical activity in later life, I have also experienced sadness at some of their stories, as well as being minded of my own inevitable ageing and mortality.

Concluding thoughts

My research journey has led me from working with elite young athletes through to older, sometimes frail and not always enthusiastic, exercise participants. My multi-method approach has been informed by the work of Goffman, who argued that it is necessary to interact with other people's everyday lives if we are to fully under-stand human interaction. In so doing, I learned the benefits of looking at a social issue from multiple angles to gain a more rounded understanding: from watching people, speaking to them, and reading what others have to say about them. And I also experienced the challenges of spending time with real people, who are not controlled substances in a science experiment, whose stories are varied and complex, and whose lives (and death) have had a powerful impact not only on my ability as a sociological researcher, but also on my own life story.

AGEING, EMBODIMENT AND PHYSICAL ACTIVITY: SOME KEY METHODOLOGICAL ISSUES

Sharon Wray

In her contribution to this book, Elizabeth Pike further develops her substantial contribution to research exploring ageing, physical activity and sport. Her reflexive approach offers insight into the complex, 'messy', and unpredictable nature of the social world we live in. It also captures the reality of people's everyday lives and the meanings they attach to the experiences and events they encounter. As Back (2007: 1) has argued, there is a need for sociologists to 'pay attention to the fragments, the voices and stories that are otherwise passed over or ignored'. In order to do this, the methodological approach and skills of the researcher need to be sensitive to the complexities of social life. Skills such as intuition, empathy, sensitivity, self-reflection and the ability to listen effectively to others are valuable research tools. These skills are evident in Pike's (2000, 2011a, 2011b, 2012) accounts of doing research with older people, which provide valuable insights into the problems and pleasures of researching their experiences of physical activity. One aim of this commentary is to show the distinctive and valuable contribution Pike's work makes to research in sport and physical activity. Another is to consider how this type of methodological approach can inform and enhance current research practice in the area of physical activity and sport.

As Pike points out, although it is becoming commonplace to 'write the researcher into the research', discussion of the personal relationships that are formed within a social research setting is often ignored. This is also commented on by Coffey (1999) who notes that research methods texts often fail to address the effects of doing social research on both the researcher and those with whom they come into contact. Yet doing social research is a personal experience that often influences both our perspectives on particular issues and our sense of who we are. As researchers we bring aspects of our intellectual, emotional and physical selves into the fieldwork setting. These personal and professional characteristics and statuses inevitably influence the interactions we have with our research participants. Such interactions are temporary and constantly undergo (re)negotiation between researcher and research participant (Gunaratnam, 2003; Wray and Bartholomew, 2010).

Aspects of past and current experience often influence a researcher's choice of research topic and interest in a topic area. Pike (this volume; see also 2000, 2012) notes how she had competed in the same sports as her research participants and had also been injured. These shared aspects of biography made it easier for her to empathize with her participants' feelings and understand how they perceived their ageing sporting bodies. However, as she points out, because she was 'at least 20 years younger' than her research participants she could not share their lived embodied experience of ageing. Nevertheless, as she comments later in the chapter, biographical differences may be methodologically advantageous. For example, it meant she was able to ask her participants to explain topics in more detail due to her lack of knowledge and experience. Subsequently she was able to gain access to rich detailed data as the research participants 'filled in' her 'missing' knowledge.

The emotional experiences that accompany the practice of doing social science research are often not discussed in research methods texts. Such an approach contradicts one of the main aims of social science research, which is to understand the reality of the social world and produce knowledge that is reliable and credible. This lack of attention to emotion is evident in sport research methods texts where the effects of emotional attachment and the subsequent emotion work this involves are often absent from methodological accounts of the research process and only discussed in relation to the research topic. This precludes attempts to include accounts of the feelings of either the researcher or the participant.

Pike's work is an exception. Her research and publications acknowledge sport and physical activity as emotionally charged pursuits (e.g. 2000, 2011b, 2012). In her chapter in this book, Pike cites two important examples to illustrate why it is important to reflect on how emotional responses influence both researcher and participant during and after the research. She discusses how during an interview a 71-year-old woman breaks down in tears and expresses feelings of sadness about 'the things I can't do anymore'. Additionally, she describes how the death of one of her research participants has a profound impact on her, particularly as she reads the transcript of their interview and has to remind herself 'that he is no longer living'. As a consequence, Pike's inclusion of the emotional aspects of doing research accomplishes two important things. First, the reliability of the knowledge that is generated is increased because it more accurately reflects 'real life'. In this respect, it captures the 'human voice' and creates accounts of the social world that are attuned to the 'embodied nature of social experience' (Back, 2007: 165). Second, it acknowledges the emotional consequences for both researcher and research participant of doing research on sport and physical activity and how these may influence the research process.

Age is a sensitive topic especially when it is linked to the physical body and appearance. Pike is aware of this and discusses the dilemmas of trying to access older people who may not want to call themselves 'old' due to the negative stereotypes associated with ageing. The desire to remain 'forever young' and the current 'war on ageing' are intimately linked to the negative portrayal of ageing that occurs in western societies (Andrews, 1999; Vincent, 2007). Importantly, for researchers these dominant discourses often shape older people's experiences of their bodies and their perceptions of their physical capabilities. This is particularly evident when researching sport and physical activity due to the focus on the body. Older bodies are often stereotyped as in decline or at risk from injury and illness (Bytheway, 1995). Research exploring physical activity in later life provides opportunities to disrupt these negative stereotypes of ageing.

Societal perceptions and expectations about women and men's bodies are also gendered. As Sontag (1972) has argued, older women's bodies tend to be judged more harshly than those of older men; in this respect they are often subjected to a 'double standard' of ageing because they are 'old' and 'female'. Consequently, it is not difficult to see why older people are reluctant to define themselves as 'old'. Hence Pike's strategy of using the category of 'retirement' to access participants who were 'at least 60 years of age' is a useful one.

The age people self-define as 'older' can be problematic. Age is a social construct that is contextually located within a particular socio-cultural and geographical setting (Maynard et al., 2008; Wilson, 2000). This means that the age at which people perceive and experience themselves as 'old' varies. For example, research has shown the age at which individuals self-define as young, midlife, or old, changes across ethnicity and culture (Maynard et al., 2008). This means it is difficult to define when different life stages actually begin and end. Further, a distinction is now made between the 'young-old' and the 'old-old' or the 'third' and 'fourth' age (Gilleard and Higgs, 2000; Laslett, 1989). This is because there are often significant lifestyle differences between those who are just entering into old age (60–65) and those who are older. The effects associated with belonging to a particular generational or age cohort further complicate this (Gilleard and Higgs, 2002; Vincent, 2005). Age cohorts are made up of people who were born into and shared a particular period in time. This means that the socio-cultural and political landscape of the time in which they grew up may define them as a distinct group in comparison to others (Gilleard and Higgs, 2002). Thus, as researchers we need to take into account how generation and cohort influence older people's perceptions and experiences of physical activity.

Pike acknowledges the importance of 'giving voice' to research participants and increasing the visibility of those who are socially marginalized. Feminist researchers have argued for an egalitarian approach to research that has the potential to empower those who participate (Stanley and Wise, 1993). Pike's (2011b) research accomplishes this through her choice of unstructured conversational interview, which is less restrictive to research participants because it allows them to choose the topics/issues they feel are relevant. This may include stories about their experiences they feel are not well known to the general public. Pike's use of research methods is always responsive to the needs of her research participants. For example, she (2011b) asks those who are unable to attend face-to-face interviews to write down their experiences of the ageing process and the role of exercise. This generates detailed accounts that capture the life-course experiences of older women. Additionally, Pike (2011b, 2012) used participant observation of Masters swimming training sessions, over a two-year period, to explore the social interactions taking place within this group and setting. Her choice of method is influenced by Goffman's (1959, 1967) view that human behaviour is best understood through observing the interactions that take place between individuals within a particular social setting.

Her choice of research methods increases the visibility of her participants' experiences and, as Pike suggests, may have the potential to disrupt public discourse on physical activity and later life and bring about socio-political change. Additionally, she notes how some of her research participants said they 'appreciated someone taking an interest in their stories' and how, as a consequence of talking to her, they had become more aware of their own lifestyles and the potential for change. This suggests her research participants felt empowered to change their lives as a consequence of taking part in the research.

The use of written documentation on sport and physical activity, such as media articles, reports and policy documents, is a useful way of gaining access to socio-cultural and medicalized representations of ageing and physicality. Pike (2011a: 214) undertakes a linguistic analysis of policy documents, reports and media articles 'that promote the perceived benefits of physical activity' for older people in her work exploring the active ageing agenda. She applies Cohen's (1972) theoretical ideas about folk devils and moral panics to this topic in order to reveal how the documents 'perpetuate stereotypes of the aging population through presenting an idealized way of growing old' (Pike, 2011a: 214). Significantly, Pike's methodological approach captures how, through language, older people are positioned as 'at risk' and/or in need of expert intervention to enable them to age 'healthily.' Additionally, it shows how ageing is constructed as a social and medical problem and the emphasis that is placed on participation in exercise and the adoption of a 'healthy' lifestyle as a solution to this.

Currently, there is a proliferation of self-help anti-ageing and health promotion literature that promotes exercise and physical activity as ways of delaying and preventing the onset of an ageing body (Wray, 2007). Much of this documentation emphasizes consumer-led self-care with the emphasis on individual, as opposed to state, responsibility for health. In the case of older people there is a 'positive ageing' policy agenda that seeks to encourage them to partake in regular physical activity. In her work, Pike has commented critically on the individualistic healthist discourse in policy documents that links exercise and physical activity to the prevention of ageing (e.g. 2011b, 2012). Although the 'message' of such types of documentation is proactive, it is nevertheless underpinned by negative (often medicalized) understandings of what it means to grow older. As Pike points out, examination of these types of documentation is crucial if we are to gain insight into the contextual factors that influence why older people view physical activity as an anti-ageing strategy, and the way in which ageing is still constructed as a social problem. Subsequently, an analysis of different documentary sources may help us to understand the socio-cultural context in which experiences of ageing and perceptions of the older body are played out.

In summary, this commentary has shown the distinctive and valuable contribution Pike's research and scholarship has made to the topic of physical activity and the ageing body. It has focused on five main topics: writing the researcher into the research; emotions and emotional work as part of the research process; the disruption and dismantling of stereotypes of ageing; research as an instrument of socio-political change; and finally the use of written documents in order to understand the relationship between personal experience and the social and political landscape within which they are embedded. In all of these areas Pike's sensitive reflexive approach is able to capture the embodied emotional reality of undertaking research exploring physical activity in later life.

8

RESEARCHING *INNER-CITY SPORT: WHO PLAYS, AND WHAT ARE THE BENEFITS?*

Ken Roberts

The project: Aims and methods

This project commenced in 1986 with on-site interview surveys of 4,354 adult players (age 16 and over) in seven sports at 46 indoor centres in six UK cities (Roberts and Brodie, 1992). The samples were selected from players who arrived at times distributed throughout the opening hours and throughout the weeks of survey work at each centre. One question in the interviews was whether the players would be willing to take part in further stages of the research. From among the volunteers, quota samples (structured by age, sex, place and sport) totalling 1,387 were visited then re-interviewed in their homes in 1987. At this stage, 292 non-participants, recruited from neighbourhoods adjacent to some of the centres, were added to what became a panel. In addition to the interviews, the home visits included a set of tests and measurements of height, weight, blood pressure, grip strength, lung function and flexibility. Out of the 1,679 (1,387 + 292) who were interviewed and tested at home, 372 accepted invitations to visit a local sports centre for a further set of tests. These were repeats of the height, weight, hand grip, flexibility and blood pressure measurements, plus aerobic capacity, waist and hip measurements, skinfold thickness, and blood cholesterol. From the 1,679 respondents in 1987, 1,275 were re-interviewed and retested in their homes in 1988, and 244 attended the sports centres again for a repeat of the 1987 tests.

The players were from 46 centres which were selected to permit comparisons between participants in the same sports in facilities that were under public, voluntary sector and commercial management, wet and dry, large and small, old and recently built. The plan was to see whether any combinations of types of provider, centres and sports were particularly effective in attracting and retaining particular socio-demographic groups. The project had a longitudinal dimension partly to see whether any specific sports, types of centres and/or local authority policies were particularly successful in attracting former non-players, retaining existing players or increasing their frequency of participation. However, the main point of the longitudinal design was to see whether changes in levels of sport participation between 1987 and 1988 would be related to changes in the respondents' health and fitness test scores. We expected to find cross-sectional relationships (frequent participants in the more energetic sports would score better than other players), but this evidence cannot demonstrate the direction of causality as convincingly as a longitudinal design. Cross-sectional relationships may be explained by sport making people fitter and healthier, or it might be that fit and healthy people are the most likely to become involved and to remain in sport. Experimental, laboratory-type studies with elite and non-elite players had been able to demonstrate the efficacy of sport. Would this hold among ordinary players who were playing in their ordinary ways rather than as instructed by an experimenter?

The project was unusual (possibly unique) in several ways. It was unusually large in terms of the total sample size. It was also unusual in its longitudinal design, and the number of items of information (physical measurements and answers to questions) that could be gathered in the three rounds of survey work.

The fieldwork was distributed between six different cities (Belfast, Camden in London, Cardiff, Chester, Glasgow and Liverpool). This was in order to maximize the chances that the findings would be perceived (by potential users of the research results and other audiences) as relevant in all parts of the UK, in capital and other cities, and also to permit comparisons between local authorities with different sport policies and practices. These included:

- different local mixes of recently built and older facilities;
- concentration of provision in major centres as opposed to dispersion between a larger number of neighbourhood facilities;
- efforts to target specific socio-demographic groups;
- efforts to develop partnerships with the voluntary and commercial sectors.

Respondents were from seven sports (badminton, indoor bowls, keep fit, martial arts, snooker, football, and weights). The sports were chosen so that the aggregate samples would contain adequate numbers of men and women in different age groups, and to permit comparisons between energetic and non-energetic, and competitive and recreational sports.

We knew that if the project design could be implemented successfully, the research would break new ground in addressing all the questions outlined above. Previous sport research in the UK had comprised:

- successive cross-sectional surveys (mainly as part of the General Household Survey) measuring levels of sport participation across the entire population, and within different socio-demographic groups;
- user surveys conducted independently by various local authorities;

- experimental studies measuring physiological and psychological changes attributable to playing sport;
- a large number of small (typically unfunded) enquiries into the motivations, barriers to participation, and gratifications reported by specific groups of sport participants and non-participants.

The case for the *Inner-City Sport* study was that this kind of large-scale, longitudinal enquiry would advance knowledge in ways that would not be possible by simply adding to previous types of projects. This rationale was accepted by the funding body (the Health Promotion Research Trust), so the expensive (around £500,000 in total) project commenced in 1986. Fieldwork continued throughout 1987 and 1988, which was followed by analysis and report writing, which continued beyond the formal end of the project in 1990. In addition to the two principal investigators, the co-authors of the book, there were four research staff employed throughout, plus additional assistants during the periods of fieldwork. The research also had its own dedicated project secretary.

Fieldwork

The data-gathering parts of the project were surprisingly problem free. In a large project it is impossible for a principal investigator to be hands-on during 95 per cent of the fieldwork, so there may have been occasions when equipment was damaged and needed repair, and when survey sessions needed to be retimed on the spot, but any such difficulties were resolved on the spot.

All the local authorities and centre managements who were approached were cooperative. We achieved all the target numbers of interviews and tests. Businesses are usually hesitant about admitting researchers into their premises. They sometimes fear the disclosure of trade secrets, and may also fear that staff will suspect that they are being spied on by managements. Sport facility managements were different in these respects. They appeared to welcome research which would produce hard evidence of the benefits of sport about which they were already confident, and they were also confident that their staffs, members and players would understand the aims and the potential value of the research.

We had wondered whether the samples would be willing to participate in physical tests, given the researchers' total lack of medical qualifications, but in practice we found that people were enthusiastic. They were far more interested in the tests and their results than in the questions about their education, employment and lifestyles. Non-response is often a problem in social surveys nowadays. People often suspect that a 'survey' is really a sales tactic. If people take part, they are often reluctant to provide precise information about their levels and sources of income, and other matters which they regard as private. We found that sport players do not feel this way about their physical condition, and the face-to-face fieldwork created confidence that the research was genuine (not selling). Most of those who were invited accepted the invitation to visit a local sports centre for further tests.

Our experience was that the tests improved retention rates between the successive phases of the research. Most respondents were playing sport fairly regularly. Our questions found that gains in health and fitness were among the benefits that most expected. Hence their interest in their own test scores, how these compared with the general population and with the scores of other players.

The principal investigators had wondered whether it would be difficult to recruit research staff who could handle the sociological and physical sports science aspects of the project, but in practice this was not a problem. Three out of the four research staff initially appointed were sports studies graduates who were familiar with and comfortable when handling all aspects. The social science graduate was able to opt out of those parts of the fieldwork that involved administering physical health and fitness tests.

The fieldwork was completed on schedule, and all data were entered in SPSS files during the initial two and a half years of the project. This left 18 months for analysis and report writing. The latter, needless to say, continued beyond the formal end of the project in 1990.

There were personnel issues (anticipated issues) which arise in the course of all projects where staff are on temporary contracts, and where the principal investigators cannot commit 100 per cent of their working time and attention to one project. Two of the original research staff left before the project ended. They were replaced by staff who were able to work on data analysis, but any research project really needs staff who are there from beginning to end. Both the principal investigators were heads of university departments during the project. Both had teaching duties, and were also responsible for overlapping research projects. Ideally, every researcher would like to take on projects consecutively, with an interval in between, but those who wish to remain research active know that they must respond to opportunities as these arise.

The key question, especially in retrospect, is not whether the research design could be executed (it could) but whether it delivered the intended outcomes. Did the project answer the questions that it addressed? Did it progress the knowledge base for further research and sport policy development?

The design of the project was inevitably a compromise between the normal inclinations of physical and social sports scientists. If the research had been split into two independent projects, the likelihood is that each would have followed its investigator's normal inclinations. Sport scientists tend to favour quasi-laboratory studies, and being able to control a small number of variables that are measured precisely. Sociologists who undertake quantitative research tend to opt for large representative samples when funding allows this (see below), and their normal preference is for research instruments that measure large numbers of variables which can be controlled in multivariate analysis. However, it was the compromises that were responsible for the main additions to knowledge that the project achieved. These depended on the characteristics of the achieved sample, the longitudinal research design, and the combination of socio-psychological and physical measurements that was obtained.

Sport and society

Social scientists, whatever their fields of study, will normally prefer a representative sample of a known population (of a country, town or neighbourhood) rather than a sample of users of particular facilities (sport facilities in our case) or all facilities in a given territory. Population samples make it possible to make statements about the proportions of males and females, in different age groups and social classes, who are using different (types of) centres and playing different sports. For assessing trends over time, social scientists' preference will normally be for sequential cross-sectional studies, not a panel design in which there will be problems of attrition and the expense of securing, then maintaining, the cooperation of known panellists, and which will miss the effects of inward and outward migration, and cohort replacement (the result of ageing and eventual deaths).

User surveys are most useful for facility managers. They learn whom they are serving and, most likely, the users' assessments of the facilities. They will learn the exact proportions of users who are male and female, in different age groups and so on, but they will not be able to establish accurately the extent to which such groups are over- or under-represented unless they have independent knowledge of the population in the catchment area which is unlikely to be co-terminus with any politico-administrative boundaries.

Inner-City Sport needed to conduct user surveys to obtain sufficient numbers from specific socio-demographic groups who were playing specific sports in particular types of centres, in order to compare the profiles of players of the same sports at different types of facilities and in local authorities with different kinds of sports policies and provisions. The panel design was necessary in order to investigate whether changes over time in levels of sport participation were related to changes in the respondents' health and fitness scores. People may be able to recall past levels of sport participation, but they are unlikely even to know what their blood pressure and grip strength scores would have been 12 months previously.

The advantages of a panel design for social scientists usually lie not so much in the longitudinal character of the evidence that can be collected as in the sheer quantity of information that can be obtained from each respondent, over three rounds of fieldwork in the case of *Inner-City Sport*. We were able to obtain 32 measurements of health and fitness, and to administer a stress questionnaire on two occasions, as well as (on one occasion each) gather a wealth of information about the individuals' backgrounds, education, employment, dietary habits, smoking, alcohol consumption, and other leisure activities and lifestyle practices.

Whatever the design of the study, we knew that much of our new evidence would simply confirm what was already known. The footballers tended to be males, females were the majority in keep fit classes, and older players were better represented in indoor bowls than in any other sport. We already knew, and simply confirmed, these matters. Profiles of players in different sports and overall participation rates in the various socio-demographic groups were already known from the first generation of sport participation surveys that had commenced in the 1970s.

However, there were some surprises in our evidence, mostly due to the panel design. We had not anticipated that there would be so many changes in sport behaviour between 1987 and 1988. We knew that the overall sport participation rate had been rising slowly and steadily since the General Household Survey began its time series in 1973. However, our evidence revealed far more volatility in people's sporting lives than had previously been indicated. Around a half of the non-participants who were added to the survey panel in 1987 had started to play sport during the following year. They had not necessarily become long-term or frequent players, but their sport careers had restarted. We are inclined to attribute this to the research itself, especially the health and fitness tests. We may have made an accidental discovery: survey questions about sport combined with health and fitness tests could be more effective than publicising facilities and programmes in restarting lapsed players, especially when they know that their health and fitness will be tested again in 12 months' time.

Very few of the initial participants lapsed from sport during the period of our fieldwork, but we were surprised by how many changed their frequency of play (some change was anticipated and needed in order to test for health and fitness outcomes), and also that there were so many changes in mixes of sports. We will return below to the latter point.

The main additions to social science knowledge about sport participation in *Inner-City Sport* arose from the detailed sport biographies that the research collected. Respondents were asked to recall all the sports that they had played regularly in each year of their lives from age ten onwards. The starkest conclusion to be drawn was that by their late 20s most people were either locked in or locked out of sport. Virtually everyone had played some sport regularly while they were at secondary school. Afterwards there was a steady and steep drop-out which levelled off among those who were still playing in their mid-20s. They were most likely to remain regular players for many more years. Those who had dropped out, in contrast, were unlikely to return and resume playing on a regular basis. We have noted above that the survey itself may have restarted some sport careers that had lapsed, but we doubt whether these returners would have continued to play regularly for much longer. In 1987 they knew that they would be re-interviewed and re-tested in 1988. The main difference in teenage sport participation between those who stayed in and those who dropped out was not so much in the sheer amount as in the variety of sports that the former group had been playing regularly. This appeared to have been important because, as we have just seen above, many players had changed their mixes of sports between 1987 and 1988.

It was also clear from our evidence that becoming a regular long-term sport player was quite demanding. This applied in terms of time – not so much the total number of hours and minutes spent actually playing as the manner in which this required sport to be a principal activity throughout an evening or afternoon several times each week. The financial costs were also significant and probably prohibitive for people whose household budgets left little to spare beyond necessities. Also, regular sport participation required a mixture of social and technical (sport) skills.

Those aged 25-plus who possessed the necessary combinations of skills and money, and who were currently playing regularly, were effectively locked into sport through sheer routine, social commitments and the benefits (immediate enjoyment and anticipated health and fitness gains) that they were experiencing. Those who had lapsed from sport confronted technical, social, financial and time barriers if they were to return.

We also found that the sporting lives of women and players from the lower socio-economic strata were relatively fragile. Both groups were spending less money and playing fewer sports than their comparators. This was especially true for working-class women who were the socio-demographic group that was most likely to reduce its participation between 1987 and 1988. The probable trends with age seemed to be towards wider differences in levels of participation by gender and social class.

Health and fitness

The normal preference of sports scientists who make physiological measurements is to conduct controlled experiments. Ideally they start with groups matched for age, sex and any other social and psychological variables that are deemed relevant and are especially careful to match by initial measurements of health, fitness and/or performance. One group is then given an experimental exercise or training regime and the experiment ends with a repeat of the health, fitness and/or performance measurements to see whether the experimental group has improved its scores relative to the control group. This type of experiment normally finds that the exercise or training regime has made a difference. Different exercise or training regimes can be compared, researchers can establish whether the efficacy of different regimes varies between different kinds of players, which enables individual athletes to be recommended to adopt the most appropriate regime.

The aim in *Inner-City Sport* was to simulate the experimental situation by starting with a sufficiently large sample to permit comparisons across a battery of health and fitness measurements while holding socio-demographic variables and types of sports constant but varying frequency of participation. The full battery of measurements was applied in 1987 and 1988. On each occasion it was possible to search for relationships in the cross-sectional evidence. The intention thereafter was to see whether changes in the respondents' health and fitness scores between 1987 and 1988 were related to changes in their levels and types of sports participation. Positive results would be powerful evidence that normal everyday sport confers similar health and fitness benefits to those indicated in laboratory-type experiments.

Suffice it to say that the cross-sectional evidence in 1987 and 1988 exhibited some but not all of the expected relationships between levels of sport activity and the health and fitness measurements. However, it was impossible to find any connections whatsoever between changes in sports participation between 1987 and 1988 and changes in the respondents' health and fitness scores.

In both 1987 and 1988 we took 32 separate measurements of respondents' health and fitness, and we also administered a previously validated set of questions that measured psychological stress. Analysis of the relationships between the 32 indicators showed that health and fitness were multi-dimensional: there was not a simple continuum. Four underlying health and fitness factors were identified:

- strength
- cardiovascular health
- freedom from illnesses and injuries
- self-assessed health.

Stress was an additional factor which was not closely related to any of the above.

The factors that we identified will be partly products of the indicators that were employed. A shorter, longer or different set of indicators could have revealed different factors. Also, our total sample was not representative of any wider population. A general population sample might have revealed entirely different factors. Our factors distinguish between types and levels of health and fitness among a sample of (mainly) sports-active adults. However, our evidence that health and fitness are multi-dimensional is (tentatively) generalizable.

In both 1987 and 1988 there were clear cross-sectional relationships between levels of energetic sport participation (that is, in the five energetic sports covered in the research) and self-assessed health and strength, but no relationships with either cardiovascular health or freedom from illnesses and injuries. Changes in levels of energetic sport participation between 1987 and 1988 were unrelated to any of the changes that were recorded in the sample's health and fitness scores. Playing sport and taking less energetic exercise tended to reduce stress levels, but playing sport was typically part of an overall active (harried) leisure profile which increased stress. These two processes were tending to cancel out each other's effects.

The respondents whose sport behaviour had changed between the 1987 and 1988 surveys might have made the changes close to 12 months before or only shortly before the 1988 interviews and tests. Our research design was unable to control the periods throughout which new patterns of sports behaviour had been maintained. We could simulate, but we could not reproduce accurately, the conditions in a controlled laboratory-type experiment. In any case, it could be that the changes in sport behaviour that had occurred would need to be maintained for longer than 12 months in order to impact on the individuals' health and fitness. Also, the changes in sports behaviour between 1987 and 1988 were usually modest. People had not changed from playing every day to not at all or *vice-versa*. Some respondents who were already playing regularly and frequently had started playing slightly more or less frequently, often in a different mix of sports. Initial non-participants who resumed playing had typically become occasional participants and were already leading fairly active rather than wholly sedentary lifestyles. Changes in levels of sport participation that are sustained over many years may well make a difference to specific dimensions of the players' health and fitness, as indicated in our cross-sectional evidence. However, the changes that occur from year to year in the course of adults' normal sporting lives seem to make absolutely no short-term difference.

The interviews gathered evidence about aspects of respondents' lifestyles apart from their participation in energetic sports. Two of the sports from which the samples of players were drawn – snooker and indoor bowls – were non-energetic. Respondents were also asked about other exercise, their diets, and tobacco and alcohol consumption. Each was related cross-sectionally to a specific combination of the health and fitness factors:

- other exercise improved self-assessed health and reduced stress;
- a healthy diet including fresh fruit and vegetables was associated with better cardiovascular and self-assessed health, and freedom from illnesses and injuries;
- not smoking improved cardiovascular and self-assessed health, and strength;
- nil or low alcohol consumption was related to better cardiovascular health and freedom from illnesses and injuries.

The apparent health effects of these lifestyle variables, and participation in energetic sports, were additive. Each made a difference independently of the others. So however healthy other aspects of their lifestyles, people could further improve their health and fitness by playing more sport, taking more non-energetic exercise, giving up smoking, drinking less and improving their diets. However, even in combination, these lifestyle variables did not eliminate health and fitness differences by sex, age and socio-economic status.

There was a tendency for the same individuals to have adopted all the health-related behaviour patterns. This appeared to be due to a health and fitness con-sciousness which was measured with its own battery of questions. People were most likely to engage in all the desirable health and fitness practices if they attached high value to their health and believed that how they lived could make a difference. This meant that people who were playing energetic sports quite or very frequently, typi-cally led healthy lifestyles in other respects, and would thereby be improving their scores on all the health and fitness factors that we identified. Typical year-to-year changes in these individuals' sport participation in the normal course of their lives could impact on only some of the health and fitness factors. Moreover, all the dimensions of health and fitness were shown to have numerous lifestyle and other determinants, some associated with age, sex and socio-economic status. Given this context, ordinary year-to-year changes in sports behaviour could not be expected to yield major (even measurable) gains or losses in the health and fitness of those concerned.

Sport policy

In the mid-1980s, when the *Inner-City Sport* project was planned, there were hopes of a cheap fix – a way of managing the resources available for sport so as to achieve a quantum leap in participation that would add life to people's years as well as years to their lives. Since the 1960s there had been a steady rise in participation, attri-butable to the investment of public funds in new indoor sports facilities. By the mid-1980s financial constraints on local authorities meant that any further rise in sport participation would have to be achieved through the better management of existing resources. Ever since the nineteenth-century beginnings, advocates for modern sport had claimed to be able to deliver all manner of social benefits, and had claimed government support on this basis. Governments had always justified channelling funds and other resources (originally playing fields and swimming baths) to sport as means of improving public health, reducing crime and diminishing the risks of civil disorder. The 1981 riots in inner-cities throughout England had been followed by the construction of new sports centres, in Brixton (London), Toxteth (Liverpool) and Moss Side (Manchester), among other places. A response to sectarian conflict in Northern Ireland had been the construction of 14 new indoor sport facilities in Belfast between 1977 and 1984. Sport has never won more than modest public support in terms of time spent playing or watching, money spent or participation rates (playing and watching), but has still generated enormous cultural traction. Most people have become followers and want their teams and athletes to win. They have believed that it is a 'good thing' if children and young people participate in sport instead of just 'hanging around' on the streets or remaining 'couch potatoes' at home. So governments have never been criticized for spending on sport. This has always been a relatively cheap, practical and uncontroversial way of addressing pressing social problems.

In 1976 the (Labour) government of the day had announced that 'the party' was over and ever since then local authorities throughout Britain had faced increasingly severe financial constraints. Sport, leisure and recreation, like all other departments, were seeking better value for money. By the late 1980s public leisure services were being exposed to a new (for them) market philosophy. They had begun 'targeting' and after 1989 they were required to open the management of their sport and leisure facilities to competitive tendering. These changes were underway while the *Inner-City Sport* project was in process.

Inner-City Sport can be regarded as part of the search for a quick fix. Its unequivocal answer had to be that no such fix was available. User profiles in the different sports varied according to local demography rather than local authority policies and the practices of centre managers. Targets and special campaigns could create spikes, but not sustained higher levels of participation, and were more likely, as was a continuation of new building, to simply shift players between facilities. The most effective forms of partnership had been practised for over 100 years: public provision of facilities and voluntary organization of sports teams and leagues. Commerce was never going to fill more than specialist niches – for particular types of fitness and training regimes, snooker, and exercise in a hotel environment, for example. Commerce could provide niche forms of individual exercise for people who were able and willing to pay, but could not handle competitive sports where the ruling principle had to be that 'you play if you are good enough'.

The evidence in *Inner-City Sport* implied that further raising levels of public participation through supply-side initiatives, if possible at all, would be a long haul, achieved through cohort replacement. Since most people were effectively locked into or out of sport by their late 20s, raising overall participation rates would depend on retaining more young adult players. The evidence from Belfast indicated that this could be achieved by locating high-quality facilities in neighbourhoods throughout a city, and operating these facilities with generous subsidies and low user charges. The rest of the UK replied that the Belfast model was unhelpful: that the resources to replicate the Belfast 'experiment' throughout the UK would never be available. By the 1990s Belfast itself was realizing that it had built some long-term problems – a network of ageing sports centres all in need of refurbishment.

Inner-City Sport also demonstrated beyond any reasonable doubt that any public health benefits achieved through further rises in sport participation would be modest, at best. This is not because the benefits would be modest if people with wholly sedentary lifestyles could be transformed into several-times-a-week players. The reality is that any further increases in sport participation were, and still are, most likely to be achieved through existing players playing even more frequently, or non-participants who already lead at least moderately active lifestyles becoming occasional players. *Inner-City Sport* demonstrated the dangers of basing sport policies on the findings of quasi-laboratory, experimental studies. Its implication was, and remains, that evidence from such studies should be ignored when framing policies for the general public as opposed to sport elites. Policies will always be more realistic, capable of realizing their aims, if based on evidence from studies of normal, everyday, routine sport activity. The evidence from *Inner-City Sport* shows why the current aim of increasing the proportion of adults who play at least three times a week, for at least 30 minutes per occasion, with at least moderate energy expenditure, will not necessarily deliver any public health and fitness benefits. There would be such benefits if the additional adults reaching the threshold were from those with previously wholly sedentary lifestyles, but in practice the additional numbers who cross the threshold are far more likely to be people who previously played slightly less, for whom the gains in health and fitness will be nil.

Governments are still keen to use sport in efforts to improve public health, but expectations about the pace of any increases in participation are modest, as in the targets currently set by Sport England and monitored through the Active People Surveys. A one per cent increase in participation per year is regarded as success. Since the 1990s Britain (and many other countries) has been alerted to an obesity crisis. Children have grown fatter and appear to have become less active, not through playing less sport, but more plausibly due to changes in diet and lack of exercise when they are not playing sports. Public health promotion now encompasses the encouragement of healthy eating, reduced tobacco and alcohol consumption as well as more sport. Also, twenty-first century sports policies and social science sport researchers have other preoccupations.

Sociology and sport

With hindsight we can now recognize that the *Inner-City Sport* project was conceived and executed during the dying years of an era of social democracy. This era was born after the Second World War when Western countries strengthened their welfare states. An expectation throughout the following decades was that state welfare would grow forever stronger and wider. One prospect at that time was the progressive transformation of opportunities to appreciate the arts, to play sport and enjoy the countryside from privileges of the few into rights of citizenship. The UK Sports Council's single policy following its foundation in 1965 was 'Sport for All'. From 1973 onwards progress was tracked with a battery of questions that was included in successive rounds of the General Household Survey. Sociologists investigated the sources of inequalities in participation rates, identified barriers, and sought ways in which these might be overcome for various socio-demographic groups – the working class, the unemployed, young people, women, ethnic minorities, senior citizens. In the 1980s it was unclear whether Thatcherism was a temporary pause or a long-term break with social democracy. By the 1990s the consensus was that Western countries had entered new times, described by a variety of words all prefixed by 'post' – post-industrial, post-modern, post-welfare. Subsequently, the leading questions for sociology have been about how sport is being transformed in the latest new era.

Final verdicts must still await historical distance, but one new issue has been about the implications of the individualization of biographies. Is this producing shifts in the character of sports and how these are played? Is there a shift out of clubs and teams towards individual exercise, recreation/fun and lifestyle sports including extreme sports? The sociological gaze has shifted away from participation rates onto the cultural dimension of sports – meanings, motivations and identities.

Another set of issues has arisen from the various ways and extent to which commerce has entered sport. Top sports are now played for global media audiences. Sponsors have become crucial. How does this change the social composition of fans and the character of fandom? Commerce has created new niches in the health and fitness industries, and now offers a variety of sport holiday packages. Clothing, footwear, gambling and the media have deepened their links to sport's continuing cultural traction. Government sport policies have been reoriented accordingly. Sport is now treated as an industry, a major source of jobs and a potential source of exports.

The evidence from *Inner-City Sport* remains valid and relevant, but the project itself, 20-plus years on, has the appearance of a not-to-be-repeated landmark from a bygone era.

ROBERTS' AND BRODIE'S *INNER-CITY SPORT*: AN UNDISCOVERED GEM?

Ken Green

It may seem strange in a book about exemplars of research offering a distinctive contribution to the study of sport to describe Roberts' and Brodie's *Inner-City Sport* as an undiscovered gem but that is, I think, how it should be viewed. This is not to say that the study and the book that emanated from it have been entirely overlooked but, rather, that the significance of *Inner-City Sport* has remained largely hidden from the eyes of those having most to learn from it, namely, the many students and practitioners of school physical education (PE), sports development and the like and, for that matter, academics in these fields. If I am correct in this assertion, then the significance of *Inner-City Sport* cannot be measured, straightforwardly, in terms of its impact upon academic understanding, let alone professional practice. Instead, its significance lies in the impact it *could* have on students, academics and practitioners – specifically in terms of the light the study throws upon what might be termed the 'recipe' for becoming 'locked in' to sport.

Before I elaborate, however, I want to take a brief detour down Memory Lane. I first met Ken Roberts in 1991 when I began lecturing on a PE degree programme at what was then Chester College of Higher Education (now the University of Chester). I had inherited a rag-bag of a course on leisure and sport. Hidden among trips to leisure centres and swimming pools were a handful of lectures on the sociology of leisure delivered by someone who, I was soon to discover, was considered the founding father of the sociology of leisure as well as a prominent researcher and writer on youth and class, among other areas. A year later *Inner-City Sport* was published and I immediately came to view it as *the* study with which those of us involved in PE and sport as academics, teachers or coaches needed to engage if we were to gain a better appreciation of our potential roles as promoters of sporting participation during childhood, youth and beyond. In this regard, I must admit to being a disciple – having spent the best part of the intervening 20 or so years spreading the message for *Inner-City Sport*, albeit with mixed results!

So *why* was *Inner-City Sport* so important and *what* was (or, for that matter, *is*) its distinctive contribution to the field of PE and sport? In short, *Inner-City Sport* was, and remains, important in several ways. First, the nature of the study and, in particular, its size and scope. It was unusually large and broad, ranging from the sample size (over 4,000 adults, 16+) through the number of indoor sports centres (46) to the six cities utilized, which included the main cities – Belfast, Cardiff, London and Glasgow – of each of the four countries of the UK, some of which were noted for being ethnically, socially, economically and politically diverse, not to say troubled (Belfast, Liverpool and inner-city London). Thus, the size and character of the data-set were significant. Second, and as Ken himself points out in his essay, the study broke new ground in combining social and physical dimensions of participation, from sporting biographies through to measures of physical fitness. Partly as a consequence of one and two, the third and, to my mind, most distinctive contribution was, unsurprisingly, the findings. It is these, therefore, that I want to concentrate on in the remainder of this commentary.

What, then, did we stand to learn from *Inner-City Sport*? There were numerous nuggets that could inform and shape our understanding of sports participation and, by extension, professional practices. Among other things, the study demonstrated that any public health benefits achieved through increases in sport participation would, at best, be modest. In addition, it provided evidence for the role that sports facilities might play among marginal players (that is, those who participate irregularly in sport), alongside data to support the view that raising levels of sports participation through investment in facilities would require the kind of long-term political planning and commitment for which successive governments had shown, and continue to show, little appetite or inclination. The study (as Roberts observes) also confirmed what was already known – especially with regard to the significance of social divisions (in the form of age, class and sex in particular) and inequalities for sports participation (and, for that matter, health). *Inner-City Sport* also provided the nuanced empirical research to support the intuition that regular sport participation required a combination of social as well as technical (sport) attributes (what sociologists might call 'capitals'). Consequently, becoming a regular long-term sports player was likely to prove highly unlikely among those who lacked the economic (disposable income), cultural (physical and sporting skills as well as familiarity with and knowledge of the custom and practices associated with particular sports) and social (knowing people who might form a link to sport) resources. Thus, it transpired that those who had lapsed from sport confronted (often insurmountable) economic (financial), social (time but more importantly people with whom to play) and also technical (their sporting skills had inevitably diminished) barriers if they were to return.

The importance of these findings notwithstanding, in the remainder of this commentary I want to focus on one particular aspect of the insights from *Inner-City Sport* which I consider to be of particular significance: that is, those related to what is often termed 'lifelong participation' in sport. Among the many and varied justifications for PE and youth sport, there is a broad consensus around the desirability of one particular purpose: the promotion of a lifelong commitment to participation in sport and physical activity. Since the identification of the so-called 'Wolfenden gap' in the early 1960s, the end of compulsory schooling has been commonly viewed as a critical point at which a significant amount of 'drop-out' (or, at the very least, 'drop-off') from sport and physical activity is likely to occur and subsequently gather pace. What stands out about much of the literature related to the promotion of so-called active lifestyles and lifelong participation among young people is the general dearth of a sociological perspective on the topic. At one level, this should not be seen as altogether surprising for there has long been a tendency to study (interrelated) aspects of people's lives – and, for that matter, people themselves – in isolation. Thus, the field of sports-related studies often splinters into separate studies of sport, leisure and PE. Indeed, the sports science degree programmes that have developed out of the former Certificate of PE degree programme are conventionally multi-disciplinary rather than inter-disciplinary courses. Yet it is axiomatic that, as Roberts (1999: 226) puts it, 'society is not neatly divided into sports players, tourists ... It is the same people who do all these things'. Equally apparent to those in the PE and youth sport communities is the fact that the PE, sporting and leisure dimensions of young people's lives cannot be easily disentangled.

Inner-City Sport was an integrated study of those who had become 'committed' to sport as adults. It provided substantial empirical support for the taken-for-granted belief that childhood and youth are the life stages where the foundations for long-term uses of leisure are laid. Childhood and youth tend, to paraphrase Roberts, to be the main stages for the formation of sporting and physical activity capital. Roberts and Brodie found that virtually all those who play regularly between the ages of 16 and 30 become, as it were, 'locked in' to sport and are frequently 'established on continuous sports careers which ... are unlikely to be disrupted for many more years' (1992: 37). Thus most people are effectively locked into or out of sport by their late 20s. Those aged 25-plus who possessed the necessary combinations of skills and money, and who were currently playing regularly, were effectively locked into sport through sheer routine, social commitments and the benefits (immediate enjoyment and anticipated health and fitness gains) that they were experiencing. Indeed, they were likely to remain regular players for many more years. Those who had dropped out, in contrast, were unlikely to return and resume playing on a regular basis. In short, individuals become locked in 'by their desire to repeat satisfying experiences derived from physical recreation in the past' and by becoming 'bound into social networks in which sport activity [is] normal' (Roberts and Brodie, 1992: 39).

As well as providing substantial empirical evidence reinforcing the significance of childhood and youth, as well as social divisions, for attachment to sport beyond school and into adulthood, *Inner-City Sport* had something new to offer. For the first time we were able to glean from an empirical study just what the contours of the 'secure foundations' for long-term adherence to sport might look like. In short, 'wide sporting repertoires' were revealed as the recipe for encouraging adherence to sport: more specifically, the introduction of youngsters to a variety of sports and physical recreations in which they acquired degrees of competency and pleasure/ enjoyment. The key to adherence was not, it turned out, being good at sport or even spending a long time playing sport. While these might help, more fundamental was the development of a portfolio or repertoire of sports. Sporting repertoires made it more likely that youngsters would sustain participation through the various life-stage transitions that tend to unhinge sporting involvement. Thus, the chief characteristics of the committed minority who became 'locked in' to sport tended to be that they had been 'active in several (usually three or more) games (or activities) throughout their sports careers' (Roberts and Brodie, 1992: 37) and, as a consequence, typically possessed a wide sporting repertoire. The point about such repertoires was that 'whatever their reasons for dropping out of particular sports, where the individuals played several games their entire sports careers were less vulnerable' (Roberts and Brodie, 1992: 44), especially during periods of transition, such as from school to work.

It is worth dwelling on the finding that adherence tends not to be a matter of simply being good at, playing a lot or merely enjoying particular sports. Indeed, as Roberts and Brodie observed, 'Most children enjoy games and there are thousands of inactive adults who can recall being quite good at particular sports when at school' (1992: 41). For many youngsters, these early experiences tend not to be translated into a habitual commitment to sport and physical activity in later life; far from it – for a good number the end of compulsory schooling still signals a steady, sometimes rapid, withdrawal from involvement. What 'tracks' from childhood and adolescence through to adulthood is not so much the level as the breadth of activity. It is 'the number of different sports' young people played regularly and in which 'they became proficient during childhood and youth' (Roberts and Brodie, 1992: 42) that makes the difference. This 'richness' is, then, the chief characteristic that marks out the early sports socialization of those adults destined to become 'locked in' to sport. This richness is especially important when one appreciates just how volatile youngsters' involvement in sport can be: they chop and change and experiment.

My conviction that Ken Roberts' work more generally had potentially profound significance for our understanding of young people's engagement with sport – in their spare time as well as during school PE in particular – led me to publish a paper (Green, 2002) arguing the case for greater engagement among physical educationalists, via Roberts' work, with the sociologies of youth and leisure. The paper was based on the conviction that any study of young people's propensity towards ongoing involvement in sport needs to be viewed as an aspect of their lives 'in the round' and lamented the failure of those investigating (whilst typically advocating) lifelong participation through PE to make use of a sociological perspective on leisure, youth cultures and sport. Nonetheless the paper, published a decade ago, has only had 223 views during the intervening decade (this may of course, say more about the paper itself than the topic!). This alone does not, of course, justify my opening claim that *Inner-City Sport* remains an undiscovered gem. What does is the dearth of direct reference to the study (and related text) in research in the field of PE and youth sport since the 1992 publication of *Inner-City Sport: Who Plays, and What are the Benefits?*

As well as identifying key features of the participatory profiles of those young people most likely to become locked into sport, *Inner-City Sport* was future-proofed! It pointed, 20 years ago, to the shifts in the character of sports being taken up and how these are played a decade or more before this fact was widely appreciated and acknowledged. At the same time it highlighted the now readily apparent shift out of clubs and teams towards individual exercise, recreation/fun and so-called lifestyle sports. In doing so it hinted at what has become recognized as the individualization of young people's lives and their leisure and sporting biographies in particular. Last, but by no means least, I would venture to suggest that *Inner-City Sport* was also significant in terms of value for money! Although an expensive project (costing around £500,000) when compared with many UK government-funded projects (and especially those in the field of sport), it must be considered money well spent, for among other things it appears to have answered the hitherto unanswered and seemingly unanswerable question: 'What makes people stay in sport?' Thanks to *Inner-City Sport*, we now have a much clearer understanding of how childhood and youth – notwithstanding the almost unavoidable impact of social inequalities on all areas of life including sport – serve to socialize some young people into sport and others away from it. A quarter of a century on, the study may, in Ken Roberts' own words, have 'the appearance of a not-to-be-repeated landmark from a bygone era'. Be that as it may, the aims, the methodological mix and above all else the findings have as much validity and relevance to the world of PE and leisure-sport today as they did a quarter of a century ago.

9

RESEARCHING SPORT-FOR-DEVELOPMENT: THE NEED FOR SCEPTICISM

Fred Coalter

Introduction

This chapter presents some reflections on my experiences undertaking two major research projects in sport-for-development in ten countries in Africa and in two locations in India – first, to produce a user-oriented monitoring and evaluation manual (Coalter, 2006) and then to undertake a major research project exploring the impacts of participation in such programmes (Coalter, 2013; Coalter and Taylor, 2010). It is also informed by research undertaken with seven 'sport-and-conflict' programmes funded by Comic Relief in the UK (Coalter, 2011a; 2013). The chapter is not about methods but methodology and the general political, intellectual and practical environment in which sport-for-development research is undertaken.

Doing research and losing friends

A fundamental problem in undertaking research in sport-for-development is that the policy area is dominated by a mixture of interest groups, sports evangelists and conceptual entrepreneurs (Hewitt, 1998) who offer an apparent economy of remedies to deep-rooted problems via focusing on a single concept – 'sport'. This produces a potent mixture of self-interest, faith and a general lack of intellectual rigour which is reinforced by forms of 'incestuous amplification' (http://www.cybercollege.com/ia.htm) in which believers talk to believers, minimize exposure to ideas that run contrary to their own beliefs and adopt a selective perception of data and information by ignoring less than supportive research findings.

Such perspectives tend to reduce the role of research to affirming belief. For example, Johan Koss of Right to Play defines research as functioning 'to prove what we say that we do' (van Kampen, 2003: 15), or UNICEF (2006: 1) which attests to 'a shared belief in the power of sport for development [and] a shared determination to find ways to document and objectively verify the positive impact of sport'. This reflects Kruse's (2006: 8) observations about the intriguingly vague definitions of sport-for-development, with practice not based on evidence, but 'on an intuitive certainty and experience that there is a positive link between sport and development'. Or as Coakley (2011: 307) refers to it, 'unquestioned beliefs grounded in wishful thinking'. Further, a peculiar aspect of sport-for-development is that many academic critics of the supposed top-down imposition and insensitivity of 'neo-colonialist' funders seem to retain a basic *belief* in the inherent developmental potential of 'sport' (Kay, 2011; Lindsey and Grattan, 2012; Nicholls, Giles and Sethna, 2011).

This has strong parallels with Pisani's (2008) experience in the area of HIV and AIDS – an area in which many in sport-for-development claim to make a positive contribution. Pisani (2008: 288) argues that many programmes are based on false assumptions and the systematic ignoring of morally or politically uncomfortable evidence. This results in the monitoring of implementation being more important than the evaluation of outcomes.

> You almost never have to show you've prevented any infections. You can be judged a success for just doing what you said you were going to do, like build a clinic, or train some nurses or give leaflets to 400 out of the nation's 160,000 drug injectors.
>
> *(Pisani, 2008: 288)*

In such circumstances Pisani's (2008: 300) assertion that 'doing honest analysis that would lead to programme improvement is a glorious way to be hated by just about everyone' was never more true than in sport-for-development.

Rational activities and political contexts

Weiss (1993: 94) offers an analysis which suggests that some of these processes may be generic, arguing that 'evaluation is a rational exercise that takes place in a political context'. In this context policy is formulated and funding is obtained via processes of lobbying, persuasion, negotiation, alliance-building and pragmatic opportunism. This often results in:

> inflated promises [and] the goals often lack the clarity and intellectual coherence that evaluation criteria should have ... Holders of diverse values and different interests have to be won over, and in the process a host of realistic and unrealistic goal commitments are made.
>
> *(Weiss, 1993: 96)*

In a similar vein, Pawson *et al.* (2004) make the general observation that most social policy interventions can be characterised as 'ill-defined interventions and hard to follow outcomes'. However, inflated promises are most likely to occur in marginal policy areas which suffer from status anxiety and are seeking to gain legitimacy and funding from mainstream agencies – which is the case for sport-for-development (Black, 2010; Levermore, 2008). Consequently, the programmes which researchers seek to evaluate are not neutral experiments, but are the product of political decisions and strategic partnerships. In fact, in sport-for-development such partnerships often seem as important as the programmes that they deliver. In this context Weiss (1993: 96) reminds us of realpolitik by arguing that 'a considerable amount of ineffectiveness may be tolerated if a program fits well with prevailing values . . . or if it pays off political debts'. Consequently, a lack of clarity, precision and intellectual coherence regarding evaluation criteria might simply reflect political necessities and be inherent in such processes. In sport-for-development it seems that the very vagueness of the use of the term 'sport' and, most especially, 'development' are central to such lobbying and conceptual entrepreneurship (we will return to this below).

Such studied vagueness has clearly negative implications for the role and function of monitoring and evaluation. Such processes and a desire to offer funders an economy of remedies – 'development' is a catch-all notion – often result in situations where 'intermediate objectives are missing, providing targets for how much and when results were expected', and 'indicators are used in the application for funds, but not for actual monitoring and reporting', with the absence of clear targets 'making it difficult to assess performance' (Kruse, 2006: 27; see also Coalter, 2006, 2007). For example, the research I undertook in Africa and India was part of a strategic alliance between a generic aid organization and a quasi-governmental sports promotion agency. Perhaps this explains the somewhat imprecise aims 'to test the hypothesis that sport contributes to the personal development and wellbeing of disadvantaged children and young people and brings wider benefits to the community'. Although such studied vagueness might have been politically necessary, it presented problems in developing a precise monitoring and evaluation framework (Coalter, 2013).

Vague and generalized images

In sport-for-development such processes are exacerbated and reinforced because of the 'mythopoeic' character of sport. Mythopoeic concepts are pre-scientific and their demarcation criteria are not specific, but are based on popular and idealistic notions which are produced largely outside sociological analysis and which 'isolate a particular relationship between variables to the exclusion of others and without a sound basis for doing so' (Glasner, 1977: 2–3). Such, usually heroic, myths contain certain elements of truth, but elements which become reified and distorted and 'represent' rather than reflect reality, standing for supposed, but largely unexamined, impacts and processes. The strength of such myths lies in their 'ability to evoke vague and generalised images' (Glasner, 1977: 1). Such mythopoeic perspectives are attracted to particular forms of 'evidence' or testimony – what Hartmann and

Kwauk (2001: 286) refer to as selective 'heartfelt narratives, evocative images, and quotable sound bites'.

The strength of the mythopoeic nature of sport and its associated essentialist and universalizing conceptions of 'sport' are indicated by the cross-cultural nature of the beliefs in its individual impacts and social outcomes. For example, Lindsey and Grattan (2012) reject so-called positivist methodology as being intimately related to forms of neo-colonialist oppression and adopt 'decolonising, feminist-oriented, participatory action research' to explore the supposedly ignored perspectives of 'Global South voices' in a Zambian football programme. However, the seemingly standard in-depth interviews indicate that they view sport almost precisely in the same terms as the neo-colonialist oppressors – having value for its popularity, its 'associative value' and its ability to bring young people together, its ability to act as a diversionary activity to reduce crime and to enable young people to develop physically and to improve their health, as a compensatory mechanism for those who are less academically gifted and as a vehicle for various 'educational messages'. Kay (2009: 1188) warns 'Global North' researchers of the dangers of their Western Cartesian dualism and of the need for researchers 'to subvert enduring "colonial" power relationships'. However, her in-depth interviews with female participants and providers in a Delhi-based sport-for-development programme illustrate a similar and relatively standard analysis of the perceived positive impacts of participation – increased self-confidence and aspirations. Burnett (2001: 51), in South Africa, states that many respondents 'approached and interpreted change very much from a functionalist perspective, because "educational" and "functional" outcomes were held in high regard by all'. In post-war Liberia I asked a programme provider (who was being funded by a major UK charity, presumably on the basis of some definition of effectiveness) to define the desired impacts and outcomes of a football programme – his answer was 'peace'. Subsequent discussion to define 'peace' and to understand how it could be a realistic outcome of a small self-selecting football programme proved to be difficult and inconclusive.

Such widespread examples of populist faith in the functionalist and supposedly transformative properties of sport present substantial difficulties for undertaking monitoring and evaluation of programmes, in part because they limit critical thinking and the essential requirement for academic scepticism (Berger, 1971; Portes, 2000).

Programme theory and 'de-reification'

A valid and robust evaluation of a programme must be based on the definition and measurement of precisely defined impacts which, most importantly, reflect the nature of the programme processes and experiences. The measurement of arbitrarily imposed or, usually, assumed impacts (e.g. self-efficacy, self-esteem, social skills) or outcomes (e.g. changed sexual behaviour, peace, reduction in HIV and AIDS) can easily lead to a programme being regarded as 'unsuccessful' – even if the programme processes were unlikely to have delivered the desired impacts.

The development of an approach to monitoring and evaluation, which might also contribute to the improvement of programme effectiveness, requires an ability to outline a broad programme theory – a theory of change. This describes the assumptions about the nature of participants (who are frequently simply assumed to be in need of 'development'), the relationship between programme processes and participant responses, and resulting impacts (changes in values, attitudes, skills and intentions) – a *presumed* sequence of causes and effects (Weiss, 1997).

In effect there is a need to 'de-reify' sport (Crabbe, 2008), to recognize the full import of Coakley's (1998: 2) assertion that we need to regard 'sports as *sites* for socialisation experiences, not *causes* of socialisation outcomes'. Or to consider Hartmann's (2003: 134) assertion that 'the success of any sports-based social intervention program is largely determined by the strength of its non-sport components'. Or the conclusion of the International Working Group on Sport for Development and Peace – not the likeliest of critics – that 'the evident benefits appear to be an indirect outcome of the context and social interaction that is possible in sport, rather than a direct outcome of participating in sport' (Sport for Development and Peace International Working Group, 2008: 4).

'Sport' is a collective noun which encompasses a wide variety of contexts and experiences. For example, there are individual, partner and team sports; there are sports which are based on the development of cognitive and spatial skills and those based on motor skills; there are non–contact, contact and collision sports; and there are sports based on self-assessed criteria and objective norm evaluations. In this regard the President's Council on Physical Fitness and Sports (2006: 4) refers to 'the importance of not lumping all sports or sport participants together' and states that 'broad generalizations about "sports" are unlikely to be helpful'. The report refers to different types of rule structures, social interactions, developmental stimuli, subculture, micro-cultures and implicit moral norms and, importantly, the varying experiences of individuals in the same context.

However, the mythopoeic and essentialist view of sport, a quasi-religious view of transformations and a desire for simple and cheap solutions to complex and intractable problems, often result in difficulties getting programme providers (or funders) to think about 'sport' in terms of social processes and experiences which might lead to a precise set of measureable impacts – after all, 'sport is sport'. We have already noted the very traditional and reductionist views of Lindsey and Grattan's (2012) respondents and when I asked a member of a Malawian organization about the nature of the relationship between football and the reduction of HIV and AIDS, I was told, with no hint of irony, that footballers were too tired to have sex. No further discussion took place on this issue.

There are two broad and inter-connected approaches to developing programme theory. The first is for programme providers to outline systematically the various components and mechanisms and how, via a *presumed* series of causes and effects, they *might* lead to desired impacts (Weiss, 1997). In the majority of organizations discussions about desired impacts and outcomes and how these related to programme mechanisms proved to be difficult; 'sport' was taken for granted and any attempts to 'de-reify' it, to understand the elements, components, relationships and experiences which might lead to the desired impacts and outcomes were often viewed as threatening – especially where obtuse claims had been made to and accepted by funders.

A second approach is to derive a programme theory from relevant research and theory and to design a programme that contains the mechanisms and elements that have been identified as maximizing the potential to achieve the desired impacts (Coalter, 2013; Pawson, 2006). Because of the difficulties that programme providers had in articulating the processes and mechanisms, a combination of both approaches had to be used. For example, one of the claims was that taking part in sport would almost automatically lead to an improvement in 'self-confidence'. However, as Bandura (1997: 382) regards confidence as 'a catchword, rather than a construct embedded in a theoretical system' we sought to measure *perceived self-efficacy*. The added utility of such an approach is that perceived self-efficacy is a central concept in social learning theory, which underpinned most of the programmes with their role models and learning by doing. Further, theory and research tells us that perceived self-efficacy is best developed via inclusive mastery experiences, role modelling, verbal persuasion and social support (Biddle, 2006). The traditional competitive, performance-oriented approach to sport is much less inclusive and, in terms of values and attitudes, represents a different moral universe.

An additional bonus of such an approach is that it serves to broaden the definition of relevant research and knowledge and raises questions about the somewhat odd assertion that sport-for-development is a 'new field' in its 'formative stage' (Kay, 2009: 1177; Coalter, 2013). This is important because, from a social science perspective, many of the rather common-sense terms used in evangelical rhetoric present complex problems of definition and measurement. The failure to address such issues systematically reduces greatly the ability to understand fully the nature of any impacts and outcomes and our ability to compare the *relative* effectiveness of various programmes. Many of the common-sense terms used in policy rhetoric are the subject of substantial theoretical debate and there is often a lack of consensus as to how such terms should be defined and measured and their significance for 'development'.

Programme theories are based on a configurational approach to causality (Pawson, 2001), in which impacts (and most certainly outcomes) are not assured and can only be understood as being *produced* by the interaction of a particular and often complex combination of circumstances. This reflects Pawson *et al.*'s (2004: 7) contention that, 'it is through the workings of entire systems of social relationships that any changes in behaviours, events and social conditions are effected' – in such circumstances essentialist and universalizing notions of 'sport' have little analytical value. Even the most robust impact and outcome-based evaluations are often unable to *explain* either success or failure – the 'how?' and 'why?' questions. Given the variety of sport-for-development programmes, the huge diversity of socio-cultural contexts in the so-called Global South and the, often ignored, variety of participants, it is unlikely that sport-for-development can develop via an accumulation of testimonies and measured impacts and outcomes.

Families of mechanisms

This requires a shift from the universalism of the sports evangelists to the exploration of middle-range mechanisms (Pawson, 2006) – it shifts the focus from families of programmes (sport-for-development) to *families of mechanisms*. The approach holds the possibility of the development of a middle-range theory, rather than a simple accumulation of impact studies or 'heartfelt narratives' (Hartmann and Kwauk, 2011). Even more ambitiously, Weiss (1997: 154) suggests that theory-based evaluation 'can track the unfolding of events, step-by-step, and thus make causal attributions on the basis of demonstrated links. If this was so, evaluation would not need randomized control groups to justify its claims about causality'. As Pawson (2006) argues, if we shift our focus to families of *mechanisms* we might discover that apparently diverse interventions share common components.

While posing difficult intellectual and sometimes emotional problems, the adoption of this broad approach had a number of significant advantages:

- It served, partially, to de-reify sport by emphasizing the essential distinction between *necessary conditions* and *sufficient conditions* – the processes and experiences necessary to maximize the potential to achieve desired impacts and reduce potentially negative ones. However, the hold of the mythopoeic 'sport' remained strong.
- It identified and sought to explore and resolve different, often vague, assumptions held by providers, funders and researchers. Many of the programme personnel and the funders would agree that this process assisted in the development of a mutual understanding and more realistic expectations. It certainly did not correspond to the Global North neo-colonialist 'oppression' imagined by some of the liberation methodologists (Darnell and Hayhurst, 2012; Lindsey and Grattan, 2012).
- It assisted in the formulation of theoretically coherent, precise and relevant impacts related to programme contexts and processes. Out went 'tired footballers' and in came perceived self-efficacy, self-esteem and relevant information.
- It provided the potential for process-focused formative, rather than simply summative (i.e. impact), evaluation and the improvement of programmes.
- It contributed to capacity-building, to developing a greater sense of ownership, understanding, integration and an organizational ability to reflect on and analyze attitudes, beliefs and behaviour – a developmental outcome. Via an ongoing, fieldwork-based, collaborative process, most developed a better understanding of *their assumptions* as to how such programmes might and might not work. They developed more realistic assessments of what could and could not be expected and a much greater degree of ownership of their programmes. While driving to the airport, having worked with an organization developing a programme-based logic model, a young man placed his hand on my shoulder and said 'I want to thank you Fred … I now understand much better why I do what I do'. Some may view this as an indication of neo-colonialist

indoctrination, while others might see it as contribution to an increased sense of ownership, perceived self-efficacy and maybe even 'empowerment'.

One issue became clear via this approach – rarely do sport-for-development programmes rely solely on sport to address issues of personal development. Most are *sport-plus* programmes and although their core activity is sport, it is used and adapted in various ways to seek to achieve certain 'development' objectives and is often complemented by workshops and discussions about a range of topics such as HIV and AIDS, female education and empowerment, anger management and so on. In such circumstances isolating the 'sport-effect' is nearly impossible (Coakley, 2011; Hartmann and Kwauk, 2011) – in certain circumstances it might only be a 'fly-paper' to attract young people to education and training programmes. Further, the sporting activity may be much less important than the 'attractiveness factors' and social relationships which encourage people to stay with such programmes (Biddle and Mutrie, 2001; Coalter, 2013; Fox, 2000; Sandford *et al*, 2006). More fundamentally, Morris *et al.*, (2003) suggest that *any* programme where there had previously been none may be the most important factor. Of course, such approaches might not be deemed important if the required impacts are achieved, although this would seem to raise questions about the specificity of a field called 'sport-for-development'.

The programme theory/theory of change approach assisted in the agreement of more realistic potential impacts but also pointed to a fundamental and basic issue which is too often simply assumed – the nature of participants and their supposed 'development needs'.

Deficit models

The problems associated with the amorphous notion of sport are exacerbated by the vague notion of 'development'. For example, Black (2010: 122) refers to 'the inherently contentious and contested character of this ubiquitous concept' and Hartmann and Kwauk (2011: 286) refer to it as 'deeply complicated and poly-vocal'. The political advantages of the lack of clarity and precision in the use of this term are balanced, even outweighed, by its analytical opaqueness. For the purposes of this chapter it is legitimate to assume that a core assumption of, and rationale for, sport-for-development programmes is that deprived communities produce 'deficient' people who can be 'developed' through sport. This is often taken to be confirmed by post-programme in-depth interviews in which participants affirm the positive impacts of participation. However, such selective testimonies and heartfelt narratives cannot be regarded as representative of all participants in a programme – and certainly not of 'sport-for-development'. Also, such an approach contains the strong possibility of social desirability bias – the tendency of respondents to reply in a manner that will be viewed favourably by others, or which will affirm themselves. This issue is present in most research where respondents provide self-evaluations of their personal abilities and qualities. However, this may be a particular concern in sport-for-development programmes, in which vulnerable young people are dependent on programme providers for access to free programmes which they value highly. The rhetoric of such programmes systematically emphasizes notions of self-improvement and self-worth and there will be obvious pressures to provide the expected responses and to affirm the value of the programme – especially where programme providers are involved in data collection (Coalter and Taylor, 2010).

However, 'before' survey research data raise some questions about deficit assumptions (Coalter, 2013; Coalter and Taylor, 2010). The young people in these programmes were not homogeneous groups and there was a range of self-evaluations, with many expressing quite strong self-belief in their own efficacy and most within an accepted 'normal' range of self-esteem. It seems to be a reasonable assumption that living in such deprivation means that many have to develop certain levels of *perceived* self-efficacy and self-worth in order to remain positive and to survive. Further, as most programmes are self-selecting, one must assume that a certain degree of perceived self-efficacy was necessary in order to decide to participate in the first place. Of course it is possible that some of these evaluations reflect a certain self-protective element, with a degree of denial and suppression (Hunter, 2001; Jenkins, 1997). We have no way of knowing from our data, although their relative consistency across several cultures seems to indicate otherwise.

At the very least, the before-and-after survey data indicate that these respondents can be regarded as relatively normal young people living in often dreadful circumstances and they raise questions about overly-generalized deficit models. The importance of this is that the nature and extent of impacts on participants depend not only on the nature of the experience, but also on the nature of the participants and their response to the various aspects of the programmes – the key mechanism. To ignore this contains obvious ideological and pedagogic dangers. It raises important questions about how 'need' and 'development' are conceptualized and how desired impacts and behavioural outcomes are defined and measured. The need for greater clarity is also emphasized by the apparent diversity among the so-called Global South/Majority World/low-income participants – both *between* the East African participants and, most especially, between them and the Indian participants. There is a paradoxical danger of well-meaning projects being based on negative stereotypes of all young people from particular areas, with the attendant danger of misconceived provision, inappropriate performance indicators and subtle forms of racism.

How relative is relative?

Much is often made of cultural relativity and the problems of assuming the cross-cultural relevance of certain measures. For example, in the before-and-after surveys in India and Africa we used the standard Rosenberg (1965) measure of self-esteem and some have suggested that the emphasis on individualism was ethnocentric. Also, during the development phase of the project, a programme provider in the majority Muslim Senegal suggested that the concept of self-esteem was a Western, market-driven individualistic notion. It was suggested that in many communities the subordination of the self to the collective good, rather than overly individualistic behaviour, was a way of achieving status and esteem. Baumeister *et al.* (2003; 2005) also argue that even in some Judeo–Christian traditions modesty and humility are regarded as virtues, with high self-esteem being associated with pride and vainglory. A slightly different issue was raised in India. While helping to design a questionnaire, I was informed that some of the females would have difficulties in answering the survey questions, which were designed in close collaboration with the indigenous female programme providers. At first I thought that this related to language, or the complexity of the Likert scales. However, it referred to the fact that women in the slum communities were not used to being consulted or asked their opinion and they might suffer a form of cognitive disequilibrium – a disorientation relating to being asked about their attitudes and opinions and subsequent confusion about if, or how, to answer.

While such possibilities cannot be ignored, there is a considerable consistency in our data (Coalter and Taylor, 2010) across programmes and cultures and samples in which Muslims are the majority. Also, it is possible to offer some reasonable explanations for the measured differences between the various samples, where the main divide seems to be between the East African and Indian data – raising questions about politically correct, but analytically doubtful, references to the Global South or low-income countries. Finally, although there is evidence that the *average strength* of self-esteem is mediated by certain aspects of cultures, research evidence suggests that self-esteem functions in similar ways in different cultures and that, in terms of correlates of self-esteem as a psychological construct, there is substantial cross-cultural generality (Brown *et al.*, 2009).

In terms of the use of the concept of perceived self-efficacy, no programme providers raised any concerns. This seems to reflect Luszczynska *et al.*'s (2005: 439) conclusion that 'general self-efficacy appears to be a universal construct that yields meaningful relations with other psychological constructs' such as self-regulation, goal intentions and outcome expectancies. However, an interesting perspective was provided in Gulu (Northern Uganda) by a leader of sports programmes in camps for internally displaced people. Many had been subsistence farmers, but in Gulu they had been provided with free food by the World Food Programme via huge brown tents in the town. There was a fear that they were losing their agri-cultural skills, which would have made re-settlement difficult. The programme provider suggested that the respondents would deliberately underestimate their perceived self-efficacy because they would feel that they would risk losing the food programme and have to return to farming if they indicated that they had high perceived self-efficacy! However, the survey data proved him wrong.

Within the debate about cultural relativism it is worth noting the comment by Brown *et al.* (2009: 154) that 'cultural differences in the magnitude of some phenomena may not necessarily translate into functional differences between cultures' and that 'a complete understanding of culture requires understanding cultural similarities as well as cultural differences'.

The contingent nature of impacts

In addition to questioning a universalizing deficit model, the survey data also raise issues about assumptions that participation in sport-for-development programmes inevitably leads to 'personal development'. This oversimplifies the differential impact of such programmes and the strength and direction of the impacts. Reflecting previous research (Fox, 2000) the data indicate a positive general *tendency* for those with the weakest or lower-than-average scores for perceived self-efficacy and self-esteem to increase their evaluations. In two East African samples the increases in average self-efficacy scores were statistically significant, with no change in the Indian sample (Coalter, 2013; Coalter and Taylor, 2010). However, a substantial proportion of those with higher than average scores *decreased* their self-evaluations and even some with below average scores decreased their evaluation. For reasons of space it is not possible to explore explanations for such differential impacts. However, the variety of responses to the diversity of programmes clearly point to the limitations of using 'heartfelt narratives' (Hartmann and Kwauk, 2011) as a basis for illustrating the impact of programmes, or understanding programme processes. Most forms of social intervention are likely to have some positive impacts on some participants and it is relatively easy to produce *ad hominem* evidence – 'sport saved me from a life of crime'. But two questions remain: *why* did a programme work for some and not others – we are rarely presented with evidence of reduced scores or unchanged participants – and what have positive individual self-assessments to do with 'development'? (We will return to this below.)

Despite certain tendencies in the data, there was no clear and systematic 'sport-for-development effect' – did we really think that we would find such a thing? As in all forms of social intervention, the nature and extent of impacts were contingent and varied between programmes, participants and cultural contexts.

In such complex sports-plus programmes it is clear that we need to be careful about attributing any impacts simply to 'sport'. But also we need to exercise caution in attributing changes to the programme *per se*. For example, Hartmann and Kwauk (2011) refer to the difficulties in controlling for intervening and confounding variables which will also influence attitudes and behaviour. Participation in such programmes is only one of many things that people do. Therefore its impact will depend on the relative salience of the experience compared to other factors such as criminal sub-cultures, peer groups, family, wider social, cultural and religious norms, school, economic imperatives and so on. For example, in a comparison with non-participants in Kampala and Dar es Salaam there were few significant differences between participants and non-participants on key measures.

Of course, even where programmes lead to improved self-evaluations and increased knowledge or even intention to change behaviour, we are still left with the question: what has this to do with 'development'?

Displacement of scope

Issues of deficit models and differential impacts raise important issues about displacement of scope (Wagner, 1964). This relates to the process of wrongly generalizing micro-level effects to the meso and macro levels. This in part relates to old debates within social science about the relationship between structure and action, between the individual and the social or even between values, attitudes and behaviour.

However, such issues are conflated in the use of the amorphous term 'development' – everything from individual self-confidence, changed sexual behaviour, community cohesion, social capital to 'peace' and 'development'. Some argue that a neo-liberal individualistic perspective underpins sport-for-development, reinforced by the emphasis on the achievements of elite sport 'celebrity diplomats' (Black, 2010:126) to illustrate the supposed 'power' of sport (Coakley, 2011; Darnell and Hayhurst, 2012; Jeanes, 2011; Kidd, 2008). Such a perspective brings to mind Weiss's (1993) concern with a 'blame the victim approach' which ignores structures and seeks to deal with long-standing broad-gauge problems via limited-focus programmes of individual behavioural change. The key question is that, irrespective of the differential impact of participation in sport-for-development programmes, does any of this 'go beyond the touch line'? What is the relationship between measured impacts, intentions and behaviour? Even if sports participation does assist in the development of certain types of *individual* competence, efficacy, self-esteem, values, attitudes or even expressed intention to change behaviour, this cannot be taken to imply that these will be transferred to behavioural change, or wider social or community benefits. For example, the transtheoretical theory of behaviour change (Prochaska and Velicer, 1997) illustrates that the relationship between changed attitudes, intentions and subsequent behaviour is not unilinear and may often be reversed. Consequently, even if we can illustrate changes in values, attitudes and self-perceptions, we are still left with the generic methodological problem of relating this to subsequent behaviour change – which surely must be part of any definition of development?

This is most clearly seen in the area of HIV and AIDS. Some have offered positive evaluations based on sport-for-development programmes' supposed ability to change individual intentions about safe sex (Maro and Roberts, 2012; Maro et al., 2009). However, others are much more pessimistic. For example, Jeanes (2011: 13) notes that, 'HIV and AIDS education programmes delivered through sport or other mechanisms are unlikely to be effective if targeting young people as if their health behaviour is played out within a social vacuum'. Or Mwaanga's (2010: 66) comment that:

> To claim that sport can combat HIV and AIDS is not only to overstate the limited capacity of sport but also to dangerously ignore the complexity of HIV and AIDS . . . the fundamental question that confronts us . . . [is] how can we better understand the interplay between sport, with its limited capacity on one hand, and HIV and AIDS, in its full complexity, on the other.

Such perspectives are supported by many from outside the narrow sport-for-development fraternity. For example, Ungar (2006) questions the extent to which resilience can simply be regarded as an individual characteristic. He suggests that the concern should be the resilient and enabling nature of *environments*. Rather pithily he suggests that it might be better to 'change the odds' rather than try to resource individuals to 'beat the odds' in environments which frequently do not support behaviour change, or offer opportunities for 'development' (political power and influence can also be important). A peer leader interviewed in South Africa emphasised that his training had added to his employability via an increased sense of self-efficacy, improved time management, problem solving skills, programme-related administrative skills and report writing. However, when asked if this would lead to employment he said that this was unlikely, as he was not a member of the ANC (Coalter and Taylor, 2010)!

If I may slightly adjust Wagner's (1964) notion of displacement of scope, the most basic questions related to sport-for-development programmes seem to be:

- In what ways are the participants in need of 'development'?
- Does participation positively affect the combination of values, attitudes, knowledge and aptitudes contained in a notion of 'development', for all or some?
- How does the programme achieve such impacts and for whom?
- Does this result in an intention to change specific behaviours, for all or some?
- Does this lead to an actual change in behaviour, for all or some?
- Does the participants' environment enable desired changes in behaviour (Jeanes, 2011; Mwaanga, 2003; Ungar, 2006)?
- If not, how does this contribute to broader processes of social and economic development?

Some reflections on well-meaning ambition

A key assumption of the project in Africa and India was that the organizations and personnel would be relatively stable over the period of the project and beyond. This was necessary for the successful completion of the project, but also underpinned the desire to contribute to the development of an organizational philosophy of monitoring and evaluation and the required capacity. However, this proved to be a dubious assumption. In some organizations there was a lack of staff continuity, with some involved in the initial training and development work leaving at various stages in the project. This resulted in the need for training of new personnel, a lack of continuity and a lack of robust development of organizational capacity.

Second, some organizations adopted a rather pragmatic approach to what seemed to be regarded simply as another aid project funded by important strategic funders. Here the approach was one of conformity to funding agreements to collect data and on occasion this seemed to be privileged over the methodological requirements of robust research – strong advice was ignored. The opportunities for organizational development and capacity building were not grasped by all – although lack of continuity was always going to make this difficult. The few who had previously committed resources to monitoring and evaluation benefited most and were most likely to continue with the work.

Such issues raise important questions about the extent to which a robust monitoring and evaluation philosophy and practice can be embedded in under-funded and relatively unstable organizations. A further issue, which those who have struggled to teach research methods will understand, is the substantial difficulties involved in developing both a philosophy of monitoring and evaluation and relevant skills among largely untrained, if enthusiastic, and over-worked practitioners.

Third, some liberation methodologists seem to argue for a sort of politically oriented epistemological and methodological purity, although they rarely provide any empirical evidence of how this differs from traditional approaches (Darnell and Hayhurst, 2012; Kay, 2009; Lindsey and Grattan, 2012; Nichols *et al.*, 2011). In this regard I follow Hammersley's (1995: 19) position that research is a practical activity and that 'philosophy must not be seen as superordinate to empirical research [which] cannot be governed in any strict way by methodological theory'.

In the work in Africa and India, despite attempts to use validated scales and achieve inter-programme comparisons, not all programmes used the full scales or the standard response system, especially for perceived self-efficacy. The reasons for this illustrate some of the difficulties encountered in undertaking collaborative and developmental work, in a wide variety of contexts, with relatively inexperienced people supported at arm's length. First, despite prior agreement, some simply did not use all the statements in the scale. Second, some argued that the scale was too complicated for many of their participants and chose to use simple yes/no responses. While this did provide some useful information for the programme personnel in developing thinking about the meaning of 'development' and the nature of possible programme impacts, it undermined the validity of the scale and reduced inter-programme comparability. That this is not unusual in such circumstances is illustrated by the work of Woodcock *et al.* (2012) in which local Kenyan volunteers regarded questionnaires as too long and complex, even with simplified response formats, which reduced their validity. Burnett's (2001: 47) experience in her extensive and systematic work in South Africa was that:

> questionnaires were continually changed and shortened to accommodate all levels of literacy and time constraints . . . this resulted in the simplification of questions, scaling (a reduction from a five- to a three-point Likert scale) . . . The need to adapt methodology to be flexible and context-sensitive may have impacted negatively on the sophistication of results but was envisaged to be an important result in itself.

The achievement of epistemological and methodological purity in such circum-stances proved a difficult task.

Cognitive, affective and normative dimensions: An imbalance

Craib (1984) argues that social theory has three dimensions and that theorists are doing three different things simultaneously, with varying balances between them.

The *cognitive dimension* seeks to establish objective knowledge about the social world. The *affective dimension* is one in which elements of the theories embody the experience and feeling of the theorist, which means that any debate involves more than rational argument. The third dimension is *normative* – any theory of the way that the world is, is also based on assumptions about the way that the world ought to be, what sort of actions are possible or desirable. It seems to me that too often the cognitive element is compromised in sport-for-development – even academic critics of supposedly neo-colonialist policies and practices seem to retain an affective and normative belief in the inherent developmental potential of sport. In this regard Hartmann and Kwauk (2011: 289) refer to the functionalist view of sport, which underpins much sport-for-development, as being based on 'the normative vision of social life, social change, and the status quo embedded in this dominant vision'. Coakley (2011: 309) refers to 'interpretive frameworks inspired by ideology more than research and theory' which constitute widely shared visions of how social worlds could and should be organized, but 'when combined with similarly shared emotions, identities, and dominant narratives, they tend to resist change, even when evidence contradicts them'. Although tensions between normative, affective and cognitive perspectives are inevitable, within sport-for-development they are sub-optimally confused among those whose imperative is 'to make a difference' (Black, 2010).

Within this context I am reminded of Gramsci's advice to radicals – to seek to combine pessimism of the intellect with an optimism of the will. Whereas the many ever-optimistic, innovative and generous practitioners I have met illustrate a strong optimism of the will, intellectually and emotionally I am a pessimist. My pessimism relates to two issues: (i) the sheer scale of the issues implied by the amorphous term 'development' and the failure to address systematically issues of displacement of scope; (ii) neo-liberal assumptions, the evangelists, the self-interested conceptual entrepreneurs and the cloistered atmosphere of incestuous amplification in which research is reduced to the role of confirming what they already think that they know.

I accept that evaluation is, or should be, a rational exercise that takes place in a political context (Weiss, 1993). I also acknowledge that rhetoric partly reflects processes of lobbying, persuasion, negotiation and alliance-building. I understand that in marginal policy areas such processes frequently produce inflated promises, unrealistic desired impacts and outcomes which lack the clarity and intellectual coherence that evaluation criteria should have. However, a major result of this, combined with the politico-ideological nature of sport-for-development has been that 'in its contemporary manifestation, the SDP [sport-for-development-and-peace] emphasis on practice has come, for the most part, at the expense of critical and theoretically-informed reflection' (Black, 2010: 122). From my perspective this does not imply that sport-for-development needs more cross-sectional descriptive studies of limited generalizability, more heartfelt narratives or even de-colonizing, feminist-oriented, participatory action research – noble and well-mannered as this might be. Rather, as others have suggested, there is a need to step back and to reflect critically on what we and, most especially, others might already know (Coakley, 2011; Crabbe, 2008; Tacon, 2007).

If we soften Gramsci's pessimism to scepticism, I believe that this is a core requirement of academic practice and the pursuit of cognitive understanding – albeit struggling with the affective and normative components present in all social theorizing. For example, Portes (2000: 4) refers to the 'trained skepticism' of sociologists and argues that 'gaps between received theory and actual reality have been so consistent as to institutionalize a disciplinary skepticism in sociology against sweeping statements, no matter from what ideological quarter they come'. Berger's (1971: 79–80) main interest lay in the sociology of religion – oddly relevant to sport-for-development – and he sought to promote a humanistic sociology, not dissimilar to the liberation methodologists. Nevertheless he argued that:

> the sociological perspective, with its irritating interjection of the question *'says who?'* . . . introduces an element of sober scepticism that has an immediate utility in giving some protection at least against converting too readily . . . [and] makes us a little less likely to be trapped by every missionary band we encounter on the way.

Consequently, while it is not possible to escape the affective and normative aspects of social theory, academics can contribute by working to privilege the cognitive – and there are signs that this perspective is beginning to emerge (e.g. Crabbe, 2008; Jeanes, 2011; Spaaij, 2011, 2012). Such an approach can contribute to the intellectual and practical development of sport-for-development by placing it within a much wider world of knowledge and research and by theorizing its limitations as well as outlining its 'potential'.

SPORT-FOR-DEVELOPMENT: THE WORK OF FRED COALTER

Cora Burnett

When I met Fred Coalter at a United Nations workshop in 2005, he was already a leading figure in the field of sport-for-development and well versed in the social policy research area identified as 'sport plus' and 'plus sport' (Coalter, 2007). He was then Professor of Sports Policy at the University of Stirling, responsible for the Sport England/UK Sport online Value of Sport Monitor and an established author.

Coalter's work in this area has elevated the body of knowledge through critical reflection and deconstructing existing paradigms, whilst offering alternative approaches for evidence-based research and policy making. He interrogated state of the art methodology and ways of conceptualizing 'sport for good' programmes across a range of specific policy areas. He searched for mechanisms (rather than mere correlations) and re-conceptualized 'social capital' as discussed by leading theorists such as Bourdieu, Coleman and Putnam. He deconstructed and questioned the underlying assumptions of envisaged programme outcomes, and came to the realization that practices (e.g. sport clubs) cannot make unqualified claims to contribute to social capital as sport can only develop 'certain types of social capital among particular types of members' (Coalter, 2007: 57). By putting the complexity back into research, he called for a nuanced and informed way of surveying evidence.

The key factor was to move beyond limited correlations and explore the nature of social mechanisms that would shed light on the full complexity of issues (Seippel, 2006). For Coalter, theory-based approaches to evaluation needed to reduce the distance between academic research, policy makers and practitioners – bringing them together in what Pawson (2006: 169) refers to as a new way of 'sense-making'. He also drew on the insight of Pawson and Tilley (2000: 201) to illuminate a dialectical engagement between stakeholders referred to as 'teaching and learning interactions'.

In a theory of change approach, evaluations should clarify, explain and question different approaches, programme designs and modes of delivery. For Coalter, programme theories, stakeholder engagement and real-world dynamics should find a synthesis for mutual understanding and 'development'. The sequence of cause-effect should be explained, the unit of analysis clearly defined and aligned with programme design and delivery in order to offer sophisticated and nuanced understandings.

He acknowledged the complexity of real-world settings and the difficulties in measuring change which is attributable to multi-faceted social interventions encompassing a variety of mechanisms (e.g. contexts, relationships, rules, experiences and different types of participants). He never professed to have the complete solution, but it was his quest to bring scientific conduct into the equation and the search for robust evidence, tracing the 'value-chain' and processes thereof, that enriched theory building, methodological approaches and sense-making.

In his pursuit of conceptual richness and understanding, he engaged with the work of influential scholars who are critical of offering limited-focused programmes to address 'broad-gauge problems' (Weiss, 1993: 105). Pertinent questions were asked. For example: how do you measure attitude change relating to limited and relatively poorly resourced programmes focused on HIV/AIDS education?

For Coalter, theory-based evaluation should in the first instance focus on process mechanisms which go beyond simple accountability and outcome measurements (Coalter, 2006). Monitoring and evaluation should reach beyond the summative (e.g. effectiveness of intermediate impacts) and focus on the formative (e.g. examining the ways of improving and enhancing development practices). He argued that the overarching goal for programme evaluation 'is to foster transparent, inquisitive and self-cited organisational culture . . . so we can learn to do better' (Coalter, 2007: 89). He argues for a clearer understanding and evaluation of the conceptualization, design and delivery of interventions, inclusive of 'up-take' dynamics embedded in the context of the delivery of sport experiences. He refers to Pawson (2006: 31), who argued that 'all interventions are conditioned by the action of layer upon layer of contextual influences', to deconstruct political and policy rhetoric.

At many conferences, Coalter expressed discontent with the 'black box' approach to sport-for-development research where the 'treatment' and 'magical properties' are taken as a given to deliver on preconceived (and unproblematic) 'input factors'. For him, sport merely provides the 'site' for socialization outcomes and does not possess inherent magical or transformative powers (Coakley, 2011; Hartmann and Kwauk, 2011). In many of his conference presentations, he referred to logic modelling as a basis for theory-based evaluations in the search to identify the components, mechanisms, relationships and sequences of cause and effect that might lead to 'desired' impacts (Coalter, 2010). The challenge would be to identify what has been 'desired' by whom and who benefited, how and to what extent?

Moving beyond simple cause-effect (and linear) relationships, and mediating complex understandings, influenced Coalter's 'positionality'. He became increasingly outspoken against 'sport evangelists' and the 'optimism of the will', where faith is the main driving force and evidence is packaged to serve as proof of the magical transformative power of sport. He drew on Gramsci's advice to radicals to bring 'pessimism of the intellect' and to conduct work 'without illusions and without becoming disillusioned' (Coalter, 2011b: 21). Academics, he suggested, should be sceptics and their claims have to be supported by robust research evidence and coherent theory-based explanations. His critique is directed against the 'grandiose claims of self-interested conceptual entrepreneurs promulgating ideas about the supposed "power" of sport via self-reinforcing processes of incestuous amplification' (Coalter, 2013). Yet, he is sympathetic towards practitioners who are working in very trying circumstances and who have little control in changing the 'odds' (as suggested by Ungar, 2006; cited in Coalter, 2013). It is no easy task for practitioners to address the underlying causes that created 'target groups' as beneficiaries of sport-for-development work in the first place. In this regard, he distinguishes between the necessary and sufficient conditions under which potential outcomes are achievable (Coalter, 2013).

As an academic from the Global North, he capitalized on the existing knowledge base, theoretical traditions and understandings currently available there. However, his work equally draws on his experiences of African and Indian contexts of extreme poverty that came to him as a culture shock without any comparative frame of reference. The slums of Nairobi (where Coalter undertook site visits at the Mathare Youth Sport Association) provide an experience that few people can imagine. The dehumanizing face of poverty is revealed in overcrowding, filthy streets where dogs, goats and people often compete in garbage picking for survival, and is an intimidating experience for even the hardiest of anthropologists. Similar visits to India left an imprint encapsulated into an awareness of the diversity and complex social relationships at grassroots levels where interventions are delivered for 'intended change'. These experiences and his sound theoretical and scientific schooling influenced him to challenge the proverbial Global North-Global South dichotomy (Nichols *et al.*, 2011).

He rejects accusations of post-colonial, hegemonic approaches and perpetuated colonial power relations inherent in the uncritical assumption of the 'universality of methodology and its epistemological and ontological underpinnings' (Kay, 2011; cited in Coalter, 2013). As in several of his arguments, he would illuminate the mismatch of local interventions to address multi-levelled social manifestations, referred to as a displacement of scope. The unit of analysis should address unequal power relations and hegemonic practices at the appropriate level of effect. Funders who impose neo-liberal and neo-colonial oppressive practices might be guilty of such conduct but not all researchers from the Global North or researchers who have funders from the Global North are ideologically contaminated.

Coalter is critical of environmental determinism and researchers who advocate a deficit-model of recipients (being deviant and in need of donor-identified interventions). He is also critical of researchers who professed that sport-for-development is a new field of scientific inquiry, and who had ignored scholarly insights emanating from the 1900s. In this way Coalter is putting some storms back into the 'teacup', while simultaneously releasing some more profound 'storms'.

It was inevitable that Coalter would also reflect on methodological theories and methodology across qualitative and quantitative paradigms and research designs. For him research is a practical activity where methods need to be applied in close collaboration with the research participants to meaningfully capture data and mediate understandings of lived realities. Sound methodology and theory would inform the production of his manual on monitoring and evaluation (Coalter, 2006), as well as his own research practices. His work on self-efficacy according to an experimental control research design is well known and was often utilized to address the complexities of research, the foci on process, agency and centrality of an intervention.

The *Sport for Development Impact Assessment,* produced on behalf of the International Development through Sport (IDS) agency, UK Sport and Comic Relief, bears testimony to Coalter's scholarship. This research sought to test the hypothesis that 'sport contributes to the personal development and wellbeing of disadvantaged children and young people' (International Development through Sport, 2011). The project commenced in 2007 and traced the most significant programme effects in four programmes in Africa and two in India. Methodological alignment afforded inter-institutional comparisons and intra-institutional learning. However, it is the main findings (packaged strategically as lessons to be learnt) that reinforced theoretical and pragmatic understandings in terms of: (i) personal development (not all participants needed to, or did, improve their self-esteem); (ii) gender equality and women's empowerment (transferability of skills are hampered by ideology and structures); (iii) HIV and AIDS (knowledge did not translate into behavioural change); (iv) peer leader training requires mentorship and female role models for programme delivery (with peer leaders as recipients rather than 'inputs'); and (v) building monitoring and evaluation (M & E) capacity necessitated commitment and understanding of underling mechanisms of projected effect (what works and what does not work).

Fred Coalter has been a critical and sound voice in the field of sport-for-development. He does not profess armchair wisdom but earned his insights in the very contexts where he would search for 'learnings'. He has brought a new optimism for serious academics and researchers – to articulate the complexity of sport-for-development processes and the need for robust evidence. It is no easy road to (de)construct given stakeholder (unequal) relationships and dynamics where confirmation and proof are prioritized above dialogue and learning through controversies and true reflections.

10

RESEARCHING POLICY CHANGE IN SCHOOL SPORT AND PHYSICAL EDUCATION

Barrie Houlihan

This chapter describes how we conducted research on what we considered to be dramatic change in the salience of school sport and physical education to politicians from the late 1980s (Houlihan and Green, 2006). We argued that, from the 1960s to the late 1980s, school sport and physical education (PE) had experienced a prolonged period of relative neglect by government which was explained partly by the inability of PE teacher organizations to rebut effectively the criticism that PE did not provide pupils with transferrable skills and partly by the inability of PE teacher organizations to articulate a coherent and unified view of the purpose of PE, the relationship between PE and sport/games and the content of the PE curriculum. We argued that towards the end of the 1980s and into the early 1990s a number of factors combined to raise the political profile of school sport and PE. Factors included the debate over the inclusion and status of PE in the national curriculum, the appointment of John Major as Prime Minister and the establishment of the Youth Sport Trust. The aim of the research was to better understand the process of policy change in relation to school sport and PE during this period.

However, we were keen to avoid presenting a purely descriptive account of the change in policy. Rather than concentrating solely on questions relating to what happened and when it happened, we were concerned to answer questions about why and how change in policy took place. Our concern with questions of why and how in relation to policy reflected our concern to understand the broader changes that were taking place in sport policy at around the same time. Consequently, while we were concerned with practical questions of data collection, we were also concerned to identify theoretical frameworks which would not only provide a guide to the process of data collection (i.e. indicate what sort of data and sources of data might be relevant), but also provide an interpretive framework for the analysis.

The role of theory

Theory often has an unhappy relationship with empirical research. While theory can occasionally overwhelm empirical data through a valorisation of complexity over parsimony, the collection of data and their interpretation are dependent on a recognition of the necessary and productive relationship between theory and research. If used appropriately, theory will guide research by sensitizing the researcher to themes and interconnections that might otherwise be missed and also constructively challenge research findings thus ensuring a greater degree of internal validity. For our study we were concerned to explore the relationship between a range of state and non-state policy actors and needed to pay particular attention to the patterning of relationships, the nature of influence or power to affect policy and the definition and articulation of interests.

However, a challenge that all researchers face is deciding the type of theory that is likely to prove a source of insight for the particular research question. Among the most commonly used theories for analysing policy are macro-level theories such as feminism, rational choice theory, neo-Marxism and neo-pluralism. What these theories have in common is that they offer researchers a perspective from which they can interpret major social phenomena such as the distribution of power between social groups, the relationship between the state and civil society and the basis for individual action. Each macro-level theory provides a set of propositions about society and also a conceptual language to aid description and analysis. In relation to our study of changes in the status of sport and physical education it would have been possible and productive to have adopted a macro-level framework for the research and there are plenty of examples of insightful analyses of education policy, physical education policy and sport policy which have utilized macro-level theory (e.g. Azzarito and Solomon, 2006; Benn, 2005; Hargreaves, 1994; Pronger, 2002). Indeed, in the opening section of the article in which we reviewed medium-term change in the perception of the nature and value of physical education, we concluded that there were 'four potentially significant explanatory variables: (i) ideas and ideological change at both the service and governmental core policy levels; (ii) institutional arrangements; (iii) interest group activity; and (iv) the impact of key individuals' (Houlihan and Green, 2006: 77). While some of these variables, such as ideology and interest group activity, are more amenable to analysis at the macro-level, others, especially the role of individual policy actors, are far less so and in some theories, for example Marxism, are generally rejected. In summary, we concluded that while macro-level theories have the virtue of sensitizing the researcher to particular variables (e.g. ideology, social class, gender, ethnicity) and their significance at the broad societal level, they are less useful in analyzing the specific processes underpinning particular policies and policy decisions.

As a consequence of these concerns, we turned our attention to the rich body of theory available at the meso-level and which includes the advocacy coalition framework (Sabatier and Jenkins-Smith, 1993), varieties of institutionalism (Ostrom, 1999), multiple streams (Kingdon, 1984), punctuated equilibrium (Baumgartner and Jones, 1993) and policy network theory (Marsh and Rhodes, 1992). Most meso-level theories tend to be stronger in explaining early phases of the policy process such as agenda-setting rather than later phases such as policy choice and implementation. In selecting the two analytic frameworks adopted for the study (multiple streams and the advocacy coalition framework) we applied three criteria: first, that the frameworks should be capable of analyzing a number of aspects or phases of the policy process; second, that they should be internally coherent; and third, that there is evidence that they have been applied successfully to similar policy issues.

Rather than selecting one meso-level theory to act as a guide for the research, we decided to utilize the concepts and perspectives offered by two which offered contrasting explanations for policy change. The advocacy coalition framework (ACF) emphasized the importance of analysis over the medium to long term, the impact of ideology, the importance of policy learning, the role of individuals as policy brokers and the significance of inter-group/coalition competition. In contrast, the multiple streams theory drew attention to the relative openness and fluidity of the policy process, the opportunity for bargaining and deal-making, the role of policy entrepreneurs and the degree of residual randomness in public policy-making.

The findings of the research did not fit closely with either the ACF or the multiple streams theory, but having two analytic frameworks available provided us with a rich conceptual toolkit and allowed us to draw conclusions about the importance of policy learning, the significance of individual policy actors and the importance of a benign ideological context for policy change.

Research design and the selection of methods

Research design

Once we had established the theoretical foundation for the study, the next set of decisions concerned research design and the selection of appropriate methods. As regards research design, there were a number of possible options including a sub-sectoral case study (i.e. the study of a topic or issue, such as elite athlete development or disability sport participation, within a policy sector which is not designed to illuminate the policy-making processes of the whole sector), a cross-sectoral comparative case study (e.g. comparing policy processes in sport with those in the arts) and a case study of a particular policy decision (e.g. the content of the National Curriculum for PE or the reduction in funding for School Sport Partnerships [SSPs]). Yet all these options have, to some extent, to address the often strongly voiced criticisms of the use of case studies, with the central criticism being that case studies provide a weak basis for generalization. However, it was our view that an ideographic approach – that is an in-depth analysis of one case with the aim of providing as complete an explanation as possible – was appropriate given our research aims. As de Vaus (2001: 236) has observed, case studies

> achieve explanations by building a full picture of the sequence of events, the context in which they occur, and the meaning of the actions and events as interpreted by participants and their meaning as given by a context. In the

end an adequate causal explanation is one that makes sense. It involves telling a plausible, convincing, and logically acceptable story of how events unfold and how they are linked to one another.

Thus rather than attempting to control or eliminate certain variables, for example historical contextual factors, we sought to take them into account as being essential to our understanding of policy change. Although, with regard to the particular concern with generalization, our primary concern was in-depth understanding of issues of causation, we were nonetheless concerned with generalization. While generalization as understood by statisticians conducting an analysis of large datasets was not possible, we were confident that our research design would provide the basis for drawing inferences about the school sport and PE policy process and that our findings, when combined with similar research, would provide a basis for increasingly confident generalization (Hammersley and Gomm, 2000).

The decision to use a sub-sectoral case study research design was prompted by the degree to which it complemented our aim to 'provide an analysis of the dramatic change in the political salience of school sport and PE' (Houlihan and Green, 2006: 74). Such an aim implied a longitudinal focus rather than a snapshot of the policy sub-sector at a particular point in time. We needed to be able to examine policy processes over the medium to long term (see later discussion of periodization) and to examine a number of sub-sectoral decisions in order to be able to draw conclusions about change in the policy-making process. However, the other main research design options did offer the prospect of insights that we might not gain from our selected approach. Particularly attractive was a comparative research design which would have allowed us to draw conclusions about the distinctiveness of the developments in school sport and PE policy-making. Comparison with arts policy or with media policy would have been particularly attractive. However, our decision not to adopt this design was due in part to resource constraints, especially the cost of travel to conduct interviews, and in part due to a judgement that we needed to understand the changes in our focal policy sub-sector before we embarked on comparison. With this in mind, a comparative study would be a logical next step in the research. We decided against a research design that focused on a detailed study of one particular decision for two main reasons: first, that there were already a number of excellent studies of particular decisions, for example Evans and Penney's (1995) study of the formation of the National Curriculum for PE; and second, that the concepts of change and stability were central to our research aim and, therefore, while a detailed study of a particular case would undoubtedly provide insights into the distribution and utilization of power in the policy process, it would not provide insights into change in power relations.

Periodization

Our study was focused on policy change from about 1990 to around 2005, which was a period in which we argued that substantial policy change had taken place and thus marked a significant break with previous periods. While we were confident that we had identified a particular watershed in the early 1990s, periodization for the purposes of policy analysis is far from self-evident and, on reflection, we should have considered the issue more critically. Defining watersheds that mark the division of one period from another is a largely subjective process as it involves imbuing a particular event or cluster of variables with significance. However, deciding which events or what variables are significant inevitably bears the imprint of their time of origin and the closer that the researcher is to the policy under scrutiny the more likely he or she is to overestimate significance. The danger for the research process is that the erroneous imposition of a period on a series of events or policy developments can obscure analysis and can tempt the researcher to make the data fit the supposed characteristics of the period.

The particular concern for our study was that we were perhaps too ready to accept 1997 and the election of the first Labour government to hold office since 1979 as marking a break between periods. It is only with the benefit of temporal distance that this decision could be seen as being, at best, premature and, at worst, erroneous. For example, it is possible to make a strong case that the real watershed was not the election of the Labour government but was actually seven years earlier with the appointment of John Major as Prime Minister. Arguably the changes initiated by Major – the National Lottery, the restructuring of the Sports Council and the introduction of Specialist Sports Colleges (SSCs) – were of far greater long-term significance than the policy changes introduced by Labour. However, it is equally easy to construct an alternative basis for periodization, as indeed I do with co-author Iain Lindsey in a more recent analysis of British sport policy (Houlihan and Lindsey, 2012). In this study we argue that there is substantial continuity of policy, not only between the governments of Blair and Brown and those of John Major, but also between the Labour governments and those of Margaret Thatcher. We argue:

> Blair's promotion of modernisation and his emphasis on stakeholding resonate strongly with central elements of the new public management philosophy espoused by Margaret Thatcher in the 1980s. It could also be argued that the continuities stretch back even further and are part of the gradual (though admittedly unevenly paced) progression of sport from being primarily the preserve of civil society institutions to being an instrument in the government's portfolio for dealing with a range of largely social welfare issues. The transition from an Advisory Sports Council in the mid-1960s to an Executive Sports Council in the early 1970s to Action Sport from 1982, to National Demonstration Projects in the mid-1980s to *Sport: Raising the Game* in the mid-1990s followed by the plethora of more recent initiatives provide some evidence at least of a consistent policy trajectory that stretches back to the Labour government of Harold Wilson if not further back to the Wolfenden report of 1960. According to this assessment, the Thatcher years would be defined not as a break with the past, but simply a slowing in the pace at which sport was moving into a more central position in fabric of public policy.

If we had applied Hall's (1986) typology of 'orders' of policy change we might well have presented the periodization in a different manner. Hall identified three orders of change: first-order changes are to the intensity of application of an existing policy instrument such as the distribution of funding to SSPs or to SSCs; second-order changes refer to the introduction of new policy instruments such as regulating or prescribing the content of the National Curriculum for PE; and third-order changes are those that result in a change in policy objectives, for example, replacing objectives concerned to increase youth participation with objectives concerned with talent identification and development. While the application of Hall's typology might not have resulted in us making fundamental alterations to our periodization, it would undoubtedly have introduced a greater degree of subtlety into the analysis and resulted in a more nuanced temporal framework.

Document search, selection and analysis

Although semi-structured interviews were our major source of data, document analysis fulfilled two important functions: first, as preparation for the interviews; and second, as an opportunity for triangulation in relation to interview data. The type of documents with which we were concerned tended to fall into one of three categories: opinion-based articles which illustrated the debates within the PE profession regarding the relationship between PE and sport; government policy documents; and publications by professional bodies or interest groups. As with all documentary sources, we had to consider their authenticity (whether the document is genuine and from a reliable source), credibility (whether the evidence contained in the document is typical and also free from error and deliberate distortion), representativeness (whether the document is representative of the totality of documents) and meaning (whether the evidence is clear) (Scott, 1990). The assessment we made of the documentary sources we used is provided in Table 10.1. As with all documents we were aware of the political, temporal and social context within which they were produced and the extent to which context might affect authenticity, credibility, representativeness and meaning.

Once we had identified our documentary sources and assessed them according to Scott's four criteria, we then faced the task of analysing the content. As with the analysis of the interview data, we adopted a thematic content approach which involved both of us reading the documents and identifying potential themes, discussing and agreeing the emerging themes and providing them with a title or definition, and finally, coding the documents according to our themes and selecting any quotations that we might use in the article.

Interviewing

As mentioned above in the discussion of case study research design, one of the objectives of case study analysis is to provide an insider perspective on events and processes. One of the main ways of gaining an understanding of the policy process

TABLE 10.1 Evaluating documentary sources

	Authenticity	Credibility	Representativeness	Meaning
Articles by members of professional/interest groups, e.g. articles, letters and editorials in PE teachers' magazines and journals	Most of these items were expressions of the personal opinions of individual members of professional PE teachers' organizations or were 'opinion pieces' written or commissioned by the editor of a professional body's house journal. Given the source of the items, they were clearly the 'authentic' opinion of the individuals who wrote them.	None of the items reviewed had been prepared especially for me or my co-researcher so there was no possibility that the items had been written with the intention of influencing our research. However, because the items were all expressions of (sometimes very passionately held) opinions, the intention of the authors was to influence national debates and shape opinion among the profession's membership and within the wider policy network.	It was difficult to determine whether the items we identified were representative. The items that we identified were certainly not isolated examples of the expression of particular opinions about school sport and PE. In this regard we could argue that the items were representative of a strand of published opinion. More difficult is to claim that the items were representative of opinions within the PE profession as a whole. However, during our interviews we had the opportunity to check on the strength of competing views on school sport/PE among PE teachers and were reassured that the opinions expressed in the items we had selected were broadly representative of the divisions within the profession.	In general, the opinions expressed in the items identified were clear and logically consistent. Most of the items were dealing with only a limited range of issues and were often quite short, so the scope for extended reflection and analysis by the authors was limited.

(Continued)

TABLE 10.1 (Continued)

	Authenticity	Credibility	Representativeness	Meaning
Government policy documents, e.g. National Curriculum for PE, *Sport: Raising the Game* and *Game Plan*	Given that these items were produced by government departments or by non-departmental public bodies, we were very confident about the authenticity of the documents.	At one level these documents were highly credible. However, as with most, if not all, policy documents, there are degrees of credibility. Government policy documents in their diagnosis of a problem tend to place more blame on previous governments or external policy actors than on their own previous management of the problem. Also, when a document outlines a new policy, there is always a need to distinguish between statements of aspiration (which can often be literally incredible) and commitments to action.

The main policy documents we reviewed had more than their fair share of highly ambitious aspirational statements, but also provided evidence of resource commitment. Consequently, we considered the government policy documents to have high credibility (at least relative to typical government policy statements in the area of sport). | As the policy documents were official documents published by government departments or other units within government, they were certainly representative of the views of the relevant minister and of the Prime Minister. However, whether they were representative of the Cabinet and especially of the priorities within the education ministry is more open to question. Nevertheless, we felt confident in assuming that the documents had sufficient support from senior members of the government for them to be considered as representative of the government's views on school sport and PE. | In general, the meaning of the policy documents was clear particularly in terms of objectives/aspirations, if rather less so in relation to the means by which they would be achieved. However, even in relation to the means outlined in the documents, there was a relatively high degree of clarity of meaning. |

	Authenticity	Credibility	Representativeness	Meaning
Publications by professional bodies or interest groups, e.g. annual reports from PE teachers' organizations or the Youth Sport Trust	These documents had a high degree of authenticity as they were all official publications by recognised organizations. In addition, many of the reports (for example annual reports) contained statements of accounts which have to conform to legal requirements. All the documents used had either been published by the organizations in hard copy or had been downloaded from their official websites.	The publications from professional bodies were credible insofar as they were not written deliberately our research. However, as was the case with government documents, they are written with an acute awareness of the potential public relations impact of the document. Consequently, these documents tend to highlight their achievements and downplay their failures.	As the documents were official publications of their respective organizations, we felt confident in accepting them as representative of the policy and opinions of the organization.	In general, the material included in the documents was clear and comprehensible.

for school sport and PE was to interview those who were integral to that process. While obtaining data from those closely involved in policy decisions is of obvious benefit, the process can often be problematic both in terms of reliability and validity. The interviews with leaders of interest groups and professional organizations and with senior civil servants highlighted some of the problems associated with elite interviewing. As Williams (2012: 161) notes, 'Interviews with powerful people are often seen as having distinct problems, because of access and a reluctance by respondents to answer questions in a straightforward way'.

One of the first decisions that we had to make was deciding who to try to interview. In the article we stated that:

> The nine interviewees were selected on the basis of their involvement in the development, implementation or analysis of school sport and PE policy within the last 15 years. Most interviewees were involved in more than one aspect of the policy process: eight interviewees were currently or had been involved in policy development and included senior civil servants or senior members of interest/professional organisations; six were currently or had been involved in implementation and included senior civil servants, senior members of interest/professional bodies; and four either were currently or had been senior academics involved in policy analysis.

The one group that we were unsuccessful in contacting were politicians. We certainly tried to contact both serving and former ministers of education, but without success. The absence of a contribution from politicians certainly raised concerns regarding the validity of the analysis which, to some extent, were alleviated by access to other sources of data regarding the views of politicians, including statements in House of Commons debates, newspaper articles and published speeches. Nevertheless, direct comments from ministers would have enhanced the face validity of our analysis.

All the other potential interviewees whom we approached agreed to be interviewed, but each posed different challenges. Two of the most noteworthy challenges related to interviewees who were civil servants and interviewees who were chief executive officers or equivalent of voluntary or governmental agencies. With regard to interviewing civil servants, we encountered two challenges: the first was our assumption that civil servants were central to decision-making and the second was trying to elicit responses that moved beyond bland statements of the obvious. Occasionally we found ourselves asking questions about particular decisions or about the perceptions of decision processes held by civil servants, only to receive responses which indicated that the decision forum was one that did not always include civil servants. Such a forum might simply involve discussions between a minister and the head of a non-governmental interest group. The lesson that we learned from this experience was the importance of designing an interview schedule which established, in as subtle manner as possible, the role of the interviewee in the decision process and the extent and nature of their influence, rather than assuming that policy decisions necessarily involve senior civil servants.

While the variability in the direct role of senior civil servants in policy-making told us much about the policy process for school sport and PE, these interviewees were also able to provide valuable insights into the relative influence of other policy actors. However, partly as a consequence of their variable involvement, but more due to the fact that they were public officials, it was difficult to elicit reflective observations on the policy process which could be construed as critical of other policy actors (and certainly not comments which were critical of present or previous ministers). However, the willingness of civil servants to 'talk us through' a number of recent policy changes, such as the expansion of the school sport partnership programme, gave us a very clear indication of who was influential and who was peripheral in policy discussions.

With the senior officers of interest groups or professional organizations, the problems were of a different order as most of these interviewees were more than happy to express opinions about the role, competence, influence and motives of other policy actors. The particular challenge that we faced with this group was deciding what weight to give their opinions, assessments and recollections. Often we were able to triangulate one interviewee's responses with those of at least two others in order to build up a picture of the policy process that we considered to be accurate. However, there were one or two occasions where we felt that we were being encouraged to adopt a particular view of a decision process or, more commonly, of the motives and competence of other policy actors which served to further the objectives of the interviewee's organization rather than give an accurate account of events and processes. However, it was always difficult to determine whether we were deliberately being steered to adopt a particular perspective on an organization or a particular interpretation of how a decision was made, or whether the responses were simply those of people who were passionate about the issues at stake in relation to school sport and PE.

Academics were interviewed not because of their direct involvement in the school sport and PE policy process, but primarily because of their ability to provide an overview of the policy sub-sector and the opportunity to use them as a sounding board for our ideas and analytical themes. However, while the academic interviewees were the most disinterested of our interviewees, it did not always follow that they were any less passionate about the way decisions were taken and the impact of those decisions. What tended to distinguish academic interviewees from non-academic interviewees was the greater degree of awareness of their attitudes and values and a greater capacity to reflect on the impact of their attitudes and values on their assessment of policy and policy-making.

With all our interviewees we were acutely aware that we would need to use the time available in the most productive way. In preparation for each interview we made every effort to gather as much background material as possible so that we only asked them for information about issues and aspects of policy-making for which there was no written source (Lilleker, 2003). In most cases we made contact with the selected interviewees by letter, on the assumption that emails and telephone calls would be easier for them and their secretaries and PAs to ignore. We assumed that a letter would at least make it on to their desks. In the letter we gave a brief outline of our research questions, how much of their time we would need and our willingness to provide assurances regarding anonymity. Rather than wait for a reply, we ended our letter with a note that one of us would contact their secretary/PA in approximately ten days' time to see if an interview would be possible and, if so, to arrange a time and place. Once the date had been arranged, we sent an email or letter confirming the arrangements for the interview and also outlining in more detail the three or four key topics that we wanted to cover.

As regards the conduct of the interview, we reminded the interviewee about the purpose of the research and told them that if we asked them for information which was available elsewhere (and which we had missed in our search) to direct us to that source in order to save their time. We did this not only to avoid wasting precious time, but also to avoid irritating our interviewee by having them provide information which, they might consider, we should already have obtained. Although our interviewees were very generous with their time, we always planned for an interview lasting no more than 40 minutes, assuming that for some busy people this would be the maximum amount of time that we could expect to be allocated and that it would be highly unlikely that we would have a second opportunity to ask them questions.

With regard to the conduct of the interviews and design of the interview schedule, we asked our interviewees for permission to record the interview, but assured them that we would send them a copy of any direct quotes that we planned to use and also the context within which their words would be set. One interviewee provided clarification in relation to the quotation that we had selected, while the others were content with the quotations we had selected and the context within which they had been used. The interview schedules were designed, as far as practicable, to cover the same themes with each interviewee, although specific questions were designed according to the particular responsibilities and experience of each interviewee. With most interviewees our opening questions were broad and invited them to reflect on the developments in school sport and PE over the previous ten or so years. Our intention in asking this type of question was two-fold. First, it was designed to put the interviewee at ease by asking an open question which was not necessarily focused on their actions or those of their organization. However, almost all our interviewees, as is usually the case with elite interviewing, were very experienced at being interviewed and were highly unlikely to feel ill at ease when faced with two academics. Our second intention in asking one or two general opening questions was, therefore, to see if they would identify issues, events, decisions and associated policy actors which we had overlooked.

From the opening questions we proceeded to narrow the focus on to specific issues, decisions etc., either working through our interview schedule or following up on responses to previous questions. Towards the end of the interview, when the interviewees had a clear idea of our particular research objectives, we always asked them to suggest other potential interviewees and we did identify one more interviewee who was mentioned by three interviewees.

All the interviews were transcribed and then subjected to thematic content analysis. Ideally we would have preferred to have had largely unstructured discussions with our interviewees which would have given greater scope for themes to emerge unmediated by the interviewers. However, because of the limited time we expected to have with each interviewee and because each interviewee, understandably, wanted to know what the interview would focus on, we had identified topics for discussion in advance and had also prepared an interview schedule. The challenge that we faced was in designing an interview schedule which would not impose an overly rigid set of themes on the interview, but would allow for the emergence of themes that we had not anticipated. However, while we considered that the topics we had identified and the interview schedule we used allowed scope for the introduction of new themes, we found that, although there was considerable refinement of our initial themes, no new major themes emerged.

Although we could simply have used our interview topics as themes for coding the data, we tried to look at the data with fresh eyes by both of us reading through the transcripts independently and identifying emergent major themes and sub-themes. We then discussed how best to describe/define each emergent theme and agreed on the following: changing values, beliefs and ideas; change in lobbying capacity/interest group activity; change in organizational infrastructure and resource dependency; and the significance of individual policy actors.

Theory and the interpretation of findings

At the start of the research process we identified the ACF and the multiple streams framework as potentially valuable frameworks for guiding the research and for interpreting the empirical data that the research generated. In practice, both frameworks were indeed useful in sharpening our focus during the data-collection phase. With regard to the subsequent analysis, the ACF was particularly useful in highlighting what was weak or absent from the policy sub-sector. Most significant was the weakness in organized lobbying capacity – an obvious prerequisite for coalition formation. However, the ACF emphasizes the importance of the steady accumulation of evidence, which proved to be an important factor in the process of policy change. The evidence provided by a range of organizations of the gradual erosion of sports opportunities for many pupils not only provided ammunition for individual lobbyists, but also helped to create a supportive context (e.g. among politicians) within which policy actors could operate.

However, although the ACF provided many useful insights, we found John Kingdon's multiple streams framework more valuable in interpreting our data. Of particular value was the emphasis given to the role of policy entrepreneurs, the importance of a sympathetic operating context for policy entrepreneurs and the opportunistic nature of policy-making within school sport and PE. The combined insights provided by the ACF and the multiple streams framework led to our conclusion that 'while individuals are an important explanatory factor their influence needs to be seen in the context of the institutional weakness of interest groups and the generalized, but largely unfocused, sympathy among politicians towards school sport and PE' (Houlihan and Green, 2006: 73).

In reviewing the value of our analytical frameworks, we resisted the temptation to attempt to construct a new framework or refine an existing framework which would better match our empirical findings. There were three reasons for this decision, the first of which was that we were confident that the utilization of the two frameworks had adequately illuminated the policy process in relation to our case and provided valuable insights. Second, we were using the frameworks as ideal types against which we could compare our particular case. Ideal types are useful especially in studying dynamic social phenomena such as sport policy-making which are particularly vulnerable to the vagaries of temporal location and socio-political context. Finally, we considered that attempting to develop a new analytic framework on the basis of one case (or, indeed, the relatively small number of studies of sport policy that were then currently available) would be unwise, although such framework development might be appropriate in the future.

YES, MINISTER: INSIGHTS FROM RESEARCH ON THE POLITICS OF POLICY CHANGE IN PHYSICAL EDUCATION AND SCHOOL SPORT

Andy Smith

2006 was a particularly memorable year for me, not least because by the middle of that year I was approaching the end of my full-time doctoral studies and desperately seeking employment to pay off the financial debt I had accrued during my time as a student, having spent seven years in higher education. Second, and most significantly for present purposes, my Ph.D. thesis, which explored the place of sport and physical activity in young people's lives (Smith, 2006), was accepted by the examiners. The scope of my doctoral research required me to examine several key aspects of physical education (PE) and school sport in England and Wales, especially young people's experiences of National Curriculum Physical Education and extra-curricular physical education, but researching processes of policy change in these contexts was not at that time the main focus of my work.

The publication of Houlihan and Green's (2006) paper, 'The changing status of school sport and physical education: Explaining policy change', preceeded the submission of my Ph.D. thesis by just three months. Since it focused on issues that were only tangentially relevant to my research, I decided to read it when I had reached a point where I would wish to do anything other than type the remaining words of my thesis! As is so often the case, this diversionary tactic impacted on me in a variety of unintended and unanticipated ways. In the immediate term, Houlihan and Green's work made me think more deeply about my findings and those of others. I also began to follow up other sources in their reference list which I had not cited in my own research, before furiously making notes about their key findings in case I was asked about the article in my *viva-voce*. Thankfully, my examiners did not expose my rudimentary knowledge of Houlihan and Green's article, but in the longer term their findings nevertheless struck a chord with me and sparked an interest in what is now a central research interest of mine as a sociologist: the relationship between politics and policy and the impacts of policy decisions, and non-decisions, on young people's sporting and non-sporting lives.

Athough the article was not written by sociologists, Houlihan and Green's work nevertheless helped widened my sociological imagination (Mills, 1959) precisely because I could relate to many of the events which they examined during their period of investigation (1990–2005). More particularly, I began to reflect on my experiences of PE and sport in and out of primary school during the time when Margaret Thatcher was in office, before entering secondary school one year after she was replaced as British Prime Minister by John Major, and then attending college and university in the period of the Blair government. These reflections did not simply focus on my personal biography, my experiences of PE and school sport (PESS), but also led me to realize that what I thought at the time were 'private troubles' could only properly be understood by recognizing that they were, in fact, widely shared 'public issues' (Mills, 1959) which were interdependent with much longer-term processes constituted by the actions of many other people, the majority of whom I had never met, over whom I had little control, but on whom I had been so heavily dependent for my previous life experiences. It was, in short, a reminder to me about why I studied sociology, why I wanted to become a sociologist; it also brought home to me personally the importance of Elias's (1978: 72) contention that:

> the figurations of interdependent human beings cannot be explained if one studies human beings singly. In many cases the opposite procedure is advisable – one can understand many aspects of the behaviour or actions of individual people only if one sets out from the study of the pattern of their interdependence, the structure of their societies, in short from the figurations they form with each other.

I include this brief contextual information not to engage in a moment of self-indulgence, but because it helps me to locate my own thoughts about the importance of the research by Barrie Houlihan and the late Mick Green (Houlihan and Green, 2006) in a broader context and because the convergence of these developments has, on reflection, had a lasting impact on me and my academic career. In the sections that follow, I want to briefly: (i) consider the major findings of their work; (ii) reflect upon the many important lessons to be gleaned from the approach taken; and (iii) examine the longer-term significance of their original study for later work in the field.

Building upon earlier analyses of the relationship between politics and policy in PESS (e.g. Evans and Penney, 1995; Kirk, 1992; Penney and Evans, 1999), Houlihan and Green (2006: 74), having identified what they described as a 'dramatic change in the political salience of school sport and PE' during the period between 1990 and 2005, sought to better understand these processes of policy change. In doing so, their findings shed important light on the complex networks of relationships that exist between a range of state and non-state policy actors, how the influence and positions of power occupied by key stakeholders affect policy, and how some individuals and groups are better able to define and articulate their interests and achieve their goals than other groups. Houlihan and Green sought to analyze their data – generated by analyses of relevant documents and interviews – through a constant interplay between empirical evidence and theoretical insights derived from two meso-level theories: the multiple streams framework and the advocacy coalition framework. These two frameworks were regarded at the outset as being potentially more useful in analyzing the specific processes underpinning particular policies and policy decisions in PESS that occurred over the medium-to-long-term. As it turned out, neither framework was deemed adequate in explaining the research findings, but the multiple streams theory was held to be particularly helpful in shedding light on the significance of individual policy entrepreneurs, the importance of a supportive ideological context for policy entrepreneurs, and the opportunistic nature of policy-making within PESS.

More specifically, Houlihan and Green's research pointed to the numerous ways in which the Youth Sport Trust (YST), in particular, helped provide the kind of institutional focus for PESS that was said to be lacking prior to the mid-1990s and how, during the period under investigation, that organization was able to obtain a greater capacity to define policy priorities in the area. Of particular importance, however, was the entrepreneurial role played by the then Chief Executive of the YST, Sue Campbell, who was better able to persuade civil servants and government ministers (in the Department for Culture, Media and Sport and the former Department for Education and Skills) that PESS can have a prominent role in 'achieving broader educational objectives such as whole school improvement, community development and affecting personal behavioural and attitudinal change among pupils' (Houlihan and Green, 2006: 82) that occupied the ideological high ground at the time. Indeed, even though much of the 'evidence' cited on behalf of PESS was largely impressionistic, anecdotal and underpinned by heavily ideological perceptions of the supposed worth of PESS to young people, it was sufficient to persuade the more sceptical politicians and senior civil servants in other policy areas, especially education, precisely because it was consistent with their prevailing ideological predilections.

By identifying the success which Campbell and others appeared to have in convincing government and civil servants to invest in PESS by generalizing their policy interests to incorporate non-sporting goals, Houlihan and Green's study provided valuable evidence of the continued marginalization of PESS even though there existed an increasingly supportive political context and commitment to the policy sector. Indeed, despite the significant financial and political investments that were made in PESS at the time of Houlihan and Green's research, there was little evidence of a strong political commitment to PESS as a policy priority worthy of investment for its own sake. One of the key insights provided by Houlihan and Green's research, then, is that the political interest in, and salience of, PESS is often stimulated to a large extent by non-sport decisions taken by a coalition of actors in broader, generally more powerful, policy sectors (e.g. education). As is common in other policy sectors, for government ministers and civil servants to be persuaded to make political and financial investments in PESS, the evidence which is presented needs to confirm what they already believe, or will accept, and must be considered within the scope of government and permitted by party ideology.

To facilitate their analysis, Houlihan and Green constructed what was at first sight a particularly useful model of periodization for the purposes of policy analysis in which they identified a watershed in sport policy in the early 1990s, followed by a second in 1997 when the first Labour government for 18 years took office. While a notoriously difficult task, Houlihan and Green's decision to divide long-term, dynamic and complex policy processes into a series of phases was intended to provide readers with a useful heuristic device through which to conceptualize the significant continuities and changes that characterized those processes. As Houlihan himself now admits in this volume, however, with the benefit of hindsight this decision 'could be seen as being, at best, premature and, at worst, erroneous'. It is probable that some readers will have indeed found something with which to disagree having read the original analysis, but as all good scientists endeavour to do, Houlihan has subsequently modified his explanation on the basis of a re-reading of his own data and original explanation in his more recent work with Iain Lindsey (Houlihan and Lindsey, 2012). The modification of one's original ideas for legitimate purposes such as this is a crucial lesson for any researcher – whether a novice undertaking their first project or those engaged in world-leading research – to learn, for this is one means by which science develops. It is also one means by which researchers are able to contribute to the development of a fund of social scientific knowledge that gradually 'becomes *more extensive, more correct, and more adequate*' (Elias, 1978: 53; original emphasis).

Another important lesson to be derived from Houlihan and Green's study is primarily a methodological one, namely, the difficulties researchers frequently encounter when seeking to investigate particularly sensitive matters with participants (such as civil servants) who operate in highly political social contexts (such as major political parties or government departments). First, there is the problem of gaining access to, and consent from, a sample of suitable participants. It is undoubtedly the case that the personal reputation and contacts of the two researchers, particularly Houlihan, helped them to gain access to key stakeholders and secure interviews with civil servants, senior officers of interest groups and professional organizations, and appropriately qualified senior academics. Interestingly, though, Houlihan and Green were unsuccessful in contacting both serving and former ministers of education, which meant they were constrained to study politicians' thoughts and actions by relying on the interpretations other interviewees gave of their involvement in recent policy changes. A central problem of which Houlihan and Green needed to remain mindful was avoiding uncritically accepting the interpretations their interviewees themselves gave for their own and others' thoughts and experiences. Taken on their own, these can often be misleading and even contradictory and may involve, on the part of the participants themselves, different degrees of deliberate falsification or retrospective rationalizations that serve to bolster preferred impressions about their own and others' actions. Consequently, Houlihan and Green sought to triangulate their interview data by comparing the responses given with other publically available sources of information such as government minutes and policy documents.

In the seven-year period since Houlihan and Green's initial attempt to make processes of policy change in PESS more accessible to social scientific examination, their article has rarely been outside the top five 'most read' papers ever published in *Sport, Education and Society*. Their ideas have also come to be widely integrated and studied by researchers across the globe and a search on Google Scholar suggests that their article has been cited around ten times on average in each year since its original publication. That Houlihan and Green should properly be regarded as having made an important and distinctive contribution to our knowledge of sport policy is further indicated by the impact their initial ideas have had on several high-profile discussions of the politics and policy of PESS since Mick Green sadly passed away. For example, when the Conservative-led Coalition government in Britain took the decision, in October 2010, to withdraw funding for the national infrastructure of School Sport Partnerships (SSPs), which had attracted over £2 billion of investment since 2002, research undertaken by Barrie Houlihan was quoted approvingly by the opposition in a House of Commons debate on school sport funding (*Hansard*, 30 November 2010). Such was Houlihan's standing in the field and his commitment to challenging the selective use of evidence by the Coalition government in relation to PESS he was also invited by *The Times* newspaper to contribute an article based on the research he undertook on the efficacy of the SSP programme in bringing about change in young people's participation in PESS (Houlihan, 2010). More recently, Houlihan was again asked by the media – this time, the *Guardian* newspaper (Wintour, 2012) – to comment on many of the unsubstantiated claims made by the British Prime Minister, David Cameron, in relation to the alleged failure of SSPs to promote competitive sport among young people in school-based PE.

Despite Houlihan's evidence to the contrary, it will perhaps come as no surprise that ideology continues to trump evidence, for the Coalition government has continually reasserted the need to promote competitive sport (underpinned by an ideology of competitive individualism) as a key policy objective for PE, whilst marginalizing other policy goals and interests more explicitly associated with the subject. This will sound all too familiar to readers of Houlihan and Green's original article, since it was this observation that helped provide the starting point for their influential analysis.

It has been some seven years since I first read Houlihan and Green's article and as I write this sentence a strange sense of *déjà vu* has returned: I know more now – about myself and my understanding of the study of policy change in PESS – than when I first started thinking about and writing this commentary. While politicians and other interested parties may fail to recognize the potential of social scientific research of the kind undertaken by Houlihan and Green, I am safe in the knowledge that it does have value, it can make people think more critically about themselves and their work, and it most definitely deserves to be included in a volume that includes classic works from some of the most distinguished scholars in the field of sports studies.

REFERENCES

Introduction

Adler, P. (1999) 'The sociologist as celebrity: The role of the media in field research', in A. Bryman and R. Burgess (eds) *Qualitative Research*, vol. IV, London: Sage.

Babbie, E. (2005) *The Basics of Social Research* (3rd edn), Belmont, CA: Thomson Wadsworth.

Brackenridge, C. (1999) 'Managing myself: Investigator survival in sensitive research', *International Review for the Sociology of Sport*, 34: 399–410.

Brackenridge, C. (2007) 'Managing the research project', in C. Brackenridge, A. Pitchford, K. Russell and G. Nutt, *Child Welfare in Football*, London: Routledge.

Bryman, A. (2008) *Social Research Methods* (3rd edn), Oxford: Oxford University Press.

Bryman, A. and Burgess, R. (eds) (1999) *Qualitative Research*, 4 vols, London: Sage.

Denscombe, M. (2010) *The Good Research Guide for Small-Scale Social Research Projects* (4th edn), Maidenhead: Open University Press.

Dunbar, K. and Fugelsang, J. (2005) 'Causal thinking in science: How scientists and students interpret the unexpected', in M. Gorman, R. Tweney, D. Gooding and A. Kincannon (eds) *Scientific and Technical Thinking*, Mahwah, NJ: Lawrence Erlbaum Associates.

Frost, P. and Stablein, R. (eds) (1992) *Doing Exemplary Research*, Newbury Park, CA: Sage.

Gersick, C. (1992) 'Time and transition in my work on teams: Looking back on a new model of group development', in P. Frost and R. Stablein (eds) *Doing Exemplary Research*, Newbury Park, CA: Sage.

Gilbert, N. (2008) *Researching Social Life* (3rd edn), London: Sage.

Merton, R.K. (1957) *Social Theory and Social Structure*, New York: Free Press.

Merton, R.K. (1963) 'Introduction', in M.W. Riley, *Sociological Research I: A Case Approach*, New York: Harcourt, Brace & World.

Merton, R.K. and Barber, E. (2006) *The Travels and Adventures of Serendipity: A Study in Sociological Semantics and the Sociology of Science*, Princeton, NJ: Princeton University Press.

Meyer, G., Barley, S. and Gash, D. (1992) 'Obsession and naïveté in Upstate New York: A tale of research', in P. Frost and R. Stablein (eds) *Doing Exemplary Research*, Newbury Park, CA: Sage.

Morgan, D. (1999) 'The British Association Scandal: The effect of publicity on a sociological investigation', in A. Bryman and R. Burgess (eds) *Qualitative Research*, vol. IV, London: Sage.

Riley, M.W. (1963) *Sociological Research I: A Case Approach*, New York: Harcourt, Brace & World.

Roy, D. (1999) 'The study of southern labor union organizing campaigns', in A. Bryman and R. Burgess (eds) *Qualitative Research*, vol. I, London: Sage.

Sparkes, A. (2002) *Telling Tales in Sport and Physical Activity*, Champaign, IL: Human Kinetics.

Sugden, J. and Tomlinson, A. (1999) 'Digging the dirt and staying clean', *International Review for the Sociology of Sport*, 34: 385–97.

Sutton, R. and Rafaeli, A. (1992) 'How we untangled the relationship between displayed emotion and organizational sales: A tale of bickering and optimism', in P. Frost and R. Stablein (eds) *Doing Exemplary Research*, Newbury Park, CA: Sage.

Townsend, K. and Burgess, J. (eds) (2009) *Method in the Madness: Research Stories You Won't Read in Textbooks*, Witney, Oxford: Chandos Publishing.

Van Maanen, J. (1988) *Tales of the Field*, Chicago, IL: University of Chicago Press.

1 Researching the world of professional football and Commentary

Anderson, L. (2009) 'Writing a new code of ethics for sports physicians: Principles and challenges', *British Journal of Sports Medicine*, 43: 1079–82.

Brackenridge, C., Pitchford, A., Russell, K. and Nutt, G. (2007) *Child Welfare in Football*, London: Routledge.

British Medical Association (2003) *Medical Ethics Today: The BMA's Handbook of Ethics and Law*, London: BMJ Books.

Elias, N. (1987) *Involvement and Detachment*, Oxford: Blackwell.

Football Association (2001) *Guidelines for Medical and Support Staff Involved in Professional Football Relating to Confidentiality of Information Governing Players*, London: The Football Association.

Giulianotti, R. (2004) 'Civilizing games: Norbert Elias and the sociology of sport', in R. Giulianotti (ed.) *Sport and Modern Social Theorists*, Basingstoke: Macmillan.

Hargreaves, J. (1992) 'Sex, gender and the body in sport and leisure: Has there been a civilizing process?', in E. Dunning and C. Rojek (eds) *Sport and Leisure in the Civilizing Process*, Basingstoke: Macmillan.

Malcolm, D. (2011) 'Sports medicine, injured athletes and Norbert Elias's sociology of knowledge', *Sociology of Sport Journal*, 28: 284–302.

Malcolm, D. and Safai, P. (2012) *The Social Organization of Sports Medicine: Critical Socio-Cultural Perspectives*, London: Routledge.

Malcolm, D. and Scott, A. (2011) 'Professional relations in sport healthcare: Workplace responses to organisational change', *Social Science and Medicine*, 72: 513–20.

Malcolm, D. and Sheard, K. (2002) '"Pain in the assets:" The effects of commercialization and professionalization on the management of injury in English rugby union', *Sociology of Sport Journal*, 19: 149–69.

Merton, R.K. (1957) *Social Theory and Social Structure*, New York: Free Press.

Roderick, M. (1998) 'The sociology of risk, pain and injury: A comment on the work of Howard L. Nixon II', *Sociology of Sport Journal*, 15: 64–79.

Roderick, M. (2004) 'English professional soccer players and the uncertainties of injury', in K. Young (ed.) *Sporting Bodies, Damaged Selves: Sociological Studies of Sports Related Injuries*, Oxford: Elsevier.

Roderick, M. (2006a) *The Work of Professional Football: A Labour of Love?*, London: Routledge.

Roderick, M. (2006b) 'A very precarious "profession": Uncertainty in the working lives of professional footballers', *Work, Employment and Society*, 20: 245–65.

Roderick, M. (2006c) 'Adding insult to injury: Workplace injury in English professional football', *Sociology of Health and Illness*, 28: 76–97.

Roderick, M., Waddington, I. and Parker, G. (2000) 'Playing hurt: Managing injuries in English professional football', *International Review for the Sociology of Sport*, 35: 165–80.

Safai, P. (2003) 'Healing the body in the "culture of risk": Examining the negotiation of treatment between sports medicine clinicians and injured athletes in Canadian intercollegiate sport', *Sociology of Sport Journal*, 20: 127–46.

Scott, A. (2012) 'Sport and exercise medicine's professional project: The impact of formal qualifications on the organization of British Olympic medical services', *International Review for the Sociology of Sport*, DOI: 10.1177/1012690212461909.

Theberge, N. (2008) 'The integration of chiropractors into healthcare teams: A case study from sports medicine', *Sociology of Health and Illness*, 30: 19–34.

Theberge, N. (2009) '"We have all the bases covered." Constructions of professional boundaries in sport medicine', *International Review for the Sociology of Sport*, 44: 265–82.

Waddington, I. (1996) 'The development of sports medicine', *Sociology of Sport Journal*, 13: 176–96.

Waddington, I. (2000) *Sport, Health and Drugs: A Critical Sociological Perspective*, London: E. & F.N. Spon.

Waddington, I. (2002) 'Jobs for the boys? A study of the employment of club doctors and physiotherapists in English professional football', *Soccer and Society,* 3: 51–64.

Waddington, I. (2012) 'Sports medicine, client control and the limits of professional autonomy', in D. Malcolm and P. Safai (eds) *The Social Organization of Sports Medicine*, London: Routledge.

Waddington, I. and Roderick, M. (2002) 'The management of medical confidentiality in English professional football clubs: Some ethical issues and problems', *British Journal of Sports Medicine*, 36: 118–23.

Waddington, I., Roderick, M. and Parker, G. (1999) *Managing Injuries in Professional Football: A Study of the Roles of the Club Doctor and Physiotherapist*, Centre for Research into Sport and Society, Leicester: University of Leicester.

Waddington, I., Roderick, M. and Naik, R. (2001) 'Methods of appointment and qualifications of club doctors and physiotherapists in professional football: Some problems and issues', *British Journal of Sports Medicine*, 35: 48–53.

2 *Darwin's Athletes*: A retrospective after 15 years and Commentary

Baldwin, J. [1955] (1983) *Notes of a Native Son*, Boston, MA: Beacon Press.

Baldwin, J. (1961) *Nobody Knows My Name: More Notes of a Native Son*, New York: Dell.

Bass, A. (2002) *Not the Triumph but the Struggle: The 1968 Olympics and the Making of the Black Athlete*, Minneapolis, MN: University of Minnesota Press.

Carrington, B. (2010) *Race, Sport and Politics*, Los Angeles, CA: Sage.

Cashmore, E. (1990) *Making Sense of Sport*, London: Routledge.

Clark, K. (1965) *Dark Ghetto: Dilemmas of Social Power*, New York and Evanston, IL: Harper Torchbooks.

Clarke, J. (ed.) (1968) *William Styron's Nat Turner: Ten Black Writers Respond*, Boston, MA: Beacon Press.

Cohen, P. (2010) 'Culture of poverty makes a comeback', *New York Times*, 17 October.

Cose, E. (1997) 'The house that Jack built', Newsweek. Available online at: www.thedailybeast.com/newsweek/1997/04/13/the-house-that-jack-built.html. Accessed 13 April 1997

Cunliffe, M. (1970) 'Black culture and white America', *Encounter*, 34: 30–1.

Duneier, M. (1992) *Slim's Table: Race, Respectability, and Masculinity*, Chicago, IL and London: The University of Chicago Press.

Early, G. (1998) 'Performance and reality: Race, sports and the modern world', *The Nation*, 10/17 August.

Edwards, H. (1969) *The Revolt of the Black Athlete*, New York: Free Press.

Edwards, H. (1973) 'The black athlete: 20th century gladiators for white America', *Psychology Today*, November 1973.

Edwards, H. (1988) 'The single-minded pursuit of sports fame and fortune is approaching an institutionalized triple tragedy in Black society', *Ebony*, 43: 138–40.

Edwards, H. (1992) 'Are we putting too much emphasis on sports?', *Ebony*, 47: 128–30.

Eitzen, D. (2003) *Fair and Foul: Beyond the Myths and Paradoxes of Sport*, New York: Rowan & Littlefield.

Elkins, S. (1959) *Slavery: A Problem in American Institutional and Intellectual Life*, Chicago, IL: University of Chicago Press.

Elkins, S. (1975) 'The slavery debate', *Commentary*, 60: 40–54.

Fanon, F. [1952] (1967) *Black Skin, White Masks*, New York: Grove Press.

Glazer, N. and Moynihan, D. (1970) *Beyond the Melting Pot: The Negroes, Puerto Ricans, Jews, Italians, and Irish of New York City*, Cambridge, MA: The MIT Press.

Gross, S. and Bender, E. (1971) 'History, politics and literature: The myth of Nat Turner', *American Quarterly*, 23: 487–518.

Guttmann, A. (2003) 'Sport, politics and the engaged historian', *Journal of Contemporary History*, 38: 363–75.

Hain, P. (1971) *Don't Play with Apartheid*, London: George Allen & Unwin.

Hamilton, C. (1968) 'Our Nat Turner and William Styron's creation', in J. Clarke (ed.) *William Styron's Nat Turner: Ten Black Writers Respond*, Boston, MA: Beacon Press.

Hamlin, J. (2001) 'Symposium on race in jazz/writers, musicians to debate relevance', *San Francisco Chronicle*, 29 March.

Hannerz, U. (1972) *Black Psyche: The Modal Personality Patterns of Black Americans*, Berkeley, CA: The Glendessary Press, Inc.

Harris, R. (1982) 'Segregation and scholarship: The American Council of Learned Societies' Committee on Negro Studies, 1941–1950', *Journal of Black Studies*, 12: 315–31.

Hoberman, J. (1992) *Mortal Engines: The Science of Performance and the Dehamanization of Sport*, New York: Free Press.

Hoberman, J. (1997) *Darwin's Athletes: How Sport has Damaged Black America and Preserved the Myth of Race*, Boston, MA: Houghton Mifflin Company.

Howe, I. (1968) 'Why should Negroes be above criticism?', *Saturday Evening Post*, 241: 10.

James, C.L.R. (1963) *Beyond a Boundary*, London: Stanley Paul.

Jarvie, G. (2000) 'Sport, racism and ethnicity', in J. Coakley and E. Dunning (eds) *Handbook of Sports Studies*, London: Sage.

Jarvie, G. and Thornton, J. (2012) *Sport, Culture and Society*, London: Routledge.

Jones, L. (1963) *Blues People: Negro Music in White America*, New York: William Morrow & Company.

Kardiner, A. and Ovesey, L. [1951] (1962) *The Mark of Oppression: Explorations in the Personality of the American Negro*, New York: Meridian Books.

Kelley, R. (1999) 'Judging by color?', *New York Times*, 19 September.

Kjaerum, M. (2012) 'Sport and discrimination in Europe', *Sport and Discriminations in Europe*, Paris: Sport and Citizenship.

Lapchick, R. (1975) *The Politics of Race and International Sport: The Case of South Africa*, Westport, CT: Greenwood Press.

Leonard, D. (2000) *The Decline of the Black Athlete: An Online Exclusive: Extended Interview with Harry Edwards*. Available online at: colorlines.com/archives/2000/04/the_decline_of_the_black_athletean_online_exclusive_extended_interview_with_harry_edwards.html. Accessed 20 April 2000

Markovits, B. (2003) 'The colors of sport', *New Left Review*, 22:151–60.

Martin, R. (1940) 'A doctor's dream in Harlem', *The New Republic*, 3 June, 798–800.

Massey, D. and Sampson, R. (2009) 'Moynihan redux: Legacies and lessons', *The Annals of the American Academy of Political and Social Science*, 621: 6–27.

Moynihan, D. (1965) *The Negro Family: The Case for National Action*, Office of Planning and Research: US Department of Labor.

Moynihan, D. (1968) 'The new racialism', *Atlantic*, 222: 35–40.

Myers, S. (1998) 'Hoberman's fantasy: How neoconservative writing on sport reinforces perceptions of black inferiority and preserves the myth of race', *Social Science Quarterly*, 79: 879–84.

Nelson, J. (2004) *Lost Chords: White Musicians and Their Contribution to Jazz, 1915–1945*. Available online at: www.allaboutjazz.com.

Newsweek 66 (1965) 'The Negro family: Visceral reaction', 6 December.

Patterson, J. (2010) *Freedom is Not Enough: The Moynihan Report and America's Struggle over Black Family Life*, New York: Basic Books.

Patterson, O. (1998) *Rituals of Blood: Consequences of Slavery in Two American Centuries*, New York: Basic Books.

Prudhomme, C. (1938) 'The problem of suicide in the American Negro', *Psychoanalytic Review*, 25: 187–204, 373–91.

Rainwater, L. and Yancey, W. (1967) *The Moynihan Report and the Politics of Controversy*, Cambridge, MA and London: The MIT Press.

Row, J. (2008) 'Styron's choice', *New York Times*, 7 September.

Russell, K., Wilson, M. and Hall, R. (1993) *The Color Complex: The Politics of Skin Color Among African Americans*, New York: Anchor Books.

Ryan, J. (1998) *Black and Sports – Lifeline or Noose?*. Available online at: www.SFGate.com. Accessed 20 September 1998.

Schudel, M. (2008) 'Musician Richard Sudhalter: Jazz history left bitter note', *Washington Post*, 20 September.

Scott, D. (1997) *Contempt and Pity: Social Policy and the Image of the Damaged Black Psyche 1880–1996*, Chapel Hill and London: The University of North Carolina Press.

Shropshire, K. and Smith, E. (1998) 'The Tarzan syndrome: John Hoberman and his quarrels with African American athletes and intellectuals', *Journal of Sport & Social Issues*, 22: 103–12.

Sitkoff, H. and Wreszin, M. (1968) 'Whose Nat Turner? William Styron vs the black intellectuals', *Midstream*, 11.

Small, M., Harding, D. and Lamont, M. (2010) 'Reconsidering culture and poverty', *The Annals of the American Academy of Political and Social Science*, 629, 6–27.

Spaaij, R. (2011) *Sport and Social Mobility: Crossing Boundaries,* London: Routledge.

Styron, W. (1967) *The Confessions of Nat Turner*, New York: Random House.

Styron, W. (1992) *This Quiet Dust*, London: Vintage.

Sudhalter, R. (1999) *Lost Chords: White Musicians and Their Contribution to Jazz, 1915–1945*, New York: Oxford University Press.

Time (1970) 'Moynihan's memo fever', 95, 23 March.

US News & World Report (1964) 'A liberal's advice to northern Negroes', 20 January.

US News & World Report (1970) 'Moynihan memo: Negroes are making great progress, but –', 16 March.

Valentine, C. (1968) *Culture and Poverty: Critique and Counter-Proposals*, Chicago, IL: and London: University of Chicago Press.

Vertinsky, P. (1998) 'More myth than history: American culture and representations of the black female's athletic ability', *Journal of Sport History*, 25: 532–61.

White, T. (1965) *The Making of the President 1964*, New York: Atheneum Publishers.

Wigginton, R. (2006) *The Strange Career of the Black Athlete*, Westport, CT: Praeger.

Wilkens, J. (1997) 'Shackles of sports', *The San Diego Union-Tribune*, 2 March.

Wilson, W. (2009) *More Than Just Race: Being Black and Poor in the Inner City*, New York and London: W.W. Norton & Company.

3 Habitus as topic and tool: Reflections on becoming a prizefighter and Commentary

Anderson, N. [1923] (1961) *The Hobo: The Sociology of the Homeless Man*, Chicago, IL: University of Chicago Press.

Bachelard, G. (1971) *Epistémologie*, Paris: Presses Universitaires de France.

Bensa, A. (1995) *Chroniques Kanak. L'ethnologie en marche*, Paris: Ethnies.

Blumer, H. (1966) *Symbolic Interaction*, Englewood Cliffs, NJ: Prentice-Hall.

Bourdieu, P. [1980] (1990) *The Logic of Practice*, Cambridge: Polity Press.

Bourdieu, P. (2002) 'Participant objectivation: The Huxley Medal lecture', *Journal of the Royal Anthropological Institute*, 9: 281–94.

Bourdieu, P. and Bensa, A. (1985) 'Quand les Canaques prennent la parole', *Actes de la recherche en sciences sociales*, 56: 69–85.

Bourdieu, P., Darbel, A., Rivet, J-P. and Seibel, C. (1963) *Travail et travailleurs en Algérie*, Paris and The Hague: Mouton.

Bourdieu, P. and Wacquant, L. (1992) *An Invitation to Reflexive Sociology*, Chicago, IL: University of Chicago Press and Cambridge: Polity Press.

Crossley, N. (1995) 'Merleau-Ponty, the elusive body and carnal sociology', *Body & Society*, 1: 43–63.

Damasio, A. (2010) *Self Comes to Mind: Constructing the Conscious Brain*, London: William Heinmann.

Dunning, E. (1999) *Sport Matters*, London: Routledge.

Elias, N. and Dunning, E. (1986) *Quest for Excitement*, Oxford: Blackwell.

Favret-Saada, J. [1978] (1980) *Deadly Words: Witchcraft in the Bocage*, Cambridge: Cambridge University Press.

Foucault, M. (1990) *The Care of the Self: The History of Sexuality, vol. 3*, London: Penguin.

Gans, H. (1995) *The War Against the Poor*, New York: Pantheon.

Geertz, C. (1974) *The Interpretation of Cultures*, New York: Basic Books.

Goffman, E. (1989) 'On fieldwork', *Journal of Contemporary Ethnography*, 18: 123–32.

Hastrup, K. (1995) *A Passage to Anthropology: Between Experience and Theory*, London: Routledge.

Hughes, E. (1994) *On Work, Race, and the Sociological Imagination*, Chicago, IL: University of Chicago Press.

Jenkins, R. (1991) *Pierre Bourdieu*, London: Routledge.

Johnson, M. (1987) *The Body in the Mind*: Chicago, IL: University of Chicago Press.

Katz, M. (ed.) (1993) *The 'Underclass' Debate: Views from History*, Princeton, NJ: Princeton University Press.

Manning, P. (2005) *Freud and American Sociology*, Cambridge: Polity Press.

Manning, P. (2009) 'Three models of ethnographic research: Wacquant as risk-taker', *Theory & Society*, 19: 756–77.

Marcus, G. (1998) *Ethnography through Thick and Thin*, Princeton, NJ: Princeton University Press.

Mellor, P.A. and Shilling, C. (1997) *Reforming the Body, Religion, Community and Modernity*, London: Sage/Theory, Culture & Society.

Reed-Danahay, D. (ed.) (1997) *Auto/Ethnography: Rewriting the Self and the Social*, New York: Berg.

Shilling, C. [1993] (2012) *The Body and Social Theory* (3rd edn), London: Sage/Theory, Culture & Society.

Shilling, C. and Mellor, P.A. (1996) 'Embodiment, structuration theory and modernity: Mind/body dualism and the repression of sensuality', *Body & Society*, 2: 1–15.

Shilling, C. and Mellor, P.A. (2011) 'Retheorising Emile Durkheim on society and religion: Embodiment, intoxication and collective life', *The Sociological Review*, 59: 17–42.

Wacquant, L. (1985) *L'École inégale. Éléments de sociologie de l'enseignement en Nouvelle-Calédonie*, Paris and Nouméa: Editions de l'ORSTOM with the Institut Culturel Mélanésien.

Wacquant, L. (1989) 'Corps et âme: notes ethnographiques d'un apprenti-boxeur', *Actes de la recherche en sciences sociales*, 80: 33–67.

Wacquant, L. (1995a) 'The pugilistic point of view: How boxers think and feel about their trade', *Theory & Society*, 24: 489–535.

Wacquant, L. (1995b) 'Pugs at work: Bodily capital and bodily labor among professional boxers', *Body & Society*, 1: 65–94.

Wacquant, L. (1995c) 'Protection, discipline et honneur: une salle de boxe dans le ghetto américain', *Sociologie et sociétés*, 27: 75–89.

Wacquant, L. (1996) 'L "underclass" urbaine dans l'imaginaire social et scientifique américain', in S. Paugam (ed.) *L'Exclusion: L'état des Savoirs*, Paris: Éditions La Découverte.

Wacquant, L. (1997) 'Three pernicious premises in the study of the American ghetto', *International Journal of Urban and Regional Research*, 21: 341–53.

Wacquant, L. [1992] (1998a) 'Inside the zone: The social art of the hustler in the black American ghetto', *Theory, Culture & Society*, 15: 1–36.

Wacquant, L. (1998b) 'The prizefighter's three bodies', *Ethnos: Journal of Anthropology*, 63: 325–52.

Wacquant, L. (1998c) 'A fleshpeddler at work: Power, pain, and profit in the prizefighting economy', *Theory, Culture & Society*, 27: 1–42.

Wacquant, L. (2001) 'Whores, slaves, and stallions: Languages of exploitation and accommodation among professional fighters', *Body & Society*, 7: 181–94.

Wacquant, L. (2002a) 'Taking Bourdieu into the field', *Berkeley Journal of Sociology*, 46: 180–86.

Wacquant, L. (2002b) 'Scrutinizing the street: Poverty, morality, and the pitfalls of urban ethnography', *American Journal of Sociology*, 107: 1468–532.

Wacquant, L. [2000] (2004a) *Body & Soul: Notebooks of an Apprentice Boxer*, New York and Oxford: Oxford University Press.

Wacquant, L. (2004b) 'Habitus', in J. Beckert and M. Zafirovski (eds) *International Encyclopedia of Economic Sociology*, London: Routledge.

Wacquant, L. (2005a) 'Carnal connections: On embodiment, membership and apprenticeship', *Qualitative Sociology*, 28: 445–71.

Wacquant, L. (2005b) 'Shadowboxing with ethnographic ghosts: A rejoinder', *Symbolic Interaction*, 28: 441–47.

Wacquant, L. (2008) *Urban Outcasts: A Comparative Sociology of Advanced Marginality*, Cambridge: Polity Press.

Wilson, W. (1978) *The Declining Significance of Race: Blacks and Changing American Institutions*, Chicago, IL: University of Chicago Press.

Wilson, W. (1987) *The Truly Disadvantaged: The Inner City, the Underclass, and Public Policy*, Chicago, IL: University of Chicago Press.

4 Mischief managed: Ticket scalping, research ethics and involved detachment and Commentary

Atkinson, M. (2000) 'Brother, can you spare a seat: Developing recipes of knowledge in the ticket scalping subculture', *Sociology of Sport Journal*, 17: 151–70.

Atkinson, M. (2003) *Tattooed: The Sociogenesis of a Body Art*, Toronto: University of Toronto Press.

Atkinson, M. and Young, K. (2008) *Deviance and Social Control in Sport*, Champaign, IL: Human Kinetics.

Elias, N. (1956) 'Problems of involvement and detachment', *British Journal of Sociology*, 7: 226–52.

Elias, N. (1987) *Involvement and Detachment,* Oxford: Basil Blackwell.

Gold, R. (1958) 'Roles in sociological field observation', *Social Forces*, 36: 217–223.

Hathaway, A. and Atkinson, M. (2003) 'Active interview tactics in research on public deviance: Exploring the two cop personas', *Field Methods*, 15: 161–85.

Hollander, P. (1999) 'Saving sociology?', *Sociological Inquiry*, 69: 130–47.

Humphreys, L. (1970) *Tearoom Trade: Impersonal Sex in Public Places*, Piscataway, NJ: Transaction Publishers.

Stebbins, R. (1996) *Tolerable Difference: Living with Deviance*, New York: McGraw-Hill.

Sugden, J. (2012) 'Truth or dare: Examining the perils, pains, and pitfalls of investigative methodologies in the sociology of sport', in K. Young and M. Atkinson (eds) *Qualitative Methods on Sport and Physical Culture*, London: Elsevier.

van den Hoonaard, W. (2001) 'Is research-ethics review a moral panic?', *Canadian Review of Sociology and Anthropology*, 38: 19–36.

van den Hoonaard, W. (2002) *Walking the Tightrope: Ethical Issues for Qualitative Researchers*, Toronto: University of Toronto Press.

Wacquant, L (2004) *Body & Soul: Notes of an Apprentice Boxer*, Oxford: Oxford University Press.

Woodward, K. (2006) *Boxing, Masculinity and Identity: The 'I' of the Tiger*, London: Routledge.

Woodward, K. (2008) 'Hanging out and hanging about: Insider/outsider research in the sport of boxing', *Ethnography*, 9: 536–60.

Woodward, K. (2012) *Sex Gender and the Games,* Basingstoke: Palgrave.

Woodward, K. and Woodward, S. (2009) *Why Feminism Matters: Lost and Found*, Basingstoke: Palgrave MacMillan.

Woodward, K. and Woodward, S. (2012) 'Being in the academy: A cross generational conversation', *Equality, Diversity and Inclusion: An International Journal*, 31: 435–51.

5 *Bodybuilding, Drugs and Risk*: Reflections on an ethnographic study and Commentary

Adler, P. and Adler, P. (1987) *Membership Roles in Field Research*, London: Sage.

Becker, H. (1963) *Outsiders: Studies in the Sociology of Deviance,* New York: Free Press.

Bloor, M. (1978) 'On the analysis of observational data: A discussion of the worth and uses of inductive techniques and respondent validation', *Sociology*, 12: 545–52.

Bloor, M. (1997) 'Addressing social problems through qualitative research', in D. Silverman (ed.) *Qualitative Research: Theory, Method and Practice*, London: Sage.

Bloor, M. and Wood, F. (2006) *Keywords in Qualitative Methods: A Vocabulary of Research Concepts*, London: Sage.

Bloor, M., Monaghan, L., Dobash, R. and Dobash, R. (1998) 'The body as a chemistry experiment: Steroid use among South Wales bodybuilders', in S. Nettleton and J. Watson (eds) *The Body in Everyday Life*, London: Routledge.

Bourdieu, P. (1977) *Outline of a Theory of Practice*, Cambridge: Cambridge University Press.

Dobash, R., Monaghan, L., Dobash, R. and Bloor, M. (1999) 'Bodybuilding, steroids and violence: Is there a connection?', in P. Carlen and R. Morgan (eds) *Crime Unlimited: Questions for the 21st Century*, London: Macmillan.

Glaser, B. and Strauss, A. (1967) *The Discovery of Grounded Theory*. Chicago, IL: Aldine.

Goffman, E. (1959) *The Presentation of Self in Everyday Life*, Middlesex: Penguin Books.

Goffman, E. (1989) 'On Fieldwork', *Journal of Contemporary Ethnography*, 18: 123–32.

Hammersley, M. and Atkinson, P. (1995) *Ethnography: Principles in Practice* (2nd edn), London: Routledge.

Hastrup, K. and Elsass, P. (1990) 'Anthropological advocacy: A contradiction in terms?', *Current Anthropology*, 31: 301–11.

Kellett, P. (2009) 'Advocacy in anthropology: Active engagement or passive scholarship?', *Durham Anthropology Journal*, 16: 22–31.

Kim, Y. (2012) 'Ethnographer location and the politics of translation: Researching one's own group in a host country', *Qualitative Research*, 12: 131–46.

Klein, A. (1993) *Little Big Men: Bodybuilding Subculture and Gender Construction*, Albany, NY: State University of New York Press.

Korkia, P. and Stimson, G. (1993) *Anabolic Steroid Use in Great Britain: An Exploratory Investigation*, London: The Centre for Research on Drugs and Health Behaviour.

Lenehan, P. (1994) Editorial, *International Journal of Drug Policy*, 5: 2.

McKeganey, N. and Bloor, M. (1991) 'Spotting the invisible man: The influence of male gender on fieldwork relations', *British Journal of Sociology*, 42: 195–210.

Merton, R. (1972) 'Insiders and outsiders: A chapter in the sociology of knowledge', *American Journal of Sociology*, 78: 9–47.

Monaghan, L.F. (1999a) 'Challenging medicine? Bodybuilding, drugs and risk', *Sociology of Health and Illness*, 21: 707–34.

Monaghan, L.F. (1999b) 'Accessing a demonised subculture: Studying drug use and violence among bodybuilders', in L. Noakes, E. Wincup and F. Brookman (eds) *Qualitative Research in Criminology*, Aldershot: Ashgate.

Monaghan, L.F. (2001a) *Bodybuilding, Drugs and Risk*, London: Routledge.

Monaghan, L.F. (2001b) 'Looking good, feeling good: The embodied pleasures of vibrant physicality', *Sociology of Health and Illness*, 23: 330–56.

Monaghan, L.F. (2001c) 'The bodybuilding ethnophysiology thesis', in N. Watson and S. Cunningham-Burley (eds) *Reframing the Body*, Basingstoke: Palgrave.

Monaghan, L.F. (2002) 'Vocabularies of motive for illicit steroid use among bodybuilders', *Social Science and Medicine*, 55: 695–708.

Monaghan, L.F. (2006) 'Fieldwork and the body: reflections on an embodied ethnography', in D. Hobbs and R. Wright (eds) *The Sage Handbook of Fieldwork*, London: Sage.

Monaghan, L.F. (2013) 'Extending the obesity debate, repudiating misrecognition: Politicising fatness and health (practice)', *Social Theory and Health*, 11: 81–105.

Monaghan, L.F., Bloor, M., Dobash, R. and Dobash, R. (2000) 'Drug-taking, "risk boundaries" and social identity: Bodybuilders' talk about ephedrine and nubain', *Sociological Research Online* 5 (2). Available online at: www.socresonline.org.uk/5/2/monaghan.html

Pates, R. and Barry, C. (1996) 'Steroid use in Cardiff: A problem for whom?', *The Seventh International Conference on the Reduction of Drug Related Harm*, Hobart, Tasmania.

Roderick, M. (2003) *Work, Self and the Transformation of Identity: A Sociological Study of the Careers of Professional Footballers*, Unpublished doctoral thesis, Leicester: University of Leicester.

Roderick, M. (2006) *The Work of Professional Football: A Labour of Love?*, London: Routledge.

Scheper-Hughes, N. (1995) 'The primacy of the ethical: Propositions for a militant anthropology', *Current Anthropologist*, 36: 409–40.

Shilling, C. (2003) *The Body and Social Theory* (2nd edn), London: Sage.

Silverman, D. (1993) *Interpreting Qualitative Data: Methods for Analysing Talk, Text and Interaction*, London: Sage.

Stewart-Clevidence, B. and Goldstein, P. (1996) 'A female ethnographer in a macho milieu: Doing research on anabolic androgenic steroids', *The Journal of Performance Enhancing Drugs*, 1: 33–40.

Weber, M. (1949) *The Methodology of the Social Sciences*, Glencoe, IL: Free Press.

Williamson, K., Davies, M. and McBride, A. (1993) 'A well steroid user clinic', in H. Shapiro (ed.) *The Steroid Papers*, London: Institute for the Study of Drug Dependence.

6 *Home and Away revisited* – warts and all and Commentary

Ball, S. (1981) *Beachside Comprehensive*, Cambridge: Cambridge University Press.

Berger, P. (1963) *Invitation to Sociology*, New York: Anchor Books.

Brewer, J. (2005) 'The public and the private in C. Wright Mills' life and work', *Sociology*, 39: 661–77.

Carrington, B. and McDonald, I. (2001) (eds) *'Race', Sport and British Society*, London: Routledge.

Cole, M. (1986a) 'Teaching and learning about racism: A critique of multicultural education in Britain', in S. Modgil, G. Verma, K. Mallick, and C. Modgil (eds) *Multicultural Education – The Interminable Debate*, London: Falmer Press.

Cole, M. (1986b) 'Multicultural education and the politics of racism in Britain', *Multicultural Teaching*, 5: 20–4.

Corrigan, P. (1979) *Schooling the Smash Street Kids*, London: Macmillan Education.

Faulkner, G. (1996) 'Book review – "Sport, racism and ethnicity" (ed. G Jarvie)', *Sport, Education and Society*, 1: 123–5.

Finch, J. (1986) *Research and Policy: The Uses of Qualitative Research in Social and Educational Research*, Lewes: Falmer Press.

Fleming, S. (1991) 'Sport, solidarity and Asian male youth culture', in G. Jarvie (ed.) *Sport, Racism and Ethnicity*, London: Falmer Press.

Fleming, S. (1992a) *Sport and South Asian Male Youth*, Unpublished Ph.D. thesis, Council for National Academic Awards/Brighton Polytechnic.

Fleming, S. (1992b) 'Multiculturalism in the physical education curriculum: The case of South Asian male youth, dance and South Asian dance', *Multicultural Teaching*, 11: 35–8.

Fleming, S. (1994) 'Sport and south Asian youth: The perils of "false universalism" and stereotyping', *Leisure Studies*, 13: 159–77.

Fleming, S. (1995) *'Home and Away': Sport and South Asian Male Youth*, Aldershot: Avebury.

Fleming, S. (1997) 'Qualitative research of young people and sport: The ethics of role-conflict', in A. Tomlinson and S. Fleming (eds) *Ethics, Sport and Leisure: Crises and Critiques*, Aachen: Meyer and Meyer.

Fleming, S. (2001) 'Racial science and south Asian and black physicality', in B. Carrington and I. McDonald (eds) *'Race', Sport and British Society*, London: Routledge.

Fleming, S. (2011) 'Revisiting, deconstructing (and perhaps re-inventing) links between methods and ethics in (some) leisure research'. Keynote paper delivered to the *Leisure Studies Association Conference*, Southampton Solent University, 5–7 July 2011.

Geertz, C. (1975) *The Interpretation of Cultures*, London: Hutchinson.

Gilroy, P. (1987) *There Ain't No Black in the Union Jack: The Cultural Politics of Race and Nation*, London: Hutchinson.

Gorn, E. (1986) *The Manly Art – Bare-Knuckle Prize Fighting in America*, Ithaca, NY: Cornell University Press.

Hammersley, M. and Atkinson, P. (1983) *Ethnography Principles in Practice*, London: Tavistock.

Hargreaves, J. (1986) *Sport, Power and Culture*, London: Polity Press.

Heffer, S. (1988) *Like the Roman: The Life of Enoch Powell*, London: Weidenfield & Nicolson.

Horne, J. (2007) 'The four "knowns" of sports mega events', *Leisure Studies*, 26: 81–96.

Jarvie, G. (ed.) (1991) *Sport, Racism and Ethnicity*, London: Falmer Press.

Lacey, C. (1970) *Hightown Grammar*, Manchester: Manchester University Press.

Long, J., Carrington, B. and Spracklen, K. (1997) '"Asians cannot wear turbans in the scrum": Explorations of racist discourse within professional rugby league', *Leisure Studies*, 16: 249–60.

Magdalinski, T. (1997) 'Review article – International perspectives on race, ethnicity, identity and sport', *International Review for the Sociology of Sport*, 32: 311–14.

Miles, R. (1982) *Racism and Migrant Labour*, London: Routledge & Kegan Paul.

Mills, C.W. (1959) *The Sociological Imagination*, Harmondsworth, Middlesex: Pelican.

Mullin, C. (1990) *Error of Judgement: The Truth about the Birmingham Bombings*, London: Chatto & Windus.

Roberts, K. (1983) *Youth and Leisure*, London: George Allen & Unwin.

Scraton, S. (1987) '"Boys muscle in where angels fear to tread" – Girls' sub-cultures and physical activities', in J. Horne, D. Jary and A. Tomlinson (eds) *Sport, Leisure and Social Relations*, London: Routledge & Kegan Paul.

Sivanandan, A. (1976) *Race, Class and the State*, London: Institute of Race Relations.

Sivanandan, A. (1982) *A Different Hunger*, London: Pluto Press.

Sonstroem, R. (1978) 'Physical estimation and attraction scales: Rationale and research', *Medicine and Science in Sports*, 10: 97–102.

Sports Council (1979) *People in Sport*, London: The Sports Council.

Sports Council (1982) *Sport in the Community . . . The Next Ten Years*, London: The Sports Council.

Spracklen, K. (2008) 'The holy blood and the holy grail: Myths of scientific racism and the pursuit of excellence in sport', *Leisure Studies*, 27: 221–7.

Sugden, J. (1987) 'The exploitation of disadvantage: The occupational sub-culture of the boxer', in J. Horne, D. Jary and A. Tomlinson (eds) *Sport, Leisure and Social Relations*, London: Routlege & Kegan Paul.

Sugden, J. (1997) 'Field workers rush in (where theorists fear to tread): The perils of ethnography', in A. Tomlinson and S. Fleming (eds) *Ethics, Sport and Leisure: Crises and Critiques*, Aachen: Meyer and Meyer.

Sugden, J. (2005) 'Is investigative sociology just investigative journalism?', in M. McNamee (ed.) *Philosophy and the Sciences of Exercise, Health and Sport*, London: Routledge.

Tomlinson, A. (1986) 'Playing away from home: Leisure, disadvantage and issues of income and access', in P. Golding (ed.) *Excluding the Poor*, London: Child Poverty Action Group.

Tomlinson, A. (1997) 'Flattery and betrayal: Observations on oral and qualitative accounts', in A. Tomlinson and S. Fleming (eds) *Ethics, Sport and Leisure: Crises and Critiques*, Aachen: Meyer and Meyer.

Tomlinson, A. and Fleming, S. (eds) (1997) *Ethics, Sport and Leisure: Crises and Critiques*, Aachen: Meyer and Meyer.

Watson, B. and Scraton, S. (2013) 'Leisure studies and intersectionality', *Leisure Studies*, 32: 35–47.

Whannel, G. (1983) *Blowing the Whistle*, London: Pluto.

Whyte, W.F. (1993) *Street Corner Society* (4th edn), London: University of Chicago Press.

Willis, P. (1977) *Learning to Labour*, Aldershot: Gower.

Willis, P. (1978) *Profane Culture*, London: Routledge & Kegan Paul.

7 Methodological issues in researching physical activity in later life and Commentary

Amis, J. (2006) 'Interviewing for case study research', in D. Andrews, D. Mason and M. Silk (eds) *Qualitative Methods in Sport Studies*, Oxford: Berg.

Andrews, M. (1999) 'The seductiveness of agelessness', *Ageing and Society*, 19: 301–18.

Back, L. (2007) *The Art of Listening*, Oxford: Berg.

Barthes, R. (1967) *Elements of Semiology*, London: Jonathan Cape.

Bartholomew, M. (2012) *Health Experiences of Older African Caribbean Women Living in the UK*, Unpublished doctoral thesis, Huddersfield: University of Huddersfield.

Beames, S. and Pike, E. (2008) 'Goffman goes rock-climbing: Using creative fiction to explore the presentation of self in outdoor education', *Australian Journal of Outdoor Education*, 12: 3–11.

Bhopal, K. (2001) 'Researching South Asian women: Issues of sameness and difference in the research process', *Journal of Gender Studies*, 10: 279–86.

Birrell, S. and Donnelly, P. (2004) 'Reclaiming Goffman: Erving Goffman's influence on the sociology of sport', in R. Guilianotti (ed.) *Sport and Modern Social Theorists*, Basingstoke: Palgrave MacMillan.

Blaikie, A. (1999) *Ageing and Popular Culture*, Cambridge: Cambridge University Press.

Bytheway, B. (1995) *Ageism*, Buckingham: McGraw-Hill/Open University Press.

Chandler, D. (2007) *Semiotics: The Basics*, London: Routledge.

Coakley, J. and Pike, E. (2009) *Sports in Society: Issues and Controversies*, London: McGraw Hill.

Coffey, A. (1999) *The Ethnographic Self: Fieldwork and the Representation of Identity*, London: Sage.

Coffey, A. (2003) 'Ethnography and self: Reflections and representations', in T. May (ed.) *Qualitative Research in Action*, London: Sage.

Cohen, S. (1972) *Folk Devils and Moral Panics*, London: MacGibbon & Kee.

Denzin, N. (1989) *Interpretive Interactionism*, London: Sage.

Dionigi, R. (2006) 'Competitive sport and aging: The need for qualitative sociological research', *Journal of Aging and Physical Activity*, 14: 365–79.

Dionigi, R. (2010) 'Masters sport as a strategy for managing the ageing process', in J. Baker, S. Horton and P. Weir (eds) *The Masters Athlete: Understanding the Role of Sport and Exercise in Optimizing Aging*, London: Routledge.

Dionigi, R. and O'Flynn, G. (2007) 'Performance discourses and old age: What does it mean to be an older athlete?', *Sociology of Sport Journal*, 24: 359–77.

Dunning, E. and Waddington, I. (2003) 'Sport as a drug and drugs in sport: Some exploratory comments', *International Review for the Sociology of Sport*, 38: 351–68.

Elbaz, F. (1990) 'Knowledge and discourse: The evolution of research on teacher thinking', in C. Day, M. Pope and P. Denicolo (eds) *Insights into Teachers' Thinking and Practice*, London: Falmer Press.

Ferguson, A. and Thomas-MacLean, R. (2009) 'Messy methodological musings: Engaging in "successful" qualitative health research', *Aporia*, 1: 7–15.

Gilleard, C. and Higgs, P. (2000) *Cultures of Ageing: Self, Citizen and the Body*, Harlow: Pearson.

Gilleard, C. and Higgs, P. (2002) 'The third age: class, cohort or generation?', *Ageing and Society*, 22: 369–82.

Gitlin, A. (1990) 'Educative research, voice, and school change', *Harvard Educational Review*, 60: 443–6

Goffman, E. (1959) *The Presentation of Self in Everyday Life*, New York: Anchor Books.

Goffman, E. (1961) *Behavior in Public Places: Notes on the Social Organization of Gatherings*, New York: Free Press.

Goffman, E. (1967) *Interaction Ritual: Essays in Face-to-Face Behavior*, New York: Anchor Books.

Grant, B. and Kluge, M. (2007) 'Exploring "other body(s)" of knowledge: Getting to the heart of the story about aging and physical activity', *Quest*, 59: 398–414.

Grant, B. and O'Brien Cousins, S. (2001) 'Aging and physical activity: The promise of qualitative research', *Journal of Aging and Physical Activity*, 9: 237–44.

Griffin, R. (1998) *Sports in the Lives of Children and Adolescents: Success on the Field and in Life*, Westport, CT: Praeger Publishers.

Gunaratnam, Y. (2003) *Researching 'Race' and Ethnicity: Methods, Knowledge and Power*, London: Sage.

Hepworth, M. (2000) *Stories of Ageing*, Buckingham: Open University Press.

Hill Collins, P. (1990) *Black Feminist Thought: Knowledge, Consciousness, and the Politics of Empowerment*, Boston, MA: Unwin Hyman.

Kennedy, E. (2001) 'She wants to be a sledgehammer? Tennis femininities on British television', *Journal of Sport and Social Issues*, 25: 56–72.

Langley, D. and Knight, S. (1999) 'Continuity in sport participation as an adaptive strategy in the ageing process: A lifespan narrative', *Journal of Aging and Physical Activity*, 7: 32–54.

Laslett, P. (1989) *A Fresh Map of Life: The Emergence of the Third Age*, London: Weidenfeld & Nicolson.

Markula, P., Grant, B. and Denison, J. (2001) 'Qualitative research and aging and physical activity: Multiple ways of knowing', *Journal of Aging and Physical Activity*, 9: 245–64.

Maynard, M., Afshar, H., Franks, M. and Wray, S. (2008) *Women in Later Life Exploring Race and Ethnicity*, Maidenhead: Open University Press.

Merriam, S. (1988) *Case Study Research in Education: A Qualitative Approach*, San Francisco, CA: Jossey-Bass.

Nichols, G. (2007) *Sport and Crime Reduction: The Role of Sports in Tackling Youth Crime*, London: Routledge.

Nilsson, M., Sarvimaki, A. and Ekman, S-L. (2000) 'Feeling old: Being in a phrase of transition in later life', *Nursing Inquiry*, 7: 41–9.

Nimrod, G. (2007) 'Retirees' leisure: Activities, benefits, and their contribution to life satisfaction', *Leisure Studies*, 26: 65–80.

Phoenix, C. and Grant, B. (2009) 'Expanding the agenda for research on the physically active ageing body', *Journal of Aging and Physical Activity*, 17: 362–79.

Pike, E. (2000) *Illness, Injury and Sporting Identity*, Unpublished doctoral thesis, Loughborough: Loughborough University.

Pike, E. (2010) 'Growing old (dis)gracefully?: The gender/ageing/exercise nexus', in E. Kennedy and P. Markula (eds) *Women and Exercise: The Body, Health and Consumerism*, London: Routledge.

Pike, E. (2011a) 'The *Active Ageing* agenda, old folk devils and a new moral panic', *Sociology of Sport Journal,* 28: 209–25.

Pike, E. (2011b) 'Growing old (dis)gracefully?: The gender/ageing/exercise nexus', in E. Kennedy and P. Markula (eds) *Women and Exercise: The Body, Health and Consumerism,* London: Routledge.

Pike, E. (2012) 'Aquatic antiques: Swimming off this mortal coil?', *International Review for the Sociology of Sport,* 47: 492–510.

Pike, E. (2013) 'The role of fiction in (mis)representing later life leisure activities', *Leisure Studies,* 32: 69–87.

Plummer, K. (1983) *Documents of Life: An Introduction to the Problems and Literature of a Humanistic Method,* London: George Allen & Unwin Ltd.

Ramella, M. (2004) *Positive Futures Impact Report: Engaging With Young People,* London: Home Office.

Roper, E., Molnar, D. and Wrisberg, C. (2003) 'No "old fool": 88 years old and still running', *Journal of Aging and Physical Activity,* 11: 370–87.

Saussure, F. (1983) *Courses in General Linguistics,* London: Duckworth.

Scraton, S., Cauldwell, J. and Holland, S. (2005) 'Bend it like Patel: Centring "race", ethnicity and gender in feminist analysis of women's football in England', *International Review for the Sociology of Sport,* 40: 71–88.

Simmonds, B. (2011) *Experiences of Physical Activity in Later Life: Making Sense of Embodiment, Negotiating Practicalities, and the Construction of Identities in Rural Spaces,* Unpublished doctoral thesis, Chichester: University of Chichester.

Smith, A. and Waddington, I. (2004) 'Using "sport in the community schemes" to tackle crime and drug use among young people: Some policy issues and problems', *European Physical Education Review,* 10: 279–98.

Smith, A., Green, K. and Roberts, K. (2004) 'Sports participation and the "obesity/health crisis": Reflections on the case of young people in England', *International Review for the Sociology of Sport,* 39: 457–64.

Sontag, S. (1972) 'The double standard of aging', *Saturday Review,* 55: 29–38.

Sparkes, A. (1992) *Research in Physical Education and Sport: Exploring Alternative Visions,* London: Falmer Press.

Sport England (2000) *Young People and Sport: National Survey 1999,* London: Sport England.

Stake, R. (1995) *The Art of Case Study Research,* London: Sage.

Stanley, S. and Wise, S. (1993) *Breaking Out Again: Feminist Ontology and Epistemology,* London: Routledge.

Thompson, P. (1992) '"I don't feel old": Subjective ageing and the search for meaning in later life', *Ageing and Society,* 12: 23–47.

Tulle, E. (2008a) 'Acting your age? Sports science and the ageing body', *Journal of Aging Studies,* 22: 291–94.

Tulle, E. (2008b) 'The ageing body and the ontology of ageing: Athletic competence in later life', *Body & Society,* 14: 1–19.

Tulle, E. (2008c) *Ageing, The Body and Social Change,* Basingstoke: Palgrave MacMillan.

Vincent, J.A. (2005) 'Understanding generations: Political economy and culture in an ageing society', *The British Journal of Sociology,* 56: 579–99.

Vincent, J.A. (2007) 'Science and imagery in the "war on old age"', *Ageing and Society,* 27: 941–61.

Wilson, G. (2000) *Understanding Old Age,* London: Sage.

Wray, S. (2007) 'Health exercise and well-being: the experiences of midlife women from diverse ethnic backgrounds', *Social Theory & Health,* 5: 126–44.

Wray, S. and Bartholomew, M. (2010) 'Some reflections on outsider and insider identities in ethnic and migrant qualitative research', *Migration Letters*, 7: 7–16.

Zeilig, H. (1997) 'The uses of literature in the study of older people', in A. Jamieson, S. Harper and C. Victor (eds) *Critical Approaches to Ageing and Later Life*, Buckingham: Open University Press.

8 Researching *Inner-City Sport: Who Plays, and What are the Benefits?* and Commentary

Green, K. (2002) 'Physical education, lifelong participation and the work of Ken Roberts', *Sport, Education and Society*, 7: 167–182.

Roberts, K. (1999) *Leisure in Contemporary Society*, Wallingford: CABI Publishing.

Roberts, K. and Brodie, D. (1992) *Inner-City Sport: Who Plays, and What are the Benefits?*, Culemborg: Giordano Bruno.

9 Researching sport-for-development: The need for scepticism and Commentary

Bandura, A. (1997) *Self-Efficacy: The Exercise of Control*, New York: Worth Publishers.

Baumeister, R., Campbell, J., Krueger, J. and Vohs, K. (2003) 'Does high self-esteem cause better performance, interpersonal success, happiness, or healthier lifestyles?', *Psychological Science in the Public Interest*, 4: 1–44.

Baumeister, R., Cambell, J., Krueger, J. and Vohs. K. (2005) 'Exploding the self-esteem myth', *Scientific American*, 292: 84–92.

Berger, P (1971) *Invitation to Sociology*, London: Pelican.

Biddle, S.J.H. (2006) 'Defining and measuring indicators of psycho-social well-being in youth sport and physical activity', in Y. Vanden Auweele, C. Malcolm and B. Meulders (eds) *Sports and Development*, Leuven: Lannoo Campus.

Biddle, S.J.H. and Mutrie, N. (2001) *Psychology of Physical Activity*, London: Routledge.

Black, D (2010) 'The ambiguities of development: Implications for "development through sport"', *Sport in Society*, 13: 121–9.

Brown, J., Cai, H., Oakes, M, and Deng, C. (2009) 'Cultural similarities in self-esteem functioning. East is east and west is west, but sometimes the twain do meet', *Journal of Cross-Cultural Psychology*, 40: 1140–57.

Burnett, C. (2001) 'Social impact assessment and sport development: Social spin-offs of the Australia–South Africa Junior Sport Programme', *International Review for the Sociology of Sport*, 36: 41–57.

Coakley, J. (1998) *Sport in Society: Issues and Controversies* (6th edn), Boston, MA: McGraw-Hill.

Coakley, J. (2011) 'Youth sports: What counts as "positive development?"', *Journal of Sport and Social Issues*, 35: 306–24.

Coalter, F. (2006) *Sport-in-Development: A Monitoring and Evaluation Manual*, London: UK Sport.

Coalter, F (2007) *A Wider Social Role for Sport: Who's Keeping the Score?*, London: Routledge.

Coalter, F. (2010) 'The politics of sport-for-development: Limited focus programmes and broad gauge problems?', *International Review for the Sociology of Sport*, 45: 295–314.

Coalter, F. (2011a) *Sport, Conflict and Youth Development*, London: Comic Relief.

Coalter, F. (2011b) 'Sport for Development: Pessimism of the Intellect, Optimism of the Will', Paper presented at the *International Conference on Sport for Development and Peace: Sport as a Mediator between Cultures*, Wingate Institute for Physical Education and Sport, Israel, 15–17 September.

Coalter, F. (2013) *Sport-for-Development: What Game are We Playing?*, London: Routledge.

Coalter, F. and Taylor, J. (2010) *Sport-for-Development Impact Study*, London: Comic Relief, UK Sport and International Development through Sport.

Crabbe, T (2008) 'Avoiding the numbers game: Social theory, policy and sport's role in the art of relationship building', in M. Nicholson and R. Hoye (eds) *Sport and Social Capital*, London: Elsevier.

Craib, I. (1984) *Modern Social Theory: From Parsons to Habermas*, Brighton: Wheatsheaf Books.

Darnell, S. and Hayhurst, L. (2012) 'Hegemony, postcolonialism and sport for-development: A response to Lindsey and Grattan', *International Journal of Sport Policy and Politics*, 4: 111–24.

Fox, K. (2000) 'The effects of exercise on self-perceptions and self-esteem', in S.J.H. Biddle, K. Fox and S. Boutcher (eds) *Physical Activity and Psychological Well-Being*, London: Routledge.

Glasner, P. (1977) *The Sociology of Secularisation*, London: Routledge & Kegan Paul.

Hammersley, M. (1995) *The Politics of Social Research*, London: Sage.

Hartmann, D (2003) 'Theorising sport as social intervention: A view from the grassroots', *Quest*, 55: 118–140.

Hartmann, D. and Kwauk, C. (2011) 'Sport and development: An overview, critique and reconstruction', *Journal of Sport and Social Issues*, 35: 284–305.

Hewitt, J. (1998) *The Myth of Self-Esteem: Finding Happiness and Solving Problems in America*, New York: St Martin's Press.

Hunter, J. (2001) 'A cross-cultural comparison of resilience in adolescents', *Journal of Pediatric Nursing*, 16: 172–9.

International Development through Sport (IDS) (2011) *Sport for Development: An Impact Study*, IDS: London.

Jeanes, R. (2011) 'Educating through sport? Examining HIV/AIDS education and sport-for-development through the perspectives of Zambian young people', *Sport, Education and Society*, DOI: 10.1080/13573322.2011.579093.

Jenkins, J. (1997) 'Not without a trace: Resilience and remembering among Bosnian refugees', *Psychiatry*, 60: 40–3.

Kay, T. (2009) 'Developing through sport: Evidencing sport impacts on young people', *Sport in Society*, 12: 1177–91.

Kay, T. (2011) 'Sport in the service of international development: Contributing to the Millennium Development Goals', Paper presented to *2nd International Forum on Sport for Peace and Development*. Geneva, 10–11 May 2011.

Kidd, B. (2008) 'A new social movement: Sport for development and peace', *Sport in Society*, 11: 370–80.

Kruse, S. (2006) *Review of Kicking AIDS Out: Is Sport an Effective Tool in the Fight Against HIV/AIDS?*, Unpublished draft report to NORAD.

Levermore, R. (2008) 'Sport: A new engine of development', *Progress in Development Studies*, 8: 183–90.

Lindsey, I. and Grattan, A. (2012) 'An "international movement"? Decentering sport for development within Zambian communities', *International Journal of Sport Policy and Politics*, 4: 91–110.

Luszczynska, A., Scholz, U. and Schwarzer, R. (2005) 'The general self-efficacy scale: Multicultural validation studies', *The Journal of Psychology*, 139: 439–57.

Maro, C.N. and Roberts, G. (2012) 'Combating HIV/AIDS in Sub-Saharan Africa: Effect of introducing a mastery motivational climate in a community-based programme', *Applied Psychology: An International Review*, 61: 699–722.

Maro, C.N., Roberts, G.C. and Sorensen, M. (2009) 'Using sport to promote HIV/AIDS education for at-risk youths: An intervention using peer coaches in football', *Scandinavian Journal of Medicine and Science in Sports*, 19: 129–41.

Morris, L., Sallybanks, J., Willis, K. and Makkai, T. (2003) *Sport, Physical Activity and Anti-Social Behaviour*, Research and Public Policy Series 49, Canberra: Australian Institute of Criminology.

Mwaanga, O. (2003) *HIV/AIDS At-Risk Adolescent Girls' Empowerment through Participation in Top Level Football and Edusport in Zambia*, MSc thesis submitted to the Institute of Social Science at the Norwegian University of Sport and PE, Oslo: Norway.

Mwaanga, O. (2010) 'Sport for addressing HIV/AIDS: explaining our convictions', *Leisure Studies Association Newsletter*, 85: 61–7.

Nicholls, S., Giles, A. and Sethna, C. (2011) 'Perpetuating the "lack of evidence" discourse in sport for development: Privileged voices, unheard stories and subjugated knowledge' *International Review for the Sociology of Sport*, 46: 249–64.

Pawson, R. (2001) 'Evidence based policy (vol. 1)', in ESRC UK Centre for Evidence Based Policy and Practice, *In Search of a Method*, Working Paper 3, London: Queen Mary University of London.

Pawson, R. (2006) *Evidence-Based Policy: A Realist Perspective*, London: Sage.

Pawson, R. and Tilley, N. (2000) *Realistic Evaluation*, London: Sage.

Pawson, R., Greenhalgh, T., Harvey, G. and Walshe, K. (2004) *Realist Synthesis: An Introduction*, ESRC Research Methods Programme, Manchester: University of Manchester.

Pisani, E. (2008) *The Wisdom of Whores: Bureaucrats, Brothels and the Business of AIDS*, London: Granta Books.

Portes, A. (2000) 'The hidden abode: Sociology as analysis of the unexpected. 1999 Presidential Address', *American Sociological Review*, 65: 1–18.

President's Council on Physical Fitness and Sports (2006) *Sports and Character Development*, Research Digest Series, 7/1, Washington, DC: President's Council on Physical Fitness and Sports.

Prochaska, J. and Velicer, W. (1997) 'The transtheoretical model of health behaviour change', *American Journal of Health Promotion*, 12: 38–48.

Rosenberg, M. (1965) *Society and the Adolescent Self-Image*, Princeton, NJ: Princeton University Press.

Sandford, R., Armour, K. and Warmington, P. (2006) 'Re-engaging disaffected youth through physical activity programmes', *British Educational Research Journal*, 32: 251–271.

Seippel, O. (2006) 'Sport and social capital', *Acta Sociologica*, 49: 169–83.

Spaaij, R. (2011) 'Sport as a vehicle for social mobility and regulation of disadvantaged urban youth', *International Review for the Sociology of Sport*, 44: 247–64.

Spaaij, R. (2012) 'Beyond the playing field: Experiences of sport, social capital and integration among Somalis in Australia', *Ethnic and Racial Studies*, 35: 1519–38.

Sport for Development and Peace International Working Group (2008) *Harnessing the Power of Sport for Development and Peace*, Right to Play: Toronto.

Tacon, R. (2007) 'Football and social inclusion: Evaluating social policy', *Managing Leisure: An International Journal*, 12: 1–23.

Ungar, M. (2006) 'Resilience across cultures', *British Journal of Social Work*, 38: 218–35.

UNICEF (2006) *Monitoring and Evaluation for Sport-Based Programming for Development: Sport Recreation and Play*, Workshop Report, New York: UNICEF.

van Kampen, H. (ed.) (2003) *A Report on the Expert Meeting 'The Next Step' on Sport and Development*, NCDO: Amsterdam.

Wagner, H. (1964) 'Displacement of scope: A problem of the relationship between small-scale and large-scale sociological theories', *The American Journal of Sociology*, 69: 571–84.

Weiss, C. (1993) 'Where politics and evaluation research meet', *Evaluation Practice*, 14: 93–106.

Weiss, C. (1997) 'How can theory-based evaluation make greater headway?', *Evaluation Review*, 21: 501–24.

Woodcock, A., Cronin, O. and Forde, S. (2012) 'Quantitative evidence for the benefits of Moving the Goalposts, a sport for development project in rural Kenya', *Evaluation and Program Planning*, 35: 370–381.

10 Researching policy change in school sport and physical education and Commentary

Azzarito, L. and Solmon, M.A. (2006) 'A feminist poststructuralist view on student bodies in physical education: Sites of compliance, resistance, and transformation', *Journal of Teaching in Physical Education*, 25: 200–25.

Baumgartner, F. and Jones, B. (1993) *Agendas and Instability in American Politics,* Chicago, IL: University of Chicago Press.

Benn, T. (2005) '"Race" and sport, physical education and dance', in K. Green and K. Hardman (eds) *Physical Education: Essential Issues*, London: Sage.

de Vaus, D. (2001) *Research Design in Social Research*, London: Sage.

Elias, N. (1978) *What is Sociology?* London: Hutchinson.

Evans, J. and Penney, D. (1995) 'Physical education, restoration and the politics of sport', *Curriculum Studies*, 3: 183–96.

Hall, P. (1986) *Governing the Economy: The Politics of State Intervention in Britain and France*, Cambridge: Polity Press.

Hammersley, M. and Gomm, R. (2000) 'Introduction', in R. Gomm, M. Hammersley and P Foster (eds) *Case Study Method*, London: Sage.

Hansard HC Deb 30 November (2010) School sports funding, col. 701.

Hargreaves, J. (1994) *Sporting Females: Critical Issues in the History and Sociology of Women's Sport*, London: Routledge.

Houlihan, B. (2010) 'It's wrong to remove a child's sporting chance – schools do much more sport now than a decade ago. So why abandon a proven system?', *The Times*, 29 November 2010.

Houlihan, B. and Green, M. (2006) 'The changing status of school sport and physical education: Explaining policy change', *Sport, Education and Society*, 11: 73–92.

Houlihan, B. and Lindsey, I. (2012) *Sport Policy in Britain*, London: Routledge.

Kingdon, J. [1984] (2002) *Agendas, Alternatives and Public Policies*, Boston, MA: Little Brown.

Kirk, D. (1992) *Defining Physical Education: The Social Construction of a Post-War Subject*, London: Falmer Press.

Lilleker, D. (2003) 'Interviewing the political elite: Navigating a potential minefield', *Politics*, 23: 207–14.

Marsh, D. and Rhodes, R. (1992) *Policy Networks in British Government*, Oxford: Clarendon Press.

Mills, C.W. (1959) *The Sociological Imagination*, Oxford: Oxford University Press.

Ostrom, E. (1999) 'Institutional rational choice: An assessment of the institutional analysis and development framework', in P. Sabatier (ed.) *Theories of the Policy Process*, Boulder, CO: Westview Press.

Penney, D. and Evans, J. (1999) *Politics, Policy and Practice in Physical Education*, London: E&FN Spon.

Pronger, B. (2002) *Body Fascism: Salvation in the Technology of Physical Fitness*, Toronto: University of Toronto Press.

Sabatier, P. and Jenkins-Smith, H. (1993) *Policy Change and Learning: An Advocacy Coalition Process*, Boulder, CO: Westview Press.

Scott, J. (1990) *A Matter of Record, Documentary Sources in Social Research*, Cambridge: Polity Press.

Smith, A. (2006) *Young People, Sport and Leisure: A Sociological Study of Youth Lifestyles*, Unpublished Ph.D. thesis, Liverpool: University of Liverpool.

Williams, C. (2012) *Researching Power, Elites and Leadership*, London: Sage.

Wintour, P. (2012) 'David Cameron promises extra lottery funding for elite sport', *Guardian*, 10 August 2012.

INDEX

Page numbers in *italic* refer to tables.